D1236360

The PURPLE SHAMROCK

The Hon. James Michael Curley of Boston

The PURPLE SHAMROCK

THE HON.
James Michael Curley
OF BOSTON

By JOSEPH F. DINNEEN

M. D. ANDERSON MEMORIAL LIBRARY
UNIVERSITY OF HOUSTON

W · W · NORTON & COMPANY · INC · New York

154424

COPYRIGHT, 1949, BY

JOSEPH F. DINNEEN

First Edition

Acknowledgments are due to the Crowell-Collier Publishing Company for permission to quote from "How to Break a Political Machine," by Joseph F. Dinneen, published in *Collier's Magazine*, copyright Crowell-Collier Publishing Company, and "The Incredible Curley," by Joseph F. Dinneen, copyright Crowell-Collier Publishing Company.

To *Harper's Magazine* for permission to quote from "The Kingfish of Massachusetts," by Joseph F. Dinneen, copyright *Harper's Magazine*.

To *The New Republic* for permission to quote from "Brahmin from Boston," by Joseph F. Dinneen, copyright *The New Republic*.

PRINTED IN THE UNITED STATES OF AMERICA

Contents

5

Illustrations

Foreword

FOR MORE than a half-century James Michael Curley has been a controversial figure in Boston, an enigma on the national political scene. He is a creation of a curious society known everywhere as "The Boston Irish," as distinguished from all other Irish. Both have been, at times, difficult; and difficult to understand.

How much irreparable harm, if any, has Curley wrought in Boston? How much permanent good, if any, has he accomplished? Why does Boston tolerate him? How does he operate? How did he become what he is? What effect did environment, education and early training have upon him? What influence did he have upon the Boston Irish? What influence did they have upon him?

Some of those questions only Curley could answer. The rest are revealed in a study of the Boston Irish.

After Curley was found guilty of using the mails to defraud in Washington and received a noisy reception from his loyal followers as he stepped from a train in Boston, I talked to him. I had been Curley's critic in newspapers, in national magazines, and on the radio. He once sued me and *Harper's Magazine* for $500,000 for libel.

Curley never has been reluctant to talk to hostile critics. When a St. Louis *Post-Dispatch* reporter once opened an interview by saying, "I'm told that you're a pretty tough hombre; that you'd actually take the false teeth out of the mouths of your followers if they crossed you up," Curley grinned and disarmed him by answering: "Why not? I put them there, didn't I?"

Curley never explains himself. One of his characteristics is an exasperating failure to define or interpret equivocal statements that require amplification to be established as fact. He makes claims habitually, publicly and privately, lets them stand like unfinished stories and loses patience when he is questioned further concerning them. Often he imputes to listeners an understanding of facts and background that they do not have. His attitude seems to be that the truth of a statement should be accepted because he has made it. Any attempt to verify it is a reflection upon his integrity and an insult.

The purpose of my visit then was to have him tell his side of the story. He had not been permitted to take the stand in Washington. In many particulars, the case against him seemed to make little sense. He told me his side of the story and I reported it in the Boston *Globe*.

During the interview, Curley accused me of not being fair to him and added that reporters and writers, as a rule, never were. I told him that if he'd tell me the story of his life, I would write it as he told it, and try to be fair and objective about it. He thought it over and agreed to do so. His daughter Mary, his sons Leo, George, and Francis, and his closest and most intimate friend, Judge Daniel Gillen, were present at interviews, filled in many gaps and took part in the discussions.

This is not an authorized or approved biography. Curley

did not see it until after it was set in type, and he has been far from my only source of information, for I have been collecting material on him for more than thirty years. I have tried to be fair and objective about him. I think he is entitled to that.

I hope, too, that the story will have a larger significance. With the fall of Frank Hague in Jersey City, Curley remains as the last of the old-time bosses. But while the pattern of politics has changed—and indeed Curley played his part in the change—it has not changed completely. The lessons learned by the old-time bosses have not been lost on the new political leaders—and they should not be lost on the new voters, either.

Joseph F. Dinneen

One · The Twig Is Bent

THE TWIG was bent in a slum growth that fringed the marshes and mud flats where Boston Harbor spilled in and out with the tides. In an east wind at the ebb, the place smelled. A smothering odor of dead fish, eelgrass, fungus decay, salty brine and gas, a mixture of odors both pungent and musty, was offensive and insulting to sensitive nostrils. A few hundred yards from high-water mark in this stale, unhealthy place, a penurious government had built a city hospital, a tall brick wall fencing off the contagious wards. Roxbury at the South End line was not a good place to bring up children.

Facing City Hospital on the slimy shore were the dilapidated tenements and ramshackle rookeries of the immigrants from Galway. This was where they colonized in the haphazard, accidental arrangement of an agglomeration of refugees from a potato famine, placed and fixed as they had been herded from the ships into the arms of mill agents, ward bosses and employers hungry for cheap labor. James Michael was born in one of these tenements because the Curleys came from Galway.

Twelve-year-old Sarah Clancy and fourteen-year-old Michael Curley had arrived aboard different ships in 1864, strangers to each other and strangers in a new land, unaware that they were anonymous statistics in the greatest mass movement of population across the Atlantic and incapable of comprehending the significance of it. Boston had a population of 260,000, including 5,000 Irish immigrants, in 1847, the year before the potato famine. Ten years later, it had a population of 310,000, including 50,000 Irish. The Irish in Boston had grown from one-fiftieth to a sixth of the population and accounted for more than a third of the city's registered vote.

When the Clancys and the Curleys arrived, the Irish were entrenched and well organized. The Civil War was going on and they were in a truculent, fighting mood. A city cannot upset the racial balance of its population in so short a time without violence and there already had been considerable blood shed in clashes between the Yankees and the Irish. In the city's recent past, an Ursuline convent had been burned in Charlestown. There had been riots on Broad Street when a Yankee fire company tried to cross an Irish parade. As a result, the Boston Irish had to disband their own armed militia. The Boston Irish had sent their Fighting Ninth Regiment to the Civil War, and there had been some awkward unpleasantness because the regiment—franchised American citizens—insisted upon fighting under the Irish rather than the American flag.

From the very founding of the Massachusetts Bay Colony, the Irish had been a problem first to the Puritans and then to their somewhat more liberal Yankee-Brahmin successors. The history of the American Revolution is sprinkled with their heroes and rascals, from Commodore John Barry and General John Sullivan to the scheming, conniving Conway whom General George Washington suspected of organizing a cabal against him.

Boston Brahmins were proud of the city's age and their own Mayflower ancestry. The Boston Irish were unimpressed and indifferent to it. To them, the city was merely a place in which to work and live. As they grew in numbers and in political power and security, their horizons widened. They looked for better and more dignified employment and came upon the legend "No Irish Need Apply," a hangover from Know-Nothingism that would rankle for years as a personal insult.

Immigrants colonized first along the water front, from the mud flats by City Hospital in the South End, around its jagged outline, to the place in the North End opposite where Paul Revere set out to sound the alarm. By the very weight of their numbers they had taken over the water-front wards politically. Slowly and inexorably the horde was pushing the Yankee Brahmin ruling class back, forcing compromises and concessions from them and making deals. The political siege of the Brahmins was well under way and a loosely organized campaign to conquer the city had begun. From the beach-heads the Irish had swarmed inland, surrounding three of Boston's four hills, occupying the bases, and were beginning to swarm over them, overpopulating them, destroying real-estate values, driving the Brahmins back inch by inch. County Cork took over Copp's Hill; Kerry, Fort Hill; Donegal, Mission Hill; Meath and Mayo crept up Dorchester Heights and Galway, the flatlands to the South. The Brahmins clung to Beacon Hill.

In this simmering cauldron of population, the strong, the gifted, the talented and the educated came naturally to the top. Not all Irish immigrants were unlettered or uncultured. The Boston Irish already had a vigorous, sometimes noisy press. They had their public champions, graduates of universities either in America or in Ireland. A few of them, like John Boyle O'Reilly, were fluent and vocal and had achieved wide, even international reputations.

Sarah Clancy and Michael Curley were fair samples of the average Irish immigrant population. They were healthy and strong. Their parents had read the glittering Cunard Line posters in Galway, and had prayed, petitioned, pleaded with relatives who had come to America to send and lend money for passage so that they, too, could "come out." Parents and children had come as cheap labor to a market thirsty for them and had been swallowed up. Their education in Ireland had been skimpy and meager, picked up here and there and now and then from occasional schoolmasters. There was no hint of regal splendor, royal purple or the arrogance of the ruling class about them, or in their immediate ancestral backgrounds. They were poor, common, ordinary. They had no skills, no discernible talent.

Michael Curley, even at fourteen, was tall, had broad shoulders and bulging biceps. He was peaceable enough, but proud of his muscle. Sarah Clancy was capable of washing, cooking, sewing, the drudgery of housework. Irish immigrant girls were chambermaids, servants, domestic help, or worked in mills or sweatshops. Pitifully few men or women had opportunity for education. The parents of William Cardinal O'Connell worked at looms in a Lowell textile mill.

In the beginning the men were servile, hat-in-hand, head-bowing workers, impressed and awed by wealth, power and authority, but they became indoctrinated quickly. When rights and privileges were defined they seized upon them and used them to the limit. Eight centuries of persecution under the English gave them an historical tradition, experience and skill in turning discrimination and intolerance to their advantage.

Irish girls exchanged bad sinks, poor and little food and no luxuries in Ireland for good sinks, good and plentiful food and some luxuries in Boston. Whether this improvement was immediately worth it sometimes troubled them, but very few went back. Those who went into sweatshops balanced the good by sacrificing health for the comforts they bought.

As Irish immigrants and their progeny crowded Yankees out of successive wards, the boss emerged in each ward, either by assuming leadership or by taking the reins from someone else.

Patrick J. Maguire (P. J.—known as Pea-Jacket) was the rising boss of Ward 17, including City Hospital and the mud flats. He had been in Boston for twenty years before the Clancys and the Curleys put down their luggage in separate houses, far removed from each other and from Maguire in his domain. Very soon the elder Curley and Clancy were persuaded to register as voters. Michael Curley was considered old enough to be given a job as a hod carrier for a construction company. The Clancy and Curley women were of no importance or concern to P. J. Maguire. They could not vote.

In twenty years, P. J. had come quite a distance in Boston. He was a tailor; learned his trade under Lathrop and Godfrey, a Yankee firm; became foreman at Oak Hall Clothing House; went into business with George Jacobs as "Jacobs and Maguire," one of the first Boston Irish-Jewish combinations. There were a number of far more successful ones to follow. Before long, Jacobs disappeared from the firm. The business became "Sullivan and Maguire." There seems to be little doubt that Pea-Jacket made much more money in politics than he did in the clothing business. He saw to it, for example, that the inmates of the city prison on Deer Island were given the right to hear Mass on Sundays and holy days of obligation, and at the same time he saw to it that Sullivan and Maguire got the contract to make all the prison clothing the inmates wore. He ruled his ward with a much tighter hand than Martin Lomasney in near-by West End or P. J. Kennedy (father of former Ambassador Joseph P.) across the harbor in East Boston.

He gave Michael Curley a job as a hod carrier and ignored him for the next seven years until he was old enough to vote. During that time Michael Curley and Sarah Clancy grew up and matured. Michael was not talented or gifted in any way. He was strong, capable of defending himself physically, but he was not aggressive. Like the parents who brought him to Boston he was a follower and never a leader. He was well liked by his associates, the men with whom he worked, but he could scarcely be classified as popular. He controlled no votes; influenced none. He was an obscure voter and not a political worker. He did not nag at Maguire for advancement or a better job, and as a result he remained shelved.

He met Sarah Clancy, went about with her for years, and when he was twenty-one and she was nineteen, they were married in Saint Phillip's Church. Michael Curley's financial and social status remained the same before and after marriage. He had been a hod carrier. He remained a hod carrier, unable either because of his own failure or the failure of a political system to achieve the more lucrative job of bricklayer.

There was no honeymoon. The couple went to live in a tenement at 28 Northampton Street. In time there were three children, but only two survived, John, the older, and James Michael, born November 20, 1874, baptized and christened in Saint Phillip's. The Curleys were an obscure family in the ward, no better and no worse than hundreds of others lining the mud flats, surrounding City Hospital and the gashouse, multiplying the number that would ultimately creep up the small hill toward Saint Patrick's Church at its crest where the financially better fixed lived. The Boston Irish seemed to have an affinity for hills.

When John became old enough, he walked a mile to Dearborn Public School. When James Michael became old enough a few years later, he joined John and walked to school with him. Michael worked fourteen to sixteen hours a day and earned ten cents an hour. On that wage he moved his family around the corner to three rooms on Fellows Court where he paid eight dollars a month rent. Children crowded the neighborhood. Playgrounds were streets and mud flats; and children became familiar with and hardened to the sound of ambulance gongs leaving and returning to the hospital. They went barefoot in summer on hot cobblestone pavements; wore little else than light overalls that they could drop in a moment to swim in the cove or the ship channel. Life was not too precious and was lost often in the water or on the streets. Children fell from roofs flying kites or sleeping there on hot summer nights; and adult wakes were frequent because tuberculosis, or "the con," was a curse upon immigrants and their families.

The street-corner gang was a greater influence upon male children than the classroom and more often than not minimized the effect of home training. There were dozens of such gangs in every ward. The hangout in Curley's neighborhood was the big square at the end of the street. Church, school and home collaborated on one code of morals, while the gang taught, required and subscribed to another, epitomized in the rule: "Never tell anything to a cop."

During an era and in an environment when a penny had value, pennies were given sparsely to children. Luxuries, like sweets, were rare and tempting. The owner of a candy store or the driver of a fruit truck had to be watchful and alert. Pilfering was common. The church, the school, and usually the home disapproved of it, but the gang encouraged it and provided alibis for those under suspicion. Whatever a slum kid got away with for himself, whether it was eatable or wearable, was approved and applauded by the gang. If he got away with more than he could use, he shared. There were no Fagins. It was a voluntary and co-operative plan.

Even if church, school and parental training succeeded in keeping a child to a full degree of personal honesty, the attitude of those around him had an effect upon his conception and understanding of integrity. If a slum kid whose mouth watered for fruit was offered a peach from a stolen basket, is it reasonable to expect that his character would have been so developed at such an early age that he would refuse?

There was never enough coal to heat the three rooms on

Fellows Court, and there was never enough money. Coal was purchased in a fifty- or hundred-pound bag and stored in the kitchen. A special coal shovel, not much larger than a garden trowel, was used to spread it sparingly in the firebox of a flat-topped kitchen stove. The ashes were sifted for pieces that had not burned completely, a dusty and disagreeable Saturday-morning chore. Coal was made to burn to powder. When the bag got low, Mrs. Curley counted the lumps. Cooking and washing always were combined with house heating lest some of the value of the coal be lost. Nothing irked a householder in the poor precincts more than the realization that they were burning money. Every able-bodied boy was trained to keep his eyes open for scrapwood on dumps, in the market district, and wherever crates were unpacked. They haunted construction jobs night and day and when watchmen, workmen or foremen were not looking, carried away even expensive newel posts and new lumber with the scrap to burn in kitchen stoves and stretch out the coal supply.

Money assumed an extraordinary importance and value to people who worked hard for little of it. Enough of it would solve their problems and put them on Easy Street. All of them dreamed of having such a phenomenal surplus of it that they could be wildly extravagant and do anything they wanted, and as there seemed to be little prospect of earning it, every adult hoped for an unexpected windfall. They listened raptly to stories of inventions and accidental discoveries that had made men rich overnight, the safety pin, the return ball, the curtain roller, chemical cure-alls, oil wells and gold mines. They always were on the lookout for get-rich-quick schemes that would do the same for them. If you had the right get-rich-quick scheme—one that sounded plausible, flawless in presentation if not in operation—you could make a lot of money on the scheme.

James Michael Curley was conditioned, at least to some degree, by this common Great Expectation. When he became old enough, he sold papers. A record of having once been a newsboy is often a politician's proud boast, cited as a symbol of his humble beginning. Few city kids ever contributed much to the support of household or parents by selling papers. Usually, it was, and still is, a method of earning spending money that parents could not give them, and just as often it is, and has been, encouraged by parents to teach children the value of money by compelling or permitting them to work for it. James Michael Curley, like a good many other boys in his neighborhood, hooked rides on wagons, horsecars, omnibuses and coaches morning and night to Newspaper Row to buy his papers in mail and circulation rooms. He developed a route and corner stand, bought jelly rolls, candy, soda pop, the luxuries his parents could not afford to give him. He spent much of his profit and turned over what was left to his mother.

When he was ten years old, his father died under circumstances that were tragic. Michael Curley had a reputation in his neighborhood as a strong man. He boasted that he could lift almost anything. He had been challenged often and always had won.

One day a man on a construction job looked speculatively at a huge stone that had to be moved. "Can you lift that, Mike?" he asked.

Other men on the job looked on with interest. It was a challenge for a Hercules. "I'll bet he can't," one of them said.

"I'll bet I can," Michael Curley decided. He bent over, hooked his hands around the stone, tugged and strained, got it off the ground. Veins stood out on his forehead and neck. He dropped the stone, about four hundred pounds, and collapsed. Three days later he was dead. He was thirty-four years old.

Pea-Jacket Maguire did nothing to help the Curleys. In almost any other ward, the boss would have come to the house. There would have been money, food, a job provided for the widow, and funeral bills would have been paid, not because the ward boss was charitable and had a heart of gold, but because this kind of social service gave the whole neighborhood the impression that he was, and helped keep the people in line to vote as directed on election day. P. J. Kennedy, Martin Lomasney, John F. Fitzgerald and most of the minor ward leaders operated that way, but Pea-Jacket was close-fisted, penurious and had little time for those in his ward who would have to get from him more than they could immediately give to him.

Pea-Jacket left Sarah Curley and her two sons to shift for themselves. John Curley was twelve years old then; James Michael, ten. Mrs. Curley got a job as a scrubwoman, working nights in office buildings. John was hired by C. S. Johnson, a grocer near by, but before he could report for work, he was bitten by a spider. His face swelled and his eye closed. It was impossible for him to work. Johnson told his assistant manager that he had hired a new boy, and then left on a two weeks' vacation. James Michael decided to report for work in his brother's stead.

He turned up at the store at the appointed time on Monday morning, worked for two weeks until John recovered, and then John reported for work. Johnson recognized the boy he had hired, but the assistant manager did not, and was bewildered until John explained. John remained on the job. James Michael went back to selling papers.

When James Michael was twelve, he got a job in Stephen Gale's drugstore, sweeping, cleaning, straightening out stock, running errands, and after a short apprenticeship worked behind the counter. A drugstore in a hospital district was a busy place. He reported at seven o'clock in the morning, worked until eight-thirty; covered the mile to Dearborn School before eight-fifty; returned to the drugstore at twelve-thirty, worked till one-thirty; went back to school and was behind the counter again at four-thirty to work until eleven at night. Saturdays he worked from seven in the morning until eleven at night, and Sundays from eight in the morning until eleven at night. For that, according to his own account, he got two dollars and a half a week. His mother paid ten dollars a month rent.

He studied and did home lessons behind the counter and came to know the regular customers. Years later, he recalled that one of them, a woman, became interested in him because of the quality of his voice. "You ought to make a great preacher," she decided, and wanted to pay his way through high school and college. He said he was interested until she made it clear that by making him a great preacher she would be turning him into a Protestant minister.

John was graduated from Dearborn School and went to work full time for Johnson, the grocer. James was graduated two years later. In four years at school, he had missed only three days at the drugstore. Immediately he hired out to the New England Piano Company, a short walk from his home, as an apprentice spiral-screw-machine operator. The plant turned out twenty-five pianos a day.

"We had to work in a temperature of ninety degrees," he said later, "because of the nature of the materials. Going on in the morning, we would strip and get into overalls and old undershirts. Most of the boys chewed tobacco. They had a theory that it prevented excessive perspiration, warded off colds and tuberculosis. I worked there for nine months and went from a hundred and thirty-four pounds down to eighty pounds. The pay was seven dollars and a half a week. Then they put us on piece work. I started making twelve, fourteen and sixteen dollars a week. Promptly the boss put me back on day work, and I quit."

The workers had no union. No attempt was made to organize the place. Before he left, standing by a window, James Michael saw the top-hatted manager of the shop, a Mr. Scannell, striding across the sidewalk toward the door, and picked up a handy piece of soap used to prevent drills from burning. He threw it at the silk hat and scored a bull's-eye. Within a few minutes, the irate Scannell stomped into the room.

"Who threw that?" he demanded.

There was no answer.

"I'll give twenty-five dollars to the man who'll tell me who threw that soap," he offered.

"Make it fifty," James Michael said, "and I'll tell you."

Scannell did not make it fifty, but he knew who threw the soap.

James Michael went back to work at Johnson's grocery store as a boy of all work, assembling, wrapping and packing orders, putting them in baskets and loading them on a horse-drawn wagon. Johnson's was a big store and he drove over a long route making deliveries. This gave him a wide acquaintance among families throughout the ward. He was then an adolescent and had no idea of going into politics. He thought he would like to be a fireman and began visiting a gymnasium regularly. He was tall, developing a big frame and resembled his father. He anticipated taking civil-service examinations and enrolled in high school.

His home life had improved. It was no longer necessary for his mother to scrub floors. The combined earnings of both her sons restored Sarah Curley's family to the norm of the neighborhood. When James Michael was not in high school, he spent his evenings in the hangout of the district, One-Arm-Peter Whalen's cigar store on Northampton Street near the hospital, a casual, unorganized club where counter and pot-bellied stove were comparable to the country-store cracker barrel. Peter Whalen's was a must on the list of every politician. It was here that James Michael was indoctrinated. Here he heard the inside stories, off-the-record stories, the scandals and mysteries of ward management.

He forgot little of what he heard there, unconsciously storing it up, cataloguing and filing it away in his mind. Years later he could recite long-forgotten details about men and happenings that he had heard there. He did not immediately realize that he was sponging up an education in practical politics. He was a far better public listener than public speaker then.

Pea-Jacket was shortsighted in the management of his ward. It was one of the worst in the city. Other ward leaders could deliver their votes in predetermined blocks and amounts. Pea-Jacket never could, and as a result other ward leaders usually by-passed Pea-Jacket when they negotiated the election of a mayor. He was invited to political councils of war, but he was never dependable. Sometimes he backtracked after agreements to sell the support of his ward independently. The other leaders had little use for him, but there was not much they could do about it. They could not get rid of him.

Maguire was especially unpopular in Whalen's part of the ward, and as his territory was always being invaded by the opposition, the cigar store was the most likely place for one to get a toe hold. James Michael was enlisted in the opposition to any Pea-Jacket ticket even before he was old enough to vote. He was petitioned by both major and minor office holders to canvass for them as he made the rounds of Johnson's customers. He did so, and discovered that there was an easier way to make money and get ahead in the world than by sweating in a piano factory or driving a grocery delivery wagon, a quick short cut to riches and power.

He lost interest in the fire department and in civil-service physical examinations. He decided that he needed mental and not muscular development. He paid closer attention in night-school classes, began to read books, indiscriminately at first, and to haunt the public library. His approach to education was not professionally guided. It was blind, hit or miss, trial and error. It led in all directions, but it was determined, and for his purposes it was effective. He had found his own get-rich-quick scheme.

Two · The First Stop-Curley Combine Fails

In 1896, when James Michael Curley cast his first vote, Boston had a bicameral government. The common council, or lower chamber, was the bottom rung of the political ladder, a big, deliberative body of seventy-five members, three from each ward. A cumbersome appendage to city government, it had limited power to initiate city regulations and no power to repeal or veto. Theoretically, in collaboration with an upper-chamber board of aldermen, it approved the annual budget and extra appropriations. Its chief function was to exercise a power of suggestion, directing the consideration of aldermen and mayor to things it felt ought to be done. These recommendations, although they lacked force, were contrarily called orders. The mayor could accept them, put them into effect or reject and forget them. The council did serve, though, to call public attention to the needs of the city, and as a forum to discuss the grievances of voters.

It became a combination debating society and night school providing a training in parliamentary law and an audience of

26

members and spectators for practice in public speaking. A council showman, whether mastermind or circus clown, who publicized himself well was usually promoted from this primary grade to the upper-class board of aldermen, a more select body of nine. The only additional power the aldermen had was to screen the suggestions, or orders, of the council to the mayor. Its concurrence and added debate gave an order more weight, more popularity and more publicity, and a mayor either adopted it or felt compelled to explain why he did not at the next election if he were a candidate or supported his successor. Accepting or rejecting the order was his choice.

Both boards met one night a week. For his services a councilor was paid $300 a year, an alderman $750 a year. Without the restraining handicaps of honor, integrity and principle, a member could make much more and usually did. The system had worked well under aristocratic Brahmin rule and provided good government before the Great Immigration changed the character of the city's population.

A councilor or alderman was the first, handiest and most convenient contact of the voter with his city government. Councilors and aldermen came to know the heads of all city departments and bureaus. They became familiar with the forms and routine of city government. If a mayor was reluctant to do so because of the expense or for any other reason, orders could be introduced into the council implying a popular demand for opening a street, erecting a lamp or a telephone pole, raising the pay of a public servant or a group of them, cutting down working hours or awarding a Saturday afternoon off.

Each alderman and councilor became a local Mr. Fixit who knew just whom to see, a person usually claimed as a personal friend, to get a permit for a swinging sign or the right to store an inflammable, and his know-how was almost indispensable in getting a permit to sell liquor.

Theoretically the public servant or employee earned his

raise, reward or time off by his diligence and efficiency, and the voter was entitled to his permit, right or privilege free of charge. This had been true when Yankees were a majority of the population and had complete control of the government. The change in the system had been gradual before and during the time James Michael Curley grew to manhood, when it became the practice for the voter to reward the councilor or alderman for the time spent and skill exercised in raising the voter's pay, achieving a right or concession or securing a license. Without the interest of the alderman or councilor, the result could not have been accomplished. The voter was willing to pay, and in most cases the councilor or alderman accepted the money. Usually he rationalized his doing so and justified it by arguing that he was entitled to the fee for professional services rendered. If he spent any sum of money to be elected, he reasoned that payment from a constituent was either reimbursement or a campaign contribution for a past election or for a future election—and there was no limit to campaign contributions.

Few politicians ever admit that in the beginning they deliberately sought public office. Invariably they claim that the office sought them. James Michael Curley differed from the rest in that he always proclaimed that he deliberately chose politics as a career. After two score years in office he could say truthfully: "Public service is my business." His experience in private business was very short. He was working at politics before he was twenty. Politics interfered with his job at the grocery store. C. S. Johnson did not like to have his chief clerk soliciting votes among customers and complained of it, warning him either to give up politics or give up the grocery business. Curley had no intention of becoming a great grocer.

The leadership of his ward had changed. In the sly and cunning strategy of city politics, Pea-Jacket's rivals flattered him into accepting the chairmanship of the Democratic City Committee. He did not discover until after he had appointed

John F. Dever to succeed him as boss of Ward Seventeen that the bigger job had mysteriously become all honor and no power. He presided, but the other ward bosses of the city decided, and ran the committee.

Dever was the Boston-born son of Irish parents. His nephew Paul was to win the governorship in 1948 with Curley's support. He had been registrar of voters and secretary to Mayor Hugh O'Brien, the city's first Ireland-born mayor, elected in 1885. Curley came of age in November, 1895, and could not vote until the election of 1896 when Owen Galvin, a native-born Irish descendant and long-time office holder, then a United States Attorney, became a candidate for mayor against Thomas N. Hart. Hart, too, was of Irish descent and had been mayor six years earlier.

Curley had never been cultivated by Pea-Jacket Maguire. Dever, as Maguire's lieutenant and successor, had ignored him. When Mike Cuniff, an Irish banker and politician, dropped in at One-Arm Peter Whalen's place looking for help to defeat Hart and elect Galvin, he found James Michael Curley. Both Pea-Jacket and Dever were supporting Hart.

"You ought to be able to do a lot of good for Galvin in this ward," Cuniff suggested. "Will you put in a word for him wherever you go?"

Curley nodded. "I'll do more than that. I'll canvass the whole district."

That was his first extensive political campaign in his own ward, and his candidate was defeated. It aligned him politically against Pea-Jacket, Dever and the ward machine and caused some further embarrassment for Johnson, his employer. He gathered a small amount of political prestige as a very young voter who had antagonized the ward boss. The dissatisfied and disgruntled in the ward, an impressive minority, approved of him, even though some might have been disappointed by his youth.

Curley at twenty-two was tall with broad, square shoulders

and athletic in appearance, although not in personal inclination. He did not play football or baseball and never understood the games too well. He was quick to anger, able to
defend himself with his fists and did so occasionally. He was
not popular as a companion, wit or man about town. Neither
was he unpopular. He was a good conversationalist, a good
salesman and a good listener. His personal and family background was well known throughout the ward, and it would
serve no good purpose for him to speak of it or discuss it
there. He did not dance. He was shy and embarrassed among
women, and even at that age both he and his brother John
were still Sunday-school teachers and ushers in Saint James
Church on Harrison Avenue.

He smoked cigars, but he did not drink. He was always neat
in appearance, well dressed, courteous, the kind of young
man whom mothers in the neighborhood would hold up as
an example to their sons, saying: "Why can't you be like
James Michael Curley?" using both given names; and sons
would listen indifferently, privately acknowledging Curley's
virtues while at the same time being glad that they were not
like him. Not that they hated him for it; they didn't. His
personality was such that the praise that damns had little
effect upon them.

They knew him and sometimes must have felt sorry for
him, because he was temperamentally unsuited to the games,
dances, parties, the neighborhood activities that provided
their fun. Sometimes he must have envied them and felt sorry
for himself. He never could be a participant. He didn't enjoy
it, and because he seemed to be fitted for nothing else and
there was no other way to dispose of him, he was usually
chosen as a leader. Counted out of participation in the
schemes of local affairs, he became the ideal selection for
chairman of the committee on arrangements or general chairman of church and group minstrel shows, dances, picnics and

outings, a worker so little concerned with the fun that he could be depended upon to sell tickets, schedule entertainment, hire bands and attend to all details and chores. As a result, his name was printed on programs and he got rising votes of thanks at the next meeting—all glory and no personal enjoyment, unless glory be personal enjoyment.

He did these things for Saint James Church and for the Ancient Order of Hibernians. He must have had his future in mind when he joined the order. The wealthiest, most successful and most influential among the Boston Irish were members, usually office holders in the fraternity, while middle class and poor Irish were among the rank and file. Any division of the A.O.H. was a cross section of the Boston Irish. He joined in the same spirit that others joined the Masons or the Elks and for the same purpose, certain that he would find in its meeting rooms the men who could help him most either in politics or business. He forthwith became a busy and dependable committee worker, selling raffle tickets, raising funds, calling on the sick, writing reports and asking the most influential among them for advice, such as: "If you were my age, would you become a candidate for the common council?" an approach that would flatter almost any of them.

This kind of club work among the Irish could become a career in that day. Committee work took hours, days and weeks. The organization of a St. Patrick's Day celebration and parade—from night-before speakers through long rosters of companies, divisions and floats, housing for visiting delegations and bedding down horses, quarters for drill teams and bands, refreshments, reviewing stands, distinguished guests and protocol, to the cleanup on the day after—took perhaps a hundred hours of work. Curley enjoyed it.

Whether or not because of the advice he received at meetings of the Hibernians, he did not become a candidate for the council after he cast his first vote. He waited; and felt that he was sufficiently seasoned after he cast his second vote. Explaining, years later, how it came about, Curley described the scene this way:

"Some forgotten Warwick who frequented Peter Whalen's cigar store was the first to suggest that I stand for office.

" 'Why don't you go out for the common council?' he asked.

" 'I haven't the money to make a campaign,' I objected.

"But Whalen dipped his good hand into his pocket and came up with $10. Tom Donnellon, a city health inspector, and his brother, Mark, contributed $15 more. I made the fight on that $25 and a few more dollars of my own."

Curley, according to his own account, promptly spent the money in Max Keezer's secondhand clothing store in Harvard Square for a student's cast-off dress suit, a trade-mark that made him stand out at rallies.

He was young and inexperienced, a hesitant, repetitious and awkward speaker, fumbling for words, wearing a suit that went to Harvard at a time when its first owner might have been in Santiago among the young and able who had enlisted for the war with Spain and his audiences were remembering the *Maine*. The campaign was poorly timed. He was heckled: "Why aren't you in the service?" He explained in later years that he had tried to enlist and was turned down for hemorrhoids.

Frozen out of ward rooms and assembly halls by the ward organization, he made a thorough house-to-house canvass. There appears to be little doubt that he won the election by about five hundred votes, but he was counted out in the ward room. John Dever and his lieutenant, Charles Quirk, first of a long line of "stop Curley" combinations, had control of the election machinery.

Curley learned quickly and well and profited by experience. Public protests that he had been given a raw deal; the indignation and criticism heaped upon Dever, Quirk and Pea-

Jacket, in many cases by persons whom Curley had not known; the emotional response of voters who believed in fair play, taught him that there is a power in public sympathy that can be translated into political support. He learned that he was abysmally unskilled in oratorical technique and decided to improve it. A politician offering himself for hire to the people has only his appearance and presence, his voice and his record. A tall, heavy, impressive, authoritative stage presence and the clothes to dress the part are assets. Small stature or disfigurement are handicaps to be overcome. A voice that is strong and resonant, an ability to speak distinctly, to choose words exactly and to deliver them with finish complementary to both voice and appearance make up the ideal equipment—and Curley was only partly equipped.

He learned by trial and error that words written to be read silently have not the same ring and sometimes not the same meaning as words written or assembled to be spoken with inflection, emphasis or emotion; that the technique of oratory is far different. A printed speech can make dull reading, and exciting prose can furnish and drape a dreary lecture. He went back to the public library to read and study the orations of Gladstone, Disraeli, Burke, Daniel O'Connell, Daniel Webster, Lincoln, Edward Everett, Phillips Brooks. He had found it difficult to memorize more than twenty lines—about two hundred words of written script. He had tried to improvise extemporaneously and the result had been pitiful.

By this time, Johnson, the grocer, had had enough, but they parted friends. A politician in a grocery store can make more enemies than friends for the management. Curley got a job with the Logan & Johnson bakery supply house as a drummer, calling upon the trade in what was known as the "shoe string" route through northern Massachusetts and part of New Hampshire. His customers, he was warned, were close-fisted Yankees who bought very little. A seasoned traveling salesman taught him the trick of sitting down every morning

from eight until ten, half-filling notebooks with fictitious
orders, because a baker who saw a drummer turning over a
number of leaves would be so impressed by the volume of
sales already made that it would be easier to persuade him to
buy—a form of deception intrinsically harmless. Curley became a good salesman; did much better on the shoe-string
circuit than anyone before him, and made a comfortable
salary.

This was the first of many unimportant transient employ-
ments that were to tide him over between elections. He had
no intention of becoming a great traveling salesman, either.
His goal was an immediate one. He wanted only to be elected
to the common council, a springboard that could catapult
him into position to get control of the ward. He did not plan
his life beyond that, except for the vague idea that the common council and control of the ward must inevitably lead
somewhere, and that either or both were steps toward money.
It is doubtful that at that age he gave much thought to wider
and more extensive political power, what power would mean
and how he would use it. His ideas on its meanings were not
yet well developed. He found the honor and prestige of political office attractive only because men of honor and prestige
made money, lived luxuriously and had almost anything they
wanted. Money itself endowed them with further honor and
prestige.

As he appraised Pea-Jacket, Quirk, Dever, Cuniff, Galvin
and the politicians around him, they were no better endowed
with brains or ability than he was. Since he had been old
enough to understand he had been listening to stories of the
intrigues, the schemes, plots and betrayals that had led them
to success, and he felt sure that in that kind of contest he
had the wit, the inventiveness, enterprise and cleverness to
succeed. He accepted politics as he found it. He had no desire
to change or reform it, and saw no reason why it should be

changed or reformed. He understood it and liked it better as it was.

His first foray had brought him no close friends, no intimates. He talked the language of Roxbury gangs, although he never really could be a member of one. He had friends among them and they knew he could be depended upon to help them, but they had come to look upon him as a person apart, one who approved of them but was too preoccupied by things in which they had no immediate interest to join them.

He wore a derby hat and smoked cigars because he thought they made him look older and more mature. He was a lonely and sometimes a lonesome person. His brother John was close to him but never understood him completely. He was devoted to his mother. She understood him much better. She was stout, matronly. Her grandchildren were to remember her affectionately as "Nanny." He had moved her to a better house at 847 Albany Street. The economic status of the Curleys had already changed remarkably. Mrs. Curley could not foresee what would befall her sons in politics. She could not explain James Michael by anything she knew of her own or her husband's background. She sensed that James would go far, but she could not guess in what direction.

There is a difference between political and personal friendships, between political and personal popularity. James Michael Curley cultivated political friendships and popularity carefully and deliberately. A favor done was a vote made. One vote in a large Irish family converted all voters in that family. The family influenced relatives and neighboring families. A single vote made spread out in progression.

When Dever or Quirk failed to satisfy a complaining voter, he turned to the opposition within the ward. Many of the problems of voters were simple, trivial things that they could have solved for themselves if they knew how: a matter of getting a passport, a boarding pass or line pass at the immigration station, filling out an application for a job, providing needed references, forestalling an eviction, arranging bail, errands that trespassed upon the time and patience of Dever and Quirk. Curley made these chores his additional business. One troubled voter who had been eased brought another troubled voter with another problem. Political, not personal, friendships resulted.

Curley was concerned with their personal problem only to the extent that his interest created or converted votes. It required leg work, not genius, to solve most of them. If Curley did not know the answer, he scoured around to find it, and in the process picked up further information and a backlog of material for use in an attack upon Dever and Quirk to take the ward away from them when the time came.

He became a candidate for the common council again in 1899, dusted off the suit that went to Harvard and had it cleaned and pressed. He had more confidence, more friends, a better grip on the ward and its problems. He had been training himself to memorize longer passages. His standard, stock speech was better organized and he had learned to vary it with extemporaneous interpolations. He had added another year's experience speaking at Hibernian meetings. He had become a more formidable adversary. He could appeal to public sympathy by attacking the ward organization for counting him out.

Dever and Quirk heard about what he was doing. They listened to him and became timid. Young Lochinvar came up from the dump to taunt and ridicule them. At his rallies, he singled out men for whom he had done favors. He told what the favors were, pointed to them for confirmation, and they would nod in agreement where all could see. If he withheld details of the nature of their personal problems, he created an impression of obvious good taste in preserving a confidence and keeping sacred their private affairs.

If he said: "Where would Danny McNamara, down there

in the third row, be if he hadn't come to me in his hour of need? Where would he be, I ask you?" Danny McNamara understood fully and approved. If the audience got an exaggerated impression that Danny would have been in jail or six feet under the sod, that was politics, and McNamara did not mind. He was flattered to be identified publicly by Curley —the next councilor from the district and a rising young political leader. Many who attended the rally went home to report: "You can certainly get a lot more out of young Curley than you can get out of Dever and Quirk. Seems like it's time for a change around here."

First place on the ballot was worth an estimated 20 per cent of the total vote. The percentage was a measure of the illiterate vote and its annual decrease a gauge of progress in education. No matter how ingenious ward leaders were in making diagrams, demonstrating and illustrating on blackboards with chalk, the position of a name on the ballot, numbering candidates and providing facsimiles to be memorized, the defection, a combination of moron and protest votes, persisted. Twenty per cent could mean the difference between success and failure and was worth fighting for.

A candidate for public office, or his representative, went to the city clerk (in later years to the election department) and got nomination papers, and a day was set for filing them. The number of nominating signatures required was based upon the total party vote cast in the preceding election, usually a small and almost insignificant percentage. Signatures were never difficult for an aggressive candidate or machine to get, and position on the ballot was determined by the order of filing. The place for filing was on Milk Street, not far from City Hall.

On the night before the first day for filing, Curley, his brother John, and a group of strong-arms from the Northampton Street gang gathered at the entrance to the Milk Street building. James Michael and John sat with their backs to the door. Members of the gang formed a semicircle on the sidewalk before them and a picket was stationed at the side of the building on each flank, a force organized to defend the door against all rivals who would come to file papers. The plan was not original. It had been common strategy among candidates for more than ten years. In the morning the gang was battered and bloody, but when the registrars and clerks arrived, the two Curleys were still in possession of the door, and Curley's name appeared first on the ballot. The battle of the door grew more violent each year. It ended when ballot law regulation decreed that position henceforth would be determined by lot.

Curley was elected by such a large majority that Dever and Quirk, remembering the indignant protests of a year earlier and still smarting under Curley's sarcastic criticisms of their performance, did not have the courage to count him out. They declared him elected and he was on the way.

Three · Curley Becomes a
Ward Boss

Fifty years of unrestricted immigration had changed the character of the city's population to set the stage for James Michael Curley. When he became a city councilor in 1899, Irish and Irish descendants had expanded to 225,000 and accounted for almost half the city's total population. They had stretched the city's capacity to accommodate them, and had created its worst slums along six miles of water front, where they had first settled. They had multiplied fast, and too many continued to come from Ireland to be absorbed into the city's economy. They forced new building in the suburbs and adjacent towns and compelled expansion of the city by overcrowding it. The city continued to grow in size in proportion to their rate of increase and to the manner in which they spread out.

The first Boston Irish leaders had been employment agents or padrones among uneducated new immigrants, designated as such by employers for convenience in dealing with them, or assuming authority as spokesmen for them. In the natural course of events, these leaders discovered political power, made use of it, became ward bosses and political machines evolved. Social reforms originated with them, not because they were humanitarians, but as political devices by which they could continue to control votes and to expand and consolidate political, not social gains.

Some ward bosses had already departed the scene and others were at the peak of their power, unwittingly maneuvering themselves into a position to be toppled, when James Michael Curley came upon the stage. Those who had been deposed had served their purpose. The days of those who remained were already numbered. The first generation of American-born of Irish descent were beginning to look upon ward bosses doubtfully, skeptically, and sometimes with contempt. American-born voters of Irish descent were not, in general, like their fathers, loyal, trusting subjects of the boss.

For the first time in its history, the Boston Irish outnumbered Yankee-Brahmins in the city council, and twenty-six-year-old James Michael Curley got his first political training in a blustering majority, new to power, feeling its way, hesitant, at times fumbling and not too effective. Politics absorbed Curley. It was his sport, his release, his escape. He had no other interests. He reveled in the plots and counterplots, in the advancement and frustration of the ambitious around him. He seemed to have an uncanny instinct for it. For seven years he had listened to stories, sometimes factual, usually biased and prejudiced, tortured explanations of the segregation of Irish Catholics, a segregation that actually was either voluntary or convenient, and not discriminatory, although the fact was never acknowledged. The faults of the Yankee-Brahmins were magnified. Their virtues and the good they did in helping and protecting the Irish, particularly during the fanatic Know-Nothing era, were ignored and minimized. Deserving or not, Yankee-Brahmins had become the traditional political enemies of the Boston Irish.

When the Irish were a minority in Boston, they were clannish, closely knit, banded together and presented a solid front. Now that the battle was all but won, they talked threateningly about the Boston Brahmins to divert attention from the more interesting spectacle behind the scenes where, as always when the common danger was passed, they fell to fighting among themselves to decide who would be master. Curley had a genius for that kind of game, but the ward powers who gathered in the council chamber did not discern it soon enough. His youth misled them.

Curley attracted no attention for his oratory, either inside or outside the council chamber, but he was a busy and eager freshman, alive to every chance to introduce orders that would be popular among large groups of voters. He introduced one to provide a permanent Saturday half-holiday for city employees. Mayor Hart could not very well refuse the move without sacrificing the support of city employees. They thanked Curley for it. It became the first item in his political record. He introduced another to abolish what was known as "the vault system" in public schools by equipping the buildings with sanitary plumbing. That did not make him unpopular with the parents of schoolchildren. He introduced another to put teeth for enforcement into an eight-hour-day city ordinance. He was not anticipating becoming a candidate for mayor then. He was thinking of the votes of city employees in his own ward and of a day he could foresee when he would fight Dever and Quirk for control of the ward.

He discovered some of his shortcomings and set about correcting them. He studied and memorized the rules of order and became a good parliamentarian. He had a good voice for public speaking and realized that he did not know how to make the most of it. He was better than average, but not good. He knew of no one who could teach him technique and began his own experimentation to develop it. He was the only member of the council who would contemplate such an act

and attempt it seriously. He haunted the public library and
became a midnight-oil burner, reading histories until he fell
asleep.

His political future motivated everything he did. He quit
the bakery-supply business and got a job as an insurance agent
for the New England Life Insurance Company. In less than
a year, he and his brother John opened their own agency on
Milk Street. John had much more time for the business than
James, but James appears to have been unusually successful in
finding prospects for John among his political acquaintances.

His house on Harrison Avenue became a political headquarters, a place of pilgrimage for supplicants in the ward.
Many of them were repeaters, always in trouble, and had long
since worn out their welcome at the ward room on Hampden
Street where Dever and Quirk were weary of taking care of
them. Others shopped both places to find out where they
could get the most for nothing. Curley interviewed all comers,
never turned one away. This constant procession was sometimes a trial to his mother, who had a long report for him
when he got home each day.

She looked at her son with a strange and puzzled awe. Because of him she had come quite a distance in a short time.
He had taken her from the drudgery of scrubbing floors and
given her a life of reasonable comfort and ease. She realized
that he was now a man of importance although she could
not comprehend fully what he did or why he did it. It was
honest, as far as she knew, and he worked for what he got.

Still serving in the council in 1900, Curley wasted no time.
He became a candidate for chairman of the Democratic ward
committee. He attacked the divided leadership of Dever and
Quirk, and his statement angered Pea-Jacket, still chairman,
in name at least, of the Democratic City Committee. Pea-
Jacket characterized James Michael Curley as an overam-
bitious upstart and decided to reorganize his ward and to
teach him a lesson. It was too late for that.

Pea-Jacket did not realize how much headway Curley had made. James Michael had already divided the ward. The name of Curley became anathema to Pea-Jacket, Quirk and Dever, and not entirely because of James Michael. Another, unrelated, Thomas F. Curley, who had served Pea-Jacket faithfully for years, had been by-passed when Pea-Jacket handed the ward over to Dever and Quirk. Tom Curley wanted political advancement and felt that he should be sent to the city council. Pea-Jacket disagreed. James Michael immediately formed an alliance with his clansman, trading his support to send Tom Curley to the council for Tom's support to make James Michael Curley ward boss.

Every favor done by James Michael had placed a voter under an obligation to him, and there were too many of them for Pea-Jacket. Curley's tongue had always been sharp and sarcastic. A year's service in the council had sharpened it more. From soapboxes on street corners he criticized and ridiculed Pea-Jacket and the two men he called his puppets. He became the voice of a new and rising generation. He spoke the language of the street-corner gangs and they understood him. His persuasion divided the ward further and brought violence. He placed the old and the new in conflict, chiefly by way of pitting personalities and not so much by political methods. He was not crusading to upset the system but to change its leadership, arguing that he could do it better. Those who were under obligation to him joined enthusiastically. The indifferent and the unpledged fell in with them. There was an impressive bloc in the ward more than satisfied with the leadership of Dever and Quirk, loyal to them and to Pea-Jacket, and the inevitable older voters who resented change anyway. They, in turn, influenced younger voters, members of gangs in their families, and compelled loyalty to Pea-Jacket and his machine.

All the elements for parochial civil conflict were present. The contest was hot-tempered and at times vicious and bloody. There were gang fights at street-corner rallies, battles with sticks, clubs and sidewalk bricks, attempts by each side to prevent the other from speaking. When the dust settled and the votes were counted, James Michael Curley was boss of Ward Seventeen, elected by a slim margin of seventeen votes. There was no chance to count him out. This had been a family fight with both sides watching the ballots.

James Michael made a number of bitter personal enemies. The close friends and supporters of Pea-Jacket Maguire, Dever and Quirk would plague him from time to time for half a century. He acquired the hatred of the envious, part of the price he now learned every politician must pay in every campaign, and he got his first bath of newspaper notoriety, the youngest ward boss in the city, although by no means the youngest in its history—Pea-Jacket was only twenty-four when he took over the ward; Curley was twenty-six.

James Michael Curley was publicized as a boy wonder, tall, handsome, dark-eyed, with black hair. He packed a wallop in either right or left hand that earned the respect and admiration of tough gangsters. He had no court or police record. He was the promising young political leader with a bright future, one of the most eligible bachelors in the city, and yet he was still shy, embarrassed and tongue-tied in the presence of women.

He passed the collection box each Sunday in Saint James Church, and continued to teach Sunday school. He was on his way up to higher honors in the Ancient Order of Hibernians. No taint of scandal had ever touched him, and in the trite, ironic language of later-day politics, he was good to his mother. He was known to be studious, something of a bookworm, and sometimes astonished rally crowds by quoting poetry "like a schoolteacher." Parents and the Catholic clergy approved him without reservation. He was the most popular man in the ward, and yet few people knew or understood him.

His principles were hard to define. It is doubtful that he could have defined them himself. He had a strong, uncompromising streak of morality where women and sex were concerned. He boasted that he had never taken a dime from anyone in the ward for doing a favor, no matter how much time, effort and money he expended in achieving it, and this seems to be correct. At least such a charge was never made against him. He boasted that as a councilor or candidate for public office he had never taken a donation from a person who could not afford it, without explaining the obvious implication that he did and would take donations from those who could afford it.

Curley had accepted the system as he found it. It was his ambition to master it, not reform it. What other ward leaders had done, he would do in a larger way, even on a magnificent scale. He had vision and inventiveness. Greater skill would come in time. The vote of the ward could not be controlled by a leader who took money from the average and underpaid wage earners, and the complete vote of the ward was worth more outside the ward than whatever income might be developed within it. From the very day that he took over, his services were free to any resident.

He went to New York to examine and study Tammany. He returned with all details of its organization, a blueprint for duplicating it in his ward and a good deal of sound political advice. He adopted its name for the old ward meeting room on Hampden Street, financed it, established a treasury and assessed dues upon the members. He began collecting from merchants, tradesmen and those who did business in the ward, funds to be spent in charity. He announced that preparations for Thanksgiving and Christmas would begin thereafter in June. Politics became his full-time job. He posted a notice that he would be at the club Wednesday and Friday evenings for office hours to interview the unemployed and the needy.

Twenty to fifty residents came there each night. He was

efficient and businesslike, divided them into three batches: those who needed money, food, clothing, coal or wood; those in legal difficulty with landlords, installment houses or the police; and the unemployed. He questioned them crisply and quickly, lectured some, sympathized with others, wrote orders to butchers, grocers and fuel suppliers; called up doctors, made notes to write letters or to get in touch with creditors and handed out money sparingly. He kept a file of names with brief notes on case histories. Otherwise there was no red tape.

He instructed the second batch to meet him at the corner of Mount Pleasant Street and Blue Hill Avenue at nine o'clock the next morning and spent the next three hours in courts or police stations, arranging bail, talking with district court judges and probation officers or the district attorney. Many were juvenile cases. He had no time or patience for drunks or wife beaters. They were unreliable voters and he classified them as nuisances.

He met the unemployed in the afternoon at City Hall, handling each as an individual case. A regulation that prohibited members of the city council from soliciting employment for anyone from public corporations was more honored in the breach than in the observance. He found jobs for them in one place or another. He saved an average of twenty-five persons from criminal records, stayed an average of seven evictions or repossessions of furniture, found an average of five hundred jobs each year for the succeeding ten years. He had little time left for the insurance business, and yet he estimated that he never made less than one hundred dollars a week. Whether in salary or commission or both, that was an extraordinary income in 1901, especially considering the limited time he had to devote to the insurance business.

As a ward boss he immediately became a city councilor of much greater importance and political weight than he had been during his first year. His interests changed. Juvenile delinquents were taking up too much of his time. Teen-agers got into trouble after school hours and at night. One cause was an absence of playgrounds and clubhouses. School yards were restricted after school hours and were too small to serve neighborhoods. Children played in the streets because the dump was too uneven for games. As an immediate cure he introduced an order to prohibit admission of children under twelve to places of amusement unless accompanied by parents.

The design was to keep them off the streets. Going to a place of amusement was an excuse accepted by police when they questioned children at night. Denied the excuse, police, theoretically, would send them home. It was an involved and circuitous approach, and it didn't work. He introduced an order to raise the pay of city laborers from two dollars to two dollars and a quarter a day. There were a number of them in his ward. Personally financed public welfare was expensive. He introduced an order to transfer part of the load from ward charity to the city treasury, specifying that "temporary aid be furnished the worthy poor in times of distress without stigmatizing them as paupers."

Most early social legislation in Massachusetts came about in much the same way. The age limit children must reach, before being freed of legal obligation to attend school, was raised not because ward or city bosses thought education was good for them. It was raised to solve a different problem. As the population increased, a labor shortage disappeared and a labor surplus was created. A time came when ward bosses found it difficult to keep heads of families employed, let alone their children. When the pressure of hundreds of voting fathers for jobs for their children became disturbing, and in some cases frightening, political bosses seized upon compulsory education as an expedient. Keeping children in school until they reached the age of sixteen would defer the problem of finding work for them until the bosses found a way to cope with the problem; and they hoped education might solve it by giving children enough training to find jobs for themselves.

Ultimately ward bosses adopted the rule: one job to a family. They depended upon that one job to keep all voters in a family in line. They did not realize that respect for education was so profound among immigrants that a single high-school graduate could influence a family and sometimes an entire neighborhood; that an educated, intelligent and informed electorate would turn upon them and destroy them. Thus the first great social reform in Massachusetts did not come because the ward and city bosses were farsighted and progressive, forcing an extension of compulsory education through the legislature; they proved too shortsighted for their own good, and dug their own political graves.

The orders in council introduced by Curley may appear to be trivial, but they were in fact important. Most of them compelled reforms; and he introduced them not to keep supplicants off his neck but because he sensed that the reforms themselves would be popular and would create votes.

Equally important for his political future were the lobbyists, legpullers, logrollers and the big fellows who really ran the city. He met them first while he was in the common council. The council was Democratic, but City Hall was still Republican. Hart was a Republican mayor. The board of aldermen was Republican and Curley had a close view of a well-oiled, smooth-working Republican machine.

That was as far as he got when his term ended. He kept his agreement with Tom Curley. In the campaign of 1901, the ward dutifully nominated and elected Tom to the city council. James Michael had spent enough time in this kindergarten of politics. The next step in orderly political progress was representative in the General Court (the state legislature) and he took it.

Elected governor of the state for a second term was Winthrop Murray Crane, thirty-seven-year-old heir to the fortune of the Cranes of Dalton who manufactured the distinctive, secret formula paper used in United States currency. Henry Cabot Lodge, Senior, was United States Senator.

Proposals had been projected for the coming legislature calling for the expenditure of exceptionally large amounts of money—$5,000,000, for example, to eliminate railroad grade crossings; a topographical map of the state, undertaken at an estimated cost of $40,000, had already run into $250,000. Republican rule was beginning to show signs of wasteful extravagance. Graft and corruption were not restricted to the cities, nor were they the exclusive evils of Irish Democrats. The example was there. The city's growing pains were being felt by the state. Crane had protested during his first term that the state was interfering too much in Boston's business. He vetoed a bill to build a subway under Boston's Washington Street and insisted that the city ought to build it and lease it to the railway.

A bucket-shop bill was in prospect. National and savings banks were to be regulated. Union labor, growing fast, was feeling its strength. Seven hundred union members marched upon the State House demanding a law to permit fifty thousand voters to submit constitutional amendments directly to the people on the ballot—and got it. The legislature would be asked to legalize a ten-hour day, fifty-eight-hour week for women and children in manufacturing and mercantile establishments; and there was a proposal to liberalize Sunday laws for the sale of soft drinks and liquor.

It was clear that 1901 would be a busy year for lobbyists, for banks, stock and bond houses, railroads and railways, mill owners, merchants, wets and drys, and labor. All of these factions, except labor, were able to spend limited or unlimited amounts of money. Organized labor had votes, not money, and its growth was beginning to worry conservative legislators.

That was the outline of the legislative picture to be filled in when James Michael Curley went to the State House.

Four · From Legislature to Jail

THE STATE HOUSE opened a wider vista for the boss of Ward Seventeen. He met the most popular Brahmins of Boston, among them a few of the best intellects in the legislature. A small fish in a big pond, he had a limited field of operations. He had no important committee assignments. Though he was now a far better than average public speaker, oratory, no matter how finished and polished, influenced no votes in this assembly where legislation was guided by committees and where arguments pro and con were exhausted long before a bill reached the floor. Nevertheless even as a freshman he made an impression. He picked apart proposed legislation indiscriminately. Brahmin members could not decide whether to approve him or snub him. Some of them were to become his bitterest antagonists.

Charles H. Innes was the political leader of the Boston bluebloods. He had put together a formidable Republican machine in an outlandish combination of the best families of Back Bay and the owners and inmates of South End boarding houses and brothels. Silk- and cotton-stocking districts adjoined, and he made full use, politically, of what he had. A social-set lawyer, Innes also conducted a law school. He and Curley understood each other and got along so well from the beginning that Curley became one of Innes' law students. Curley learned a great deal from Innes. They became close friends and made deals that were mutually profitable.

Almost every member of that legislature, at some time, either would join Curley or fight against him. Their lives were to be affected in some way by him. They were to profit or lose by his later operations. A time would come when they would admire or hate him. There would be no middle ground. Yet Curley's life would be influenced but little by them. Andrew J. Peters, William S. McNary and John A. Sullivan, members of that legislature, would come back into his life later. Among the rest was a large group whom Curley would refer to publicly for half a century as "my enemies."

Curley came into the legislature with no legislative program of his own and with no preconceived opinions on legislation that he knew was to come before it, except labor. He went there chiefly to round out his education and to add another qualification to his record for future public office. He had no intention of remaining in the legislature and making a career of it. He acknowledged that he was a transient, passing through the House of Representatives for a single term, looking around, interesting himself in whatever legislation intrigued him, bills that would attract votes and whatever else came his way.

He made only one statement before taking office. "I feel it is my duty," he told his Tammany Club, "to be right on labor measures."

It was not hard for him to arrive at that decision. The American Federation of Labor was growing so fast that manufacturers, paying hands nine and ten dollars a week, an average of $449 a year, were alarmed almost to the point of panic. In six years, from 1898 to 1904, the American Federation of Labor grew in membership from 278,000 to 1,676,000. Labor in industrial Boston was on the march. Lines were

being drawn nationally in the long war then taking shape.
Curley had no hand in charting the course of labor in Boston.
He rode the crest of the wave. Anything else would have
been folly.

He voted to permit strikers to picket; to compel building
contractors to hire union labor; to protect women and children from occupational diseases and industrial accidents, and
to make mandatory the payment of overtime. He voted to
exempt Spanish War veterans from civil service. The bill was
defeated. He voted to increase the salaries of Grand Army
veterans employed at the State House. The bill passed. He
was very careful of his early record. His votes, even for lost
causes, were designed to impress the people of his ward and
of the city.

There were social evils crying for reform, but his remedies
were mild. There was, for example, an inhuman truancy law
that required the arrest and confinement of stubborn children
who were consistently absent from school. Enthusiasm for
compulsory education was so strong that children either
would be educated forcibly or go to jail. Curley presented
and secured the enactment of a law permitting the release
of truants in the event of illness or death of either parent.
It remained for a later and more enlightened legislature to
devise a sensible law.

In the meantime, with Tom Curley as his acknowledged
assistant, he was forming Ward Seventeen into a tight organization under his complete control. It differed from the New
York Tammany Hall pattern in but one detail: campaign
workers had no titles, military or otherwise; there were no
precinct captains, no lieutenants; every member of the club
was of equal rank.

Members assigned to jobs in political campaigns were told
what to do, and no matter how efficient they turned out to
be, were not advanced from one responsibility to another.
They were selected by Curley who decided and determined

their capabilities, an arrangement certain to seed a feud with
Tom Curley. From the point of view of a ward boss this was
a distinct improvement upon Tammany Hall. It nourished
no competitors and encouraged no threats to the authority
of the boss or to his uninterrupted tenure of office. It made
the Roxbury Tammany Club Curley's personal machine.
Members would be loyal to him and not to the machine. He
was the machine. There were no committees, no kitchen
cabinet, no personal advisers on policy. Curley made all decisions.

The rest was standard political-machine practice, a sure-fire
vote-winning and vote-holding line: get the jobs for the boys.
Help them when they're in trouble. Help the widows and
orphans. Take up collections to bury the destitute. Stop evictions for nonpayment of rent. Let nobody in the ward go
hungry, and be sure that everyone has a happy Thanksgiving
and Christmas.

To iron out factional differences Curley brought together
as often as he could as many of the voters of the ward as he
could persuade. He instituted annual picnics and powwows
at Centennial and Caledonian groves, inviting even those who
had moved away from the ward to return for an annual re-
union. He offered free food, races, sports, prizes, entertainment features for the kids, like a Punch and Judy show, a
Negro who could drink a pailful of water and with a twist
of his ear expel it. And there was always a "speaker of prominence" to talk at some time during the day, a political guest
selected by Curley.

The club and the State House took up all his time. He was
at the club at eight-thirty in the morning, running his free
employment service. He reported at the State House at eleven
o'clock for committee work, and never missed a session of
the legislature. He returned to the club at night to listen to
grievances and make decisions. At least twice a month, and
sometimes once a week, the clubroom was filled and an

audience looked up at him and listened, sometimes astonished, sometimes bewildered, but never bored.

He discussed education at one meeting, encouraged the
young to study hard, exhorted adolescents to buckle down,
apply themselves and prepare for college, pleaded with parents to see to it that their children did so and discussed
manners and morals. Members of the Tammany Club looked
at each other in puzzled wonder. Some were so carried away
by his words that they succumbed to an illusion that they
were in church and had to be restrained from standing and
genuflecting when he finished. He discussed the tariff, problems that were over their heads, tried to reduce them to
simple, everyday terms and watched their reactions.

He gave as much thought to his Tammany Club talks as a
preacher does to the preparation of a sermon. He wrote
speeches in longhand, memorized them, rehearsed delivery,
changed inflection and modulation until the speech suited
him, and tried out effects upon this audience. He would travel
miles to hear a good speaker.

He could gauge his progress by the attention he got and
by the response of his audiences. He spent Saturday and Sunday afternoons on Boston Common Mall, dedicated to free
speech, where any speaker, crackpot fanatic or sound re-
former, could sound off upon any subject. A speaker who
interested him was invited to appear before Tammany Club,
always persuaded, no matter what his subject, that he would
find a sympathetic and intelligent audience. Curley had a
mischievous sense of humor. Sometimes he invited speakers
on unpopular subjects, assuring them of a friendly audience,
to see what would happen and how the speaker would behave
when he found himself facing a hostile audience. A few of
these experiments ended in near riots. The hall was lighted
by gas. It was easy for anybody to throw the place into sudden darkness by blowing air into a jet outside the hall.

A speaker who opposed freedom for Ireland, described by

Curley at an earlier meeting as a Harvard professor, was hit on the head by a brass cuspidor. Curley saved another from being thrown through a window. These specimen samples were invariably stunned by the treatment they got. From the point of view of the audience this was usually very funny and good sport. The opinions of the misled but trusting evangelists were never recorded.

The clubroom became his experimental laboratory and the people in it his unsuspecting guinea pigs. He was perfecting his oratory, learning by trial and error all the things that go to make the finished public speaker.

Following his own curious method, by doing, by study, observation and comparison, Curley was learning more about the technique of public speaking than any teacher, voice coach, or established course of instruction could impart. He analyzed and classified for himself the effect upon an audience of the pitch of vocal sounds, the soothing quality of low notes, the excitement of high ones, the need for variation in modulation when an audience became restive. He experimented with the flow of syllables, speeding up and slowing down the rate of enunciation. He found that a rapid-fire delivery with lips drawn wide over bare teeth, fists clenched, eyes glaring and flashing and a torrent of fighting words could incite an audience to riot; but if, just before that peak was reached, he suddenly relaxed, smiled, smoothed his hair, pitched his voice to a low, vibrant organ note, slowed down the tempo of words and syllables, the temper of the audience subsided.

He developed his own distinctive style of oratorical showmanship. The size of audiences in Tammany Club grew. As the word spread throughout the city, people from other wards came to hear Curley speak. It was a free show and certain to be good. Anything could happen there.

One term in the House of Representatives was enough. He

took the next step, became a candidate for the board of aldermen and it was agreed that Tom Curley would go to the State Senate. Patrick A. Collins became a candidate for mayor of Boston. Collins was a potato-famine immigrant brought to the city from Fermoy, County Cork, by his widowed mother in 1848 when he was four years old. He was an errand boy in a law office at twelve, a coal miner in Ohio at fourteen. He returned to Boston at eighteen, worked his way through Harvard by upholstering chairs, was elected to the State Senate while still a student and became its youngest member in 1870 at the age of twenty-six.

He was graduated from the law school with high honors a year later and immediately was admitted to the bar. He was elected to Congress, became a power in State Democratic politics and an Irish-American leader of such stature that his name was as well known in Ireland as it was in Boston. His portrait hung beside that of Charles Stewart Parnell in the headquarters of the League of Finian Brotherhoods in Dublin. He had helped elect Grover Cleveland president, and was appointed consul general in London.

There was little doubt that he would be elected. Curley became one of his supporters, toured the city speaking for him and guaranteed to turn the vote of his ward over to him. The Ward Seventeen machine was now well oiled and nearing mechanical perfection. P. A. Collins was certain to allot him a large amount of patronage, or so Curley thought, but after Collins' election, the amount of patronage fell short of the inventory of the unemployed.

Bartholemew Fahey and James Hughes were two workers who had earned reward, and there were no jobs available for them. The Curleys could not fail. Reputation and prestige, though not at stake, would have been affected. Two letter carriers were needed in Boston, and the Post Office Department was under civil service.

Fahey and Hughes were rugged, healthy, stout enough to

walk beats, intelligent enough to deliver mail, but they were doubtful of their ability to pass the examination. Applications were filed for them. They were notified, and on the appointed day the two Curleys, James Michael and Thomas, turned up in the examining rooms in the Federal Building. James Michael impersonated Bartholemew Fahey. Tom Curley impersonated James Hughes. They were recognized by a court attendant who turned them in.

The episode attracted city-wide attention. Both were now candidates for public office. They were tried in the newspapers as well as in the courtroom, and the newspaper trial was far more dramatic than the perfunctory proceedings before Federal Judge James Lowell of the Boston Lowells. Heman W. Chapin, a Yankee lawyer, well grounded in constitutional law, defended them. He argued that two federal statutes combined to deprive the Curleys of their constitutional rights. It was seriously suggested that an applicant for a job, prevented by circumstances from taking an examination, had a right to be represented by proxy. The law did not expressly prohibit it, nor was it expressly prohibited for the proxy to assume the name of the applicant. Chapin argued that no fraud was perpetrated upon the government. The intent of the two Curleys had been only to get two jobs for two men who were capable of doing the work, and it was made clear that both men needed the jobs.

Judge Lowell listened, sentenced the two Curleys to ninety days in jail, and later denounced their effrontery in conducting campaigns for public office from their cells. However, for the second time in his political experience James Michael Curley profited by public sympathy. A transient and soon forgotten emotion among voters, it made a deep and lasting impression upon him. When all else failed, public sympathy could turn the tide of an election. He learned the lesson well and thereafter applied it as a principle of practical politics.

There is no doubt that the Curleys were favored prisoners

in Suffolk County Prison, better known as Charles Street Jail. A small way station for felons on their way to penitentiaries and a house of correction for minor misdemeanors, it had no factory or workshop and inmates employed themselves at whatever handiwork attracted them. The library was well stocked and books also could be ordered from the Boston Public Library. It was not too bad a place to be, though it did not then offer the conveniences that it would under Sheriff Dowd thirty-five years later.

Curley was thirty years old now. For nine years he had been working at politics with steady concentration. The hours had been long and the work hard. Imprisonment gave him a rest, a chance to read, to take stock of himself and to plan for the future. Politics and the public service had been an interesting and profitable profession. His mother was now well fixed. His brother John, still in the insurance business, now owned a farm in Hopkinton. Curley himself had had everything he wanted in the way of food, clothing, travel and entertainment. He had been to various conventions as a delegate of the Ancient Order of Hibernians. He was still single. He had a reputation as a champion of the poor and under-privileged, although the fact was inescapable that whatever improvement he achieved for them was a by-product of his larger ambition to be financially independent and politically powerful.

Improving the lot of the needy brought him multiplying dividends in votes. There is no doubt that he enjoyed being a benefactor to the people of his ward and that in some measure he had earned their adulation, gratitude and extravagant praise.

During that period in his life he seems to have been a genuine political Robin Hood, even though his helping hand was extended only to make sure that those he favored never would bite it, and that they would be well fed, healthy and enthusiastic enough to push him up higher politically when the chance came. He had enough money for his own needs, enough to take care of his mother, and a surplus left over to spread around where it would do him the most good politically. He did not gamble money, except on his future. He drank temperately, smoked moderately, dressed well, but not extravagantly. He still wore the dress suit that went to Harvard when making political campaigns. He had no expensive personal vices.

He saved no money, and yet money was never a problem to him. He could always get it, although he never explained precisely how or where. No ward boss has ever explained how he got money. It is known that people gave Curley money, and yet the legend is that he never asked for it or demanded it. He was always engaged in a political campaign and money could be given to him for that purpose. He was not investigated at that stage in his career.

He did a good deal of thinking about his past and future. He wondered, among other things, whether the goal was worth it, a misgiving that would continue to nag him from time to time. In another business or profession, he might have been well on his way to success and wealth after ten years. Politics had not been the short cut to riches that he had anticipated. It had led to comfort and prominence instead. Ten years' experience in any business or calling is not easily discarded. Whether he would have it or not, he was now trapped in politics and there was no escape from it any more than from the jail in which he was imprisoned. He could not now make as much money in any other business as in politics; and saving money did not suit his temperament. He could always get money without taking it out of a bank account; so he kept no bank account.

This first official blemish upon his record is either a key to his character, the origin of a further change in it, or both.

Falsifying an application blank, impersonating another and perjury could be right if the end justified these means, according to Curley's reasoning. Outside the courtroom, before his friends and followers, he defended himself on that ground, and the same defense was to crop up intermittently under similar circumstances during the rest of his public life.

Curley rationalized his conduct to his own satisfaction. In this manner, it became a matter of personal principle. Gifted with a hypnotic power of persuasion, Curley could convince others that an unlawful means to achieve an end was right, if it could be established that the end itself was just and desirable. The Fahey case thus became Curley's personal precedent, and as such often decided his behavior.

Out of a poor case in the courtroom he fashioned a good one before the people, explaining that he had deliberately, after full contemplation, broken an unjust law, interpolating as an aside his opinions of laws for the rich and laws for the poor and laws that kept honest men from getting jobs. Since a majority approved of him on election day, he correctly took it for granted that they approved of his defiance of this particular law.

Popular endorsement convinced him in this case that he was qualified to decide when, and under what circumstances, an expedient end would justify breaking a law, rule or regulation. If he were caught, and lost in court, he could always win before a bar of local public opinion where the offense would be condoned. No rules of evidence, practice or procedure prevailed there, and there was no advocate present at a rally or on a public platform to present the other side of the case.

Imprisonment also renewed an inhibition, the natural desire to keep his record clean. Now that the entry had been made, it never could be erased, and as a result, his attitude toward his record changed, a common effect as a consequence upon any person, and not peculiar to Curley. He capitalized the fault, declared that he would do it again, and was complimented and praised for his courage and his deep personal interest in the voters of his ward and characterized as a great humanitarian. What first appeared to be personal disgrace and misfortune was turned into political blessing.

There was nothing corrective in Curley's punishment. From beginning to end the whole formula could be modified to fit any transgression where it could be shown that the needy or the deserving, whether one person or the population of a whole city, benefited or were improved by what he did. That Curley benefited, too, was acknowledged, but was usually dismissed as a consideration.

Social service was still in its infancy. A few such workers were on the city payroll. The Brahmins had been responsible for that. They had been sympathetic to the new science while the Boston Irish had looked upon it contemptuously as transgressing upon the jurisdiction of the church. Elderly John Pettingell was superintendent of institutions and under the law had to visit them twice a year. When he returned to City Hall after his annual inspection of Charles Street Jail, he told a social-service worker: "I met this James Michael Curley there. He's one of the most interesting persons I've seen in all my years of service—a fine, good-looking young man. He was sitting in his cell with four books on a table beside him. I asked him what he was reading and he said: 'The Life of Thomas Jefferson.' He had already read every book in the prison library. I talked with him for half an hour.

"You're a young woman," he went on, "and I'm an old man. Years after I'm dead, you'll be hearing about that man Curley."

Five · An Alderman Marries

ALDERMAN CURLEY and Standish Willcox were the only two persons who never had to wait for a chair in Conway's barbershop not far from Saint Phillip's Church on Harrison Avenue. Any man gladly would surrender his place to Alderman Curley and wait another turn. That was easy to understand. Why they stood aside and made way for Standish Willcox was not; because following tradition in rough, tough Ward Seventeen, they should have shelled eggs upon him.

Standish symbolized in his appearance almost everything that the Ward Seventeen Irish hated. He spoke slowly, deliberately, with an unctuous, precise Oxford accent. He was tall and impressive, as straight as a ramrod with an air of one who had served with distinction in the King's fusileers at Khartoum or in the Sudan. He wore pince-nez glasses with flowing ribbon attached, and had a habit of peering under the lenses as though he were looking down his nose at a world of inferiors.

Patrons of Conway's barbershop knew almost nothing about him and would not dare inquire. They were awed by him and assumed he must be somebody important. He was

62

the only man, except for Curley, who could walk along Harrison Avenue wearing tall silk hat, Inverness cape, appropriately correct clothing beneath it including spats and carrying a malacca stick, and survive. He was suspected alternately of being an undercover British agent or a member of the United States secret service.

When Curley first heard Standish Willcox' voice in the barbershop, his sensitive ears caught the stranger's diction and he turned toward him, as their faces were being lathered, to strike up a barber-chair friendship. Curley was in an awkward position to size him up. Standish was casual and indifferent, obviously not too impressed by the alderman as a local celebrity. When Curley observed the size and appearance of Standish as they stepped out of their chairs, he was the more impressed.

They met often in the barbershop after that, and the nature of their conversations astonished and bewildered those waiting in the shop. Standish was well educated and well informed. He knew what was going on, what was happening on Beacon Hill, in Curley's ward and in City Hall. He read newspapers and magazines, and from the viewpoint of barbershop habitués, he was on the same intellectual level with the ward boss. Curley sometimes asked for opinions and listened to what he had to say. As a mystery man, Willcox piqued Curley's interest. It was he who first learned that Willcox wrote for newspapers, although what he wrote and for what newspaper or newspapers, not even Curley could discover. Standish was neither a shrinking violet nor an openly revealed lily. He could chide the ward boss good-naturedly and gently, and say things to him that others in the shop never would dare to say.

Curley could do nothing for Standish Willcox. He wanted nothing, asked for nothing. He neither encouraged nor discouraged close friendship. He did not come to meetings of the Tammany Club, but he seemed to know what went on there. He began to follow Curley's career closely, to offer a suggestion or a word of intelligent counsel now and then. Curley discovered that Standish's adroit mind often provided a missing link in inspired strategy.

"You'll be working for me yet," Curley told him.

Standish shrugged his shoulders. "Possibly."

Republicans were still a majority on the board of aldermen with such antique, historical Brahmin names as Reginald Bangs, Dudley Cotton and Harry Frothingham among them. Curley was the leader of the Democratic opposition, too skillful and too swift for all other contenders in his own party. Mercurial and unpredictable, he exasperated the orderly-minded Brahmins. They opposed him instinctively. He made use of that by having colleagues introduce orders that he fought bitterly, so that Brahmins would gang up to support it, only to learn when the order had passed that Curley had foxed them into giving him what he wanted (and appeared not to want). He got a playground in his ward that way.

All day laborers were laid off on stormy days, and there were a number of them in Curley's ward. Foremen and clerical help were paid. An order to bracket day laborers with foremen and clerical help would never pass. Curley introduced an order to economize further by laying off all foremen, who would have no workers to direct on rainy days, and all clerical help. The Brahmins would not have that, and it was defeated, so that a substitute order to pay all day laborers on rainy days could pass. The board was so bedazzled and bewildered by the constant stream of orders, by its physical inability to winnow the chaff from the wheat among them, and by Curley's parliamentary sleight-of-hand—now you see it and now you don't —that it voted for a number of things it had never intended: pensions, one day off in five for firemen, union wages for city building firemen and engineers, for visiting hours that had never been permitted in City Hospital. Never a good dancer himself, Curley introduced an order prohibiting midnight dances.

He introduced a number of humane and progressive orders that became city law. Two thirteen-year-old boys in his ward were arrested for tossing a ball in the street in violation of a city ordinance, a misdemeanor. They were fined ten dollars each, had no money, appealed their cases and were held for the October sitting of the Superior Court. Curley argued that an admonition from the judge would have been sufficient and introduced an order that the mayor be instructed to petition the General Court at its next session for legislation to authorize judges of municipal or district courts to release, on their own recognizance, minors brought before them for committing misdemeanors. The order was translated into law.

He demanded a high school specializing in shorthand, typewriting, bookkeeping and other business subjects. Out of it grew the Boston High School of Commerce. Against this, he insisted that Irish history be an elective study in all high schools. Another order resulted in a city ordinance for the sale of graves in Mount Hope Cemetery, to save the city poor from pauper burial. Another compelled the city to spend five thousand dollars a year for ice for public drinking fountains during summer months. He forced a change in the truancy law from long to short-term sentences when a fourteen-year-old boy was sent to jail for two years because he went to a circus instead of to school.

He hopped about nimbly from one cause to another and kept the mayor, the board of aldermen and the city council confused and busy. Any hint from organized labor was enough to cause an order requiring action. As a result a padrone system of using cellars, sheds, barns and stables to house contract labor was investigated and prohibited; a move to uniform all city employees was killed; City Hospital scrubwomen were raised from $2.60 a week to $6.00 a week with meals furnished; union musicians replaced the free music of army, navy and marine bands at city celebrations; and henceforth a union label had to appear on all horseshoes purchased by the city.

James Michael Curley first met Mary Emilda Herlihy at a Saint Phillip's Church minstrel show in Dudley Street Opera House. She was a slender brunette, pretty and attractive, and had a quick bright mind. Her educational, social and family background had been no better than his. She had been a parishioner in the church where James still was superintendent of the Sunday school and taught catechism. She kept house for her father, a widower on Burke Street, Roxbury. Curley singled her out and began calling at her house. He took her about with him, and soon it was publicly recognized that they were going together.

It was a strange and curious courtship because Curley's time inevitably was divided between Mary Herlihy and his constituents. His evenings with her were always interrupted by emergencies that could not wait. He was consulted at awkward times on ward or city affairs; but Mary was more than tolerant and understanding, she was genuinely interested in these problems as he relayed and outlined them to her. She turned them over in her own mind, thought about them sometimes for days and gave him her own considered opinions, usually sound, sane, intelligent and reasonable. James soon discovered that he had found a perfect companion. He told her more about himself and his problems than he had ever told any person in his life before, and he developed a wholesome respect for her judgment. She became his complete partner. No matter what problem arose, what its ramifications, the decisions involved or whether he was right or wrong, he told her fully, frankly and without restraint. If he had been wrong and hotheaded, he admitted it, and often Mary Herlihy charted the way out. He was deeply in love with her. She was a perfect balance wheel, and he needed her.

They decided to get married and picked June 27, 1906, as the day. Standish Willcox, sitting in Mike Fitzgerald's barber chair, was interrupted that morning when a boy stuck his head in the door to announce: "Alderman Curley is coming down the street, Mister Fitzgerald. Are you ready? He's due at the church in twenty minutes." Mike had just given Standish's tough beard a once-over and was lathering his face for a close shave. The rest of the chairs were occupied by lather-covered men.

Standish stepped silently out of the chair, rinsed the lather off at the washbowl and was drying his face when Alderman Curley came in. Standish looked at his watch archly, bowed slightly, indicated the chair with a wave of his hand. "My chair, Mr. Curley," he said.

Curley nodded and sat down.

"This is one of the most important days of your life," he said. "It is definitely not a time to be tardy for the kind of engagement you are about to keep."

"I've been very busy," Curley explained. "There were a number of callers at the house. I couldn't break away without offending some of them."

"Long-winded beggars, aren't they?" Standish said. "Have you got the ring, the tickets for your trip and so forth?"

The barber was rubbing lather into Curley's face. "Jimmy Norton, the best man, is looking after all the details," he said.

Standish nodded. "Nevertheless," he said, "I think I'd better follow along and help shepherd you the rest of the distance, just in case anything untoward develops."

It had been planned as a quiet wedding with only the members of immediate families and intimate friends attending. From the very beginning both he and Mary Herlihy had been determined that married life would be private, personal, entirely apart from his public life. That line had already been drawn in the ward. Political friends and followers were not invited to the ceremony and it was made clear to them that they would not be welcome at a reception following it in the bride's home.

Curley walked down the street to Saint James Rectory, where, in the presence of a small group of less than twenty, he and Mary Emilda Herlihy were married by Reverend Cornelius J. Herlihy, a relative of the bride. She wore a traveling costume of gray. Miss Alice Leonard, a close friend, was bridesmaid. They went directly from the church to the Herlihy house on Burke Street for a late-afternoon luncheon. The house was overcrowded with wedding gifts. The Tammany Club had sent a complete set of dining room furniture. Before nightfall, Mr. and Mrs. James Michael Curley were on their way to Montreal and Quebec.

He had not yet achieved such prominence or stature in Boston that his marriage would attract city-wide or extensive newspaper attention. The murder of Stanford White by Harry K. Thaw, the day before, was being headlined in big type. Pages of columns and line drawings were describing and explaining the event in minute detail. The wedding of Mary Emilda Herlihy and James Michael Curley was reported under a small, single-column head over five inches of type on page fourteen in the *Globe* where it was briefly noted that the groom was president of the Roxbury Tammany Club and leader of Ward Seventeen.

It was an unusual honeymoon. "The loyal lady expected no lifetime of moonlight and honeysuckle with James M. Curley," he said years later. "It was well for her that she had a sense of humor and unlimited courage." The wedding trip covered a good deal of territory including part of New York state. The happy couple could not pass a city hall anywhere without stopping to visit, examine, inquire, shake hands with public officials and compare notes on the administration of city government.

Wherever a crowd gathered to hear anybody speak on any

subject, the newlyweds were certain to be sitting down in front, listening intently, and the alderman from Boston was sure to ask a question at an opportune or appropriate moment, and forthwith become a participant or turn the meeting into turmoil. That happened first at the Elbert Hubbard Colony in East Aurora where the Curleys heard a Professor Jones of Toledo predict, in a lurid address, the end of the Catholic Church and of the Democratic party. This was a kind of happy accident made to order for Curley. He heckled the speaker. The speaker answered. There were a number of exchanges, and when the meeting ended, gentle, old Elbert Hubbard tugged at Curley's elbow and suggested a debate on Marxian versus Fabian socialism the following night. That suited the Curleys. They stayed over for it. Next day Curley got a book on Fabian socialism from the local library and spent the day in his hotel room reading it, memorizing telling passages. For forty-five minutes that night, he delivered a burning vindication of it and tossed the professor around handily in rebuttal. The audience gave Curley the decision. The professor suggested another date, three weeks later, but Curley declined, accepted his victory and next day they left Aurora, moved on to take in a Chautauqua or two, found no further worlds to conquer and wound up at the annual convention of the Ancient Order of Hibernians in Saratoga.

Curley was not expected at the convention. He was not listed among the speakers. He arrived in the hall in time to hear the name of Matthew Cummings placed in nomination for the presidency of the order. He knew Cummings, a well-known Boston contractor, and fifteen minutes later he was on the platform seconding the nomination in a spellbinding speech that brought the delegates out of their chairs cheering, applauding and stamping their feet. Curley and Cummings, in that order, were the heroes of the convention. Enthusiasm was such that at the end of the speech Curley found himself in the center of the stage with a silver loving cup in his hands. It had been intended for someone else, but on the spur of the moment a committee hurriedly changed its vote off stage.

The Curleys returned to Boston to make their home in a house he had bought at 114 Mount Pleasant Avenue, where Mrs. James M. Curley now took over a job that had been done for years by Curley's mother: answering the doorbell and the telephone, interviewing briefly the interminable line of voters and supplicants in the ward who came for jobs or help, making notes and appointments—her introduction to the domestic merry-go-round that is the life of the wife of a ward politician.

Until that time Curley had always made enough money to provide for his mother and to take care of all his financial obligations throughout the ward and the city. When he returned to his $750 a year job as a member of the board of aldermen, it became clear to him that his annual income would have to increase fast and to a considerable size if he were to carry on the same family and ward obligations as before marriage, and at the same time maintain a wife and the family he anticipated on a scale he envisioned for them. Whether as a result of this decision or not, friction developed within the ward.

For five years James Michael and Thomas Curley had been a partnership in its administration. They awarded common patronage among day laborers and lower-paid workers, divided patronage on better-paying executive and white-collar jobs or agreed upon selections for them. There had been occasional disputes between them, which had been ironed out, adjudicated or arbitrated by a committee of fifteen within the Tammany Club. When a Sanitary Department foreman, sponsored by Tom Curley, working under the direction of a superintendent, also sponsored by Tom Curley, began laying off teamsters and helpers in Ward Seventeen on charges of beating horses and drunkenness, the dispute between James and Tom became so bitter that it was impossible for the committee to mediate it.

James became the champion of the teamsters and helpers; Tom, the advocate of the foreman and superintendent. The ward decided the issue by electing James Michael both president of the Tammany Club and chairman of the Ward Committee, shutting out Senator Thomas Curley entirely. As a result, James Michael alone thereafter controlled all patronage in the ward and made all political decisions. He selected the candidates for whom the ward would vote in future city-wide and state-wide elections and the committee ratified his selections at perfunctory meetings. Curley determined the conditions and considerations required of a candidate in exchange for the support of the ward, and it made no difference whether the committee ratified them or not.

Marriage had a settling effect upon him, discernible to his colleagues on the board of aldermen. Whereas he had hitherto been an agitator and disturber among them, sometimes needlessly complicating orders and snarling things up for sport and amusement, now he seemed to have his mind set on a definite goal. There was grim purpose behind every move. He was now an experienced politician and parliamentarian, familiar with every device and dodge in the books. He became a careful, skillful and dexterous adversary, a thorn in the side of Mayor George A. Hibbard, a parsimonious Yankee who would rather fire employees to save expenses than add a single penny to the cost of government. His parrotlike nose was a gift to cruel cartoonists.

The character of Curley publicity changed to match the new commanding figure in the aldermanic chamber. His instinct for creating newspaper headlines blossomed and bloomed quickly. The new Curley was a man who could not be stopped, blocked or thwarted. He foresaw now that one day he could be mayor of Boston. He became such an impressive power on the board of aldermen that the other ward bosses of the city became uneasy. They did not know what had happened to Curley, but if marriage had been responsible, they soon wished fervently that he had remained single. From the floor of the aldermanic chamber, he was demanding good, clean, honest government. They were puzzled and bewildered, asking each other helplessly how Curley, a ward boss himself, could square what he was saying as a member of the board of aldermen with what they assumed he must be doing in his own ward. All ward bosses, they knew, must live. All needed almost unlimited sums of money. His practices could not differ very greatly from theirs.

When Curley singled out James Donovan, the president of the Democratic city committee and superintendent of streets under Mayor Collins, and charged him with graft, the ward bosses of the city choked, and yet Curley dragged the battle into the open to the delight of newspapers and advocates of honest government. Donovan, he said, had been and was still being paid, as head of the Democratic city committee, a salary of fifty dollars a week (a good sum in those days) to maintain friendly relations between the city and the New England Sanitary Disposal Company to continue extending a contract then in force.

"It's a deliberate and malicious lie," Chairman Donovan answered. "I've never been connected with any garbage company, know no officers or stockholders in a garbage company and have always been and am now unalterably opposed to giving out such contracts. I'm in favor of having city men collect garbage anyway, and I've never paid any attention to an assassin of character."

Nevertheless, Boston cartoonists portrayed Curley on page one as a fearless and courageous David throwing rocks labeled "Ward Seventeen Control" and "Ward Seventeen Vote" at ten Democratic city leaders, Baldwin, McNary, William and John F. Fitzgerald, Cauley, Corbett, P. J. Kennedy, Nolan, Lomasney, and a cowering Donovan in hiding, while Frothingham, labeled "Yankee Vote," and Kneeland, labeled "Labor Vote," held hands blissfully on the sidelines saying, "Never touched us," and a figure labeled "Good Government Association" cheered and threw his hat in the air.

The cartoon would look strange forty years later to generations who had looked upon Curley as anything but a crusader for good government; and yet his record as a member of the board of aldermen is remarkable. He made one headline after another, by getting out an injunction to prohibit a food concern from selling its products to the city, forcing the mayor to reinstate day laborers he had fired, extending the eight-hour day to almost all departments including hospitals; compelling the city to fireproof all its hospitals; hammering through city regulations for recognition of unions in all departments and payment of union-scale wages; investigations of public utilities and revolutionary programs for the extension of public health.

Any student or critic of city government examining Curley's record as an alderman for the three years after his marriage would conclude that he was a progressive and daring politician ready to sacrifice his future for the good of the city and its people. He had attacked ward leaders of his own race and religion mercilessly, exposed them, and had been defeated in his efforts to bring them to book. He had fought for common people and little men, made himself solid with them and incurred the enmity of every ward leader in the city. He had made himself stronger than ever in his own ward and at the same time appeared to have destroyed his chances of achieving city-wide power.

Only one man seemed to understand what he was doing. "The time is coming," Standish Willcox told him, "when I must go to work for you. I've suspected all along that it is inevitable. On a day not far away now, I will hitch my wagon to your star and follow where you lead. You don't need me now, but you'll need me soon. The time is not yet."

When James Michael Curley returned to the board of aldermen in 1910, he had been the father of four children: twins who had died, James Michael, Jr., and Mary. He had been and was still under heavy expense. On a hot day in summer that year, he was in Mike Fitzgerald's barbershop, now on School Street, being shaved. Standish Willcox was in a chair on one side of him when Curley became aware of William S. McNary of South Boston in a chair on the other side.

McNary had been a congressman two years earlier and had been defeated by Joseph O'Connell, a ward leader of suburban Dorchester whose personal organization was known as "The Red Devils." McNary had spent much of his life in politics. He had edited a business newspaper, had been in the furniture, insurance and real-estate businesses; had served in the State Legislature and was retired. He had been hurt by the defeat and hated O'Connell. He turned to Curley and said: "Jim, we've got to stop Joe O'Connell. He musn't go back to Washington." O'Connell was a lawyer, an educator, a graduate of Boston College and Harvard Law School; father of twelve children.

"Who's around to stop him?" Curley was interested.

"I thought you might," McNary said. "O'Connell's got a strong following. He's a good vote getter; but you've got your own ward in his district and I think you've got a big following outside your district."

"Why don't you have a go at it again, and take him on yourself?" Curley suggested.

"I don't want any part of it," McNary said. "I'm tired of the sound and fury of politics. I'm not interested in being a congressman again. I'm interested only in seeing to it that Joe O'Connell isn't a congressman again."

"You've been there. You've had the experience. You must have liked it and enjoyed it. O'Connell took it away from you. I haven't been thinking of going to Congress. If you want to run against him again, you'll have my ward, and I'll do what I can for you outside of it."

"No," McNary decided. "You're young. I'm satisfied with my one term. It's the next step up the ladder for you."

"You mean, you'll be with me if I run?" Curley asked.

"That would be the understanding," McNary said.

"You want me to make a decision now?"

"Not necessarily."

"But you'd like it that way."

"Yes."

"Then I'm a candidate for Congress from the Twelfth Congressional District," Curely decided.

They discussed it further and when they got out of their chairs shook hands.

Willcox got out of his chair; McNary had gone. He looked at Curley thoughtfully. "A right and proper decision, Congressman," he nodded. "My day of decision is now almost at hand."

Curley smiled. "If you're going to work for me, Standish, you might as well decide now."

"You played your drama out superbly and in complete character, Congressman," he said. "As one actor to another, let me speak my lines as I want to speak them and come upon a stage that is properly set for me. The scene is inappropriate; the audience missing or unappreciative. Shall we both waste our talents on it?"

Curley grinned. "I'll bide my time."

Curley and Willcox were drawn together first because each had a sensitive ear for good diction. Then they found that they shared a common enjoyment of great books and great authors. Even before they met, Curley's personality had interested and intrigued Willcox. After they met, Curley accepted Willcox and often was puzzled by him. That was not unusual.

As far as can be learned, Willcox was born in the whaling

city of New Bedford, perhaps around 1880, and educated in the public schools of that city. Whether he remained there or left the city to return to it later is not clear. At any rate he turned up years later as a reporter on the New Bedford *Standard*. Nothing further is known of his parents, his background, his environment or how he came by his princely manners and personal charm. There was nothing of the braggart about him, and he never explained.

He had been writing a horse column for years for the Boston *American*, mailing it each day from New Bedford. He spoke to its editors on the telephone, but never came near the office. He was paid by the inch for the space he filled, and checks were mailed to him at various addresses. His voice captivated editors and rewrite men, and he wrote beautiful prose. One day Sports Editor John Gilhooly persuaded him to come in for a visit. When he arrived, he was not recognized. Tall, commanding, authoritative, cultured and refined, he was mistaken for a personal friend of William Randolph Hearst. Members of the staff, editors and reporters who bowed, took his hat and cane and made him comfortable, could be excused for thinking that he had just left his private Pullman at the South Station, or a yacht tied up in the harbor.

It was an almost unbelievable letdown when he revealed himself.

Nevertheless, Gilhooly was so impressed by him that after a half-hour conversation he made him assistant sports editor of the *American*. Within a couple of months, Willcox was an executive editor, making up the paper in the composing room, deciding what would appear in it and what would be left out. He had been a competent and experienced make-up editor before he came to the paper.

For the next seven or eight years, he was the best-dressed, most dignified and least-known newspaperman in Boston. He maintained a strange discipline in the composing room, standing by the forms directing compositors and printers, dressed as though he were on his way to a garden party, wearing wing collar, four-in-hand or Ascot tie and formal dress. He had a habit of waving his arms occasionally to make his stiff-starched cuffs disappear up his sleeves.

He spoke his orders crisply, precisely, softly, and they were obeyed without question. It would never occur to a subordinate to twit him about his appearance. He could deliver a biting reprimand at any hint of familiarity with a long glare, not speaking a word. He appeared to know everything, correct names, long-forgotten dates, circumstances and episodes of ancient or current news importance; a walking encyclopedia of facts and statistics. He lectured proofreaders on their carelessness in gentle language that made them feel small, bite their lips and promise to do better; and to the consternation of printers he could spot a wrong font letter in a five and a half point copyright line a yard away, a feat comparable to spotting a broken strand in a piece of thread in the eye of a needle.

Throughout all of this he was affable, genial, witty, a master of dry humor. He minded his own business strictly and never pried into the affairs of his associates on the newspaper. Inevitably they made disconcerting discoveries about him. He owned a stable of trotting horses, for example. Where or how he got them, no one could find out. This, of course, was no social distinction in a day when every peddler, blacksmith and proprietor of a barn owned a trotting horse, and drove it, as did Willcox, in harness and sulky races. In the heyday of the sport, horses sold for around $250.

Just as he told his associates on the *American* nothing of his life outside the paper, so he told his friends and those he met nothing of his life on the paper. He never advertised his profession, wore a badge or admitted or acknowledged that he worked on a paper unless circumstances forced him to. He concealed the fact. He had addresses simultaneously in three sections of the city, the South End, Beacon Hill and

Back Bay. He was known in each neighborhood by his distinctive dress. In each he was believed to be a well-to-do gentleman of leisure.

Standish Willcox apparently decided after he met Curley that he would like to work with him. He had already made his estimate of him, foresaw that he would go far in city and state politics. He and Curley were alike in many ways. They were on the same intellectual plane. Each liked to speak the King's English as nearly perfectly as possible. Each was an exhibitionist, delighting in an audience, savoring drama, climax and applause. Each separated private and public life. Physically there was some resemblance. There the comparison ended. Their temperaments were entirely different. Curley could be tough. Willcox never could be anything but gentle. Curley could be popular. Willcox could not. Willcox never could be the politician, but he could be the next best thing: Curley's right-hand man with all the power and reflected glory that went with it. Curley was bold by nature. Willcox was bold because of a physical handicap that made him impervious to all opposition. He was partially deaf, though he successfully concealed that, too. He overrode all objections to what he had to say because he seldom heard them, and created the impression that he considered any objection trifling, inconsequential and not worth his consideration. It was part of the secret of his character. He sometimes glared at a person who made an innocent observation, not because of the nature of the observation, but because he didn't hear it and was exasperated. That left the observer the alternatives of repeating an inane comment in a loud voice, or shriveling up to sneak away, certain that stupidity had offended the great man. When he spoke to a group, he was blissfully unaware of heckling. When he spoke to a timid person, he could not hear a nervous or frightened response. He turned away and left the timid with no other course than to follow his instructions or accept his opinion. He rarely bent his head forward to say "I beg your pardon, I didn't hear you," or cupped his hand to an ear. If he had been able to hear perfectly, he might not have been the strange genius that he was; or the even more unusual one that he became.

Six · Congressman Curley Buys a Necklace

BOSTON HAD never seen such showmanship in a political campaign. Sometimes the voters laughed until they cried and vice versa. Rallies were balanced performances, expertly timed with a maximum of audience participation. They offered an allotted time for serious discussion for the literate of the chief political issue, a proposed restriction on immigration; and for the rest, vaudeville, music, songs, special features and unscheduled bouts in the audiences; a mixture of surprise, confusion, circus and educational enlightenment. South Boston, particularly, was rugged and lusty, and Curley was contesting for a seat in Congress against its favorite son, the very man who had persuaded Curley to become a candidate, William S. McNary. Political inconsistencies like that are common in Boston.

This is how it came about. When McNary turned up casually and apparently accidentally in Curley's favorite barbershop and suggested in an offhand manner that Curley get into a fight against O'Connell, he was interested chiefly in

The rising young politician.

Second election as mayor 1922

A happy family at Jamaicaway, 1922. Left to right: Dorothea, Leo, Mary, the May-
elect, Paul, the first Mrs. Curley, James Michael, Jr.

making Curley a candidate, not a congressman. He apparently reasoned that if Curley and O'Connell divided the vote of Dorchester and Roxbury, populous South Boston could elect McNary. In the beginning, McNary and Curley were allies. They met often, compared notes and exchanged ideas on strategy. A difference of opinion arose. They disagreed and McNary became a candidate himself. The chances are that he always intended to be a candidate; then Curley took on both McNary and O'Connell.

Between them, McNary and O'Connell bought up all the billboards in the district, hawking their political wares in bold, black type as well from every visible wall and fence. O'Connell described himself as "able, active and aggressive." McNary's pleaded: "Send a big man to do a big job." One morning the people of the district were amused to discover a long streamer pasted under each of these big posters, saying simply: "Elect a humble man, James Michael Curley."

As the campaign progressed, McNary made a big issue of his own personal honesty and integrity in his rally speeches, and becoming apprehensive that his strategy had boomeranged, paid more and more attention to Curley, attacking him on his record. Curley hired an obscure bum, dressed him as Diogenes, put a lantern in his hand and sent him stumbling through the streets of South Boston looking for the advertised honest man, McNary. A South Boston policeman arrested Diogenes on Broadway. Court Clerk William Drohan telephoned Curley that Diogenes was in jail; he had failed in his quest and had not found the honest man in South Boston.

Next morning, Curley was on hand in South Boston District Court. So, too, was a company of photographers, cartoonists and reporters. Diogenes was arraigned before Judge Fallon. Curley demanded to be heard as a witness in defense of Diogenes and protested that he should not be thrown into the Bastille for calling William S. McNary an honest man. Diogenes was released. A city of spectators grinned, and Curley as a political Barnum garnered more publicity than any candidate in the city's history.

Scollay Square was a tough section of the city when the fleet was in. South Boston was next at any time, and third on the list in that era was Roxbury Crossing, a place that got its name because a railroad once divided its main street. Curley was speaking at an outdoor rally there one night when Standish Willcox, decked out in his full trademark regalia, appeared at the outskirts of the crowd, waved his stick and called sharply: "I say, there!"

The gathering turned to look at the interrupter and made a lane for him when Curley waved and beckoned, all but bowing their heads in reverence as the apparition walked quickly through to Curley's car. Curley opened the door and Standish stepped in to sit beside him. "I'll ride along with you," he said. "Do you mind? I'm joining up, you know."

On the way to the next rally, he outlined his ideas to Curley. "My function from now on, as I see it," he said, "will be to write and direct your publicity and to assist in the preparation of your speeches, always with an eye, of course, toward headlines and editorial comment."

Curley nodded.

"And I'd like to exploit you more expertly, perhaps, in the newspapers. You have a flair for devising situations that lend themselves quite naturally to it. Diogenes, for example, was inspired genius. I think I may have a touch, or a talent, for making the most of that sort of thing, and occasionally I may be able to contribute an original idea. I'll make my own place in the presently uncertain plan of your life, if it's agreeable."

It was agreeable.

Next day, Standish dropped in on John Gilhooly. "The time has come," he said, "when we must part. I've enjoyed being here no end, but hereafter the Boston *American* and I

will go our separate ways—to our mutual advantage, no doubt.
I thought it fair to let you know."

"What's the idea?" Gilhooly asked.

"I'm to be secretary to the next mayor of Boston, James
Curley."

"Mayor?" Gilhooly was surprised. "I thought he was running for Congress."

"Don't be silly," Standish reproved. "That, my dear man,
is only a wayside station, a brief whistle-stop on the main line.
When the next election comes, he'll be chugging into City
Hall."

From that day forward, Standish Willcox was James
Michael Curley's shadow. He complemented him as a right
glove does a left. Placid and unruffled, even when others
around him were tense and excited, his demeanor was always
that of a striped-pants diplomat. He made Curley's appointments, saw to it that he kept them, represented him, greeted
and entertained his important visitors, managed his affairs,
an example of quiet, superior dignity. He could bend from
the waist with such grace to kiss the hand of a humble
washerwoman as to make her Lady for a Day. He was, among
other things, an expert on protocol, a very handy man in
every way for Curley to have around.

Curley was elected, moved his family and Standish to
Washington; but before he left Boston he abandoned forever
the cutaway coat and striped trousers that had been a charm
for more than a decade. He had worn it in every election
campaign and replaced it with the latest model. He gave it,
as a hand-me-down, to a cousin who wore it for three years
until he died. He was laid out and waked and looked very
nice in the suit that went to Harvard.

Curley came to Congress under a cloud. Even before he
arrived in Washington a movement to unseat him, founded
on the objection that he had served a term in jail for violating

a federal law, was well under way. It looked bad for Curley. He went directly to Speaker of the House Champ Clark. The crack in the Republican party that was to widen soon into the Bull Moose split was already apparent. William Howard Taft was president. Theodore Roosevelt wanted to succeed him. It looked as if 1912 would be a Democratic year. Champ Clark had his eyes on the Democratic nomination and convention. He knew that thirty-six-year-old James Michael Curley was a good public speaker and a rising power in Boston politics. They had a long talk. The petition to unseat him was pigeonholed. Curley became Clark's campaign manager in New England. A year later he had thousands of Clark campaign buttons made, toured the six Northeast states distributing them and speaking before all Democratic caucuses and state committees; but the convention nominated Woodrow Wilson.

Any proposal to restrict immigration in 1911 was certain to arouse the Boston Irish as well as the city's now substantial and fast multiplying Italian population. Public discussion of a literacy test, already in Congress, was so common that limitation of immigration was debated as class work in public and parochial schools. Opposition to it always won. Parents or grandparents came chiefly from Ireland.

Curley was dramatizing the issue. Speeches against it, under his frank, flooded the mails. As far as his followers in Boston were concerned, Curley had a finger of one hand in the dike, holding off the "interests" that wanted to restrict immigration, while he held the sluice gates open with the other to let immigrants from Ireland and Italy pour in—doing it not exactly singlehanded, but at least alone. He did hold the House of Representatives spellbound with one admirable speech, a masterpiece of rhetoric and delivery. He was showered with compliments for it by those who heard or read it.

"That was quite a speech," he thanked Standish Willcox

when he got back to his office. "It covered everything thoroughly, completely. It was well organized and well written."

"I thought so," Standish agreed. "You did a superb job. It created quite a stir—quite a sensation. It was much more effective than when it was first delivered in Congress."

Curley looked at Standish suspiciously. "It wasn't original?" he questioned.

"Not at all," Standish answered blandly. "It was sensational forty-four years ago when vaguely similar legislation was before the Congress. I came across it in my research. You repeated it verbatim."

"You mean you didn't change a single word?"

"Certainly not," Standish answered. "Why gild the lily? I wouldn't be too concerned about it if I were you. Nobody reads today's Congressional Record, let alone the Congressional Record of 1867."

Nevertheless, the literacy-test bill passed and was vetoed by President Taft. Champ Clark had placed Curley on two important committees, unusual for a novice in Congress—foreign affairs and immigration. In a canvass of members of the committee on immigration to pick a leader to support the veto, it was found that Judge Goldfogle of New York was sick and could not serve. Judge Sabbath of Chicago declined. Judge Levy of New York suggested Curley. Boston had a large Jewish population and pogroms were decimating the Jewish population of Russia. Curley and Willcox went to work, introduced showmanship into the proceedings, put on a long procession of Horatio Alger witnesses: men who came to America illiterate and penniless and who rose to positions of power, influence and wealth. He led off with a Polish assistant attorney general of Illinois and followed with a Swedish chief justice of Minnesota and a New York Italian importer. Whether it impressed the members of Congress or not, it made headlines and the veto was upheld; then, as a member of the foreign-affairs committee, Curley favored abrogation of a trade treaty with Russia because of the barbarous persecution of the Jews.

Ironically, the history of the literacy test exemplifies the force that compels a legislator to submit to the will of his constituency, even though he himself may be unwilling and his vote may be contrary to his personal interest.

Boston was experiencing the second phenomenal racial infiltration into its population. The Irish had come to the city in a tidal wave during the middle of the nineteenth century and had changed the complexion of its population suddenly, a transformation accompanied by inevitable bitterness, hatred and violence. Much of the hatred had died away, although the embers still smouldered. In the second immigration, Italians came in a slow, steady stream, regulated only by the rising price of passage charged by the steamship lines and the fluctuating demand for day labor. An insignificant puddle in the city's population at first, Italians grew to a small pond, and in 1911 to a large lake.

For more than four decades the Irish had provided brawn and brute strength. They had dug and shoveled out canals and had leveled Fort Hill with their hands, moving the soil to the Back Bay to create land for the wealthy they had displaced and for a county jail. The Irish had moved up the social and economic scale a notch or two. A small handful had even achieved inclusion in the Social Register.

Yankee Brahmins had found the Irish hard to understand. The Irish were finding the Italians just as hard to understand, and because of it could not get along with them. They could not comprehend that Italians might have similar traditions, inheritances, rivalries and enmities, and made no effort to try.

Yankee Brahmins and the Boston Irish had been able to contest in business, finance and politics; to compromise, make deals and make peace. Speaking a common language, they had comparatively little trouble getting on common ground.

Language created a different kind of problem for the Irish. They could not readily understand or be understood by Italians. Frustrated by an inability to discuss common problems, exchange ideas and talk things over, the Irish fell back upon force. That didn't work. The Italians were fighting among themselves and fighting the Irish—just as the Irish had been fighting among themselves (and still were) and fighting the Yankees. Other seaboard cities were having the same troubles. Immigration restrictions had long been threatening. Irish descendants did not want that solution, chiefly because relatives and friends were still arriving from Ireland.

Privately, politicians wished fervently that they could restrict immigration, purely for personal and selfish reasons. Italians were now channeled to heavy manual labor. They did the lifting, tugging, picking, shoveling, the heavy brawn work formerly done by the Irish; and the Irish were not reluctant to leave that labor to them. But it piled more and more supplicants for less laborious jobs for the Irish upon the politicians, and political patronage trees were becoming very bare. The orchard was all but stripped. A new construction job, for example, meant twenty jobs for Italian day laborers for every five soft jobs as timekeepers and foremen for the Irish. The Irish would not take the hard jobs in large numbers. They were above them—and the Irish had the votes.

Irish immigrants had been drilled and crammed to qualify for naturalization. No matter how illiterate, they could comply with loose legal requirements to become registered voters. The Irish could not deal with the Italians that way. Naturalization was out of the question. Italians could not be turned quickly into naturalized citizen voters. It would take ten to twenty years to educate even a small fraction of them to a point where they would be able to pay back at the polls. It was one of the most thankless political tasks in the history of ward bossism.

Nevertheless, the steady, even stream of Italian immigrants

continued, slowly working another change in the character of the city, dividing it so that a battle front moved forward a little each year. The city's Jewish population had colonized in two sections and could not be moved. Force of Italian numbers made the Irish retreat, just as force of Irish numbers had made Brahmins retreat, but the Jews remained steadfast. There were clashes between Jews and Italians and some violence, but they had the curious effect of drawing the Jews and the Irish together.

At the same time, a colony of Lithuanians got a toe hold in Irish South Boston and began to mushroom out. Later, to these was added a colony of Poles. Irish and Irish descendants in business were beginning to be plagued by cutthroat competition. Italian fishermen and lobstermen would work for less. Sometimes they worked for nothing to learn the business. Soon they were buying their own boats and going out to the banks. The T Wharf fishing fleet, once part Yankee and part Irish, became a sixth Italian, a fifth, a quarter, and a third. An industry was changing like the city.

Unable to traffic politically with the Irish or to trade with them in business, Italians found ways to barter and exchange among themselves that frustrated the Irish and made them indignant. Italians established their own economy. They took over shops abandoned by Irish storekeepers, stocked them with Italian-caught fish and lobsters, olive oil, lemons, macaroni, and Italian imports. A couple of macaroni factories appeared within the area. The Banca d'Italia took over a building. Irish customers would not buy in Italian stores and Italians would not buy in English-speaking stores. Here again language divided them.

Politically the population and the total registered vote were out of balance. A small minority of Irish and Irish descendants would for years elect office holders who would govern the Italians. Successive immigrations of Latin and Slavic races circumscribed the influence of ward bosses. For years they canceled this new population as votes and shouldered them as a luckless burden.

Curley noticed how the wives of other congressmen were dressed and decided that his wife would be dressed as well or better. He saw to that right away. He entertained, as other congressmen did, and expenses began to climb. His salary as a congressman was chicken feed. There were still expenses back home, financial political commitments that had to be met, and a ward leader away from his ward is handicapped. His income from the ward shrinks, even while he lays plans to repair and improve it. Curley found, as every new congressman does, that he could draw from the sergeant at arms against his salary and during his two terms was overdrawn regularly.

Like his constituents who waited for horses or ships to come in, for their numbers to turn up in the Louisiana or some other lottery—the quick coup that would put them on easy street instantly—Curley anticipated much the same thing, but with a far better chance that it might happen. Almost everybody in Washington played the stock market. Blue-sky laws were but faint reflections in reformers' minds. Lobbyists were tipsters and their tips had to be good. Curley was persuaded to buy Canadian Pacific. He saw a modest few thousand dollars grow quickly into a paper profit of about seventy thousand dollars, and he saw a necklace in a jeweler's window that he thought would look nice on Mrs. Curley and bought it. Had he talked to her about it first, the transaction would never have been made.

Curley was impulsive, but Mary was inclined to look before a leap, a characteristic that kept him out of much trouble and that would have kept him out of much more if she had had the opportunity to look more often. He was proud of her, and determined that she would have the best of everything. To give her the things he wanted her to have sometimes led him through strange paths, and as a result, she was continually saving him from political disaster because he seldom told her what he wanted for her, and was forever planning surprises.

The congressman went to his broker next day and ordered him to sell. Canadian Pacific was still climbing. The broker told Curley about the market, showed him ticker tape and tables, and persuaded him to wait at least until Monday morning to sell, if he still felt like it. Curley was convinced.

He woke up Monday morning to find the newspapers headlining the suicide of the president of the Canadian Pacific. The stock tumbled so fast that he was wiped out before he got to his broker.

Democrats back in Boston did not have the kind of money he needed to get out of the hole. Republicans had it. Curley took a train to Boston, rode up to Lenox to see Murray Crane, Republican leader of the state and maker of its governors. He had been governor when Curley was in the legislature, and their friendship was as vague and tenuous as might be expected between two men so far removed in so many particulars. Nevertheless, Curley sat down, talked to him and explained his circumstances. Crane, a shrewd politician, gave Curley five thousand dollars.

This did not strike Curley as unusual. Politics to him was a competitive business. He and Crane were professional politicians in opposing parties. Crane had the money and was glad to help. There was nothing that Curley could do for him, and Crane never asked Curley to do anything. Curley went back to Washington, neither sadder nor wiser, but richer.

The Washington climate did not agree with his three children. A doctor suggested that they return to Boston where the Curleys had a pretty little house with lawn, trees and a picket fence on Mount Pleasant Street. For three years Curley commuted weekends and improved his mind on these trips by reading the classics.

Curley was not happy in Congress. Two terms was too much. Congress is an ideal place to shelve a city politician. It removes him as a local power and blunts his ward influence. There is almost nothing he can do for his constituents back home. His patronage is minimized. He has few jobs to give out. He can appoint a boy to West Point or Annapolis, but the boy will get there only if he can pass a stiff examination. Sending seeds to families in tenements would make them laugh. Their planting was limited to window boxes. Curley was on the right side on immigration. That's all that concerned his voters. How he stood on tariffs or antitrust legislation interested very few of them. He could vote Republican on ninety-nine out of a hundred issues and they would never know the difference. He didn't do quite that, but Crane expressed no regrets.

Whatever he made over and above his salary did not come out of them. They assumed that he would accept money for his vote from lobbyists, that he'd run errands and do favors for big business back home, and that the character of his associates within the city would change. He could no longer get jobs or concessions from the city or its utilities, the gas, electric, telephone or transportation companies, although he might be a useful approach to United Shoe Machinery Company, cotton, wool, and textile employers, the leather business, and for federal jobs in the customs or postal service, but his field was circumscribed.

A congressman may remain in Congress indefinitely if he cares to do so. His constituents get the habit of voting for him for minor offices. They vote him into Congress, and having done so, habit and custom become so strong that they continue to vote for him even though they disapprove of his votes and actions in Congress. Boston congressmen who enjoyed life in Washington and wanted to remain there merely announced themselves as candidates for re-election and never even bothered to come home. They were sure of nomination; and that meant election because the Boston Irish would not vote for a Republican anyway.

If a congressman did not want to remain in Washington, there was only one political step upward. He had to become a candidate for mayor. It would be unthinkable for him to take a step backward into the city council or board of aldermen. He could not become a candidate for United States Senator. This was and usually is the next step for a governor.

While Curley had been in Congress, the city charter had been changed. The board of aldermen had been wiped out, and a single body, a city council of seventeen, elected by districts, had been substituted.

Curley announced himself a candidate for mayor of Boston.

Seven · The Congressman Is Elected Mayor

JOHN F. FITZGERALD was boss of the city's North End. He was eleven years older than Curley. His career paralleled Curley's in almost all respects, except that he reached each public office a decade earlier. He was a good public speaker and a good administrator although no match for Curley. Their talents were comparable, but personally they were direct opposites. Fitzgerald had a pleasant tenor voice, whereas Curley never had been known to sing in public. He was affable, genial, friendly, the kind of person upon whom a nickname is easily fastened. He was known throughout the city as Honey, Fitzy, John F. or the Little General. He was short, quick, lively and bouncy, always smiling, dwarfed by the commanding height and personality of Curley. Curley had no nickname. Few persons ever called him "Jim," except in print. He was always James Michael Curley, or merely Curley. He was serious, never a backslapper, baby kisser or gadabout.

John F. neither smoked nor drank. He loved chocolates and

hated liquor. He was born in 1863, not far from the Old North Church where Paul Revere hung out his lanterns, one of nine sons of the neighborhood grocer, and grew up to be an athlete who could not help being elected captain of the team. He was educated in near-by Eliot School and Boston Latin School, a two-letter man, baseball and football; did not go on to college, but served transient apprenticeships of various kinds. He got into politics because an Irish boy could not get a job in any bank, or a white-collar job with a railroad.

He was elected councilman, alderman, representative in the state legislature, congressman, chairman of the ward committee, a successful, popular ward boss, whose people were loyal to him. He got along well with all other ward bosses of the city and so became the first American-born son of Irish parents to become mayor. He was quick to learn and adaptable. He had a good head for figures. He was the first to introduce modern advertising techniques in political campaigns. His slogan, "A bigger, better and busier Boston," was emblazoned everywhere. He and Curley were far apart on their ideas of showmanship. John F. sang his way into the mayor's office; a song plugger for "Sweet Adeline," the theme identified him for the rest of his life. He sang it all over the world.

He gave the city a good, businesslike administration—even conservative bankers approved of him—and became the foremost salesman of the Port of Boston. City employees were his enthusiastic supporters. He raised their pay and was good to them. A natural promoter, he held an "Old Home Week," seven days of continuous celebration, invited the farmers and outlanders of New England to come to Boston, provided trade and merchandise shows for businessmen, tourists and conventioneers, put city support behind sightseeing and bought advertising space in the newspapers of other cities to sell Boston battlegrounds and historic shrines, inviting all and sundry to come to Boston and spend money. He publicized the city widely and more successfully than any mayor up to his time.

He had organized his own ward well and could deliver it down to the last vote. This loyal support was his nucleus. His daughter Rose was being courted by Joseph P. Kennedy, son of P. J. Kennedy, ward boss of East Boston. Joe Kennedy, fresh from Harvard, was then operating sightseeing buses, or rubberneck wagons, from the South Station. Fitzgerald would have the vote of East Boston. It was taken for granted that he would succeed himself as mayor, until Curley announced from Washington that he, too, would be a candidate, throwing a monkey wrench into the well-oiled Boston machine.

Tradition, practice and good political form prescribed that a candidate for mayor make known his ambition and decision to the ward bosses assembled in the Democratic City Committee, explain, try to convince them, discuss the matter and let them decide whether he was acceptable to them. After that, each ward leader would tell the candidate, usually privately, what the ward leader would expect by way of emolument and reward, stipulate his share of patronage the mayor would dispense, and make any other conditions that suited him. The candidate's private agreements with these ward leaders, accounting for disputes and disagreements among them, determined the amount of support he would get from each, and finally who would exert the most influence and boss the mayor. A candidate had to be a good trader and diplomat.

Curley consulted none of them, ignored them completely and went on to express his contempt for them. This was consistent with his treatment of them as an alderman after his marriage. He had attacked them, fought them, vanquished them, emerging as a complete contradiction: a ward boss who attacked all other ward bosses and the system that created them, while at the same time doing the things they did and benefiting by the system. Now he became the enemy of machine politicians and announced that he intended to rid Boston of them.

This had a strange effect upon all but one of Boston's ward bosses. They became afraid of Curley. They knew the nature of the things he could reveal, and after their experience with him as an alderman, they had no doubt about his courage to do it, even if it meant his political suicide. The sole exception was Martin Lomasney, boss of Ward Eight, who sat back and chortled at the discomfiture of his brother ward bosses, enjoying the show immensely. He couldn't be bluffed by Curley. He admired his colossal nerve and told him so. The most practical politician of all, he withheld his support from Curley until the last moment; then gave it to him, and discovered to his astonishment that it did him no good, and joined the anvil chorus too late.

A not uncommon paradox in politics, Curley's campaign for mayor was based on reform. He castigated all ward bosses as parasites and hypocrites, and made it clear in thundering words wherever he spoke in Boston that summer that he would have no part of them, no underhanded traffic or deals with them, no Sunday-afternoon kitchen cabinet, that he would run the city as he saw fit and take dictation from no one. He baffled the ward leaders. They could not adopt and control him. They could not get rid of him; and the louder he talked, the more timid and uncertain they became.

John F. Fitzgerald decided not to be a candidate for re-election and talked instead about becoming governor of Massachusetts. His decision was unpopular throughout the city and particularly in his own ward, where it shook the confidence of his loyal followers. They felt that John F. was unwilling to defend his title against the new champion. Whether they were right or not, John F. never acknowledged it. A panic-stricken city committee chose Thomas J. Kenny. Fitzgerald gave Kenny his support.

Kenny was a solemn, scholarly, self-educated lawyer, a demon for dry statistical details, who could break down the city budget or its financial statement for accountants but could never make it clear to people who mark crosses on ballots. He was hardly the candidate to pit against a man of Curley's appeal. He was fifty years old; Curley forty. He had been a member of the school committee, first elected by a heavy, flattering vote. He was president of the city council and, as such, acting mayor when Fitzgerald was absent from the city. He lived in South Boston. His experience and record made him available as a successor to Fitzgerald.

Curley ignored him, too.

The quality and quantity of showmanship at Curley indoor and outdoor rallies improved in each campaign. Public theater as he moved swiftly around the city during the fall of 1913 was superior to that of his first campaign for Congress. The crowds who turned out to hear him were enormous. The crowds who turned out to hear Kenny, pathetic. Curley was followed and surrounded everywhere he went by members of his Tammany Club in a motorcade. He had staff singers and entertainers. Spectators never were bored while waiting for the main event. Curley's entrance, oratory, histrionics and his nightly curtain were certain to be dramatic; and there were plenty of sideshows.

He was fighting the interests (whatever they were) and the entrenched political machine. Everywhere he went he promised to throw the politicians out of City Hall and give it back to the people. His followers were invading city neighborhoods where other gangs held allegiance to their own local ward bosses. This caused street fights almost everywhere and there usually were special details of police on hand to preserve order. The show was entertaining and exciting.

All candidates for major offices making public appearances in other than their own wards were careful to protect themselves by recruiting dependable strong-arm men skilled in various techniques for silencing hecklers, garroting, brass knuckles, lead pipes, socks of sand and BB shot or bare fists. Hecklers were not graded or typed. The sincere, intelligent, provocative questioner and the disturbing catcaller were lumped together, sometimes appearing indifferently on hospital casualty lists.

Heckling was an accepted device, occasionally spontaneous, sometimes planned. "Stealing" a rally from the opposition by mounting a soapbox in the middle of a rival's speech and carrying on a competitive discussion was the ultimate in heckling. It required the greatest courage and skill; but this would have been rare meat for Curley and none would dare try it.

One heckler followed Curley from rally to rally. He was big, weighed about 250 pounds. He stationed himself behind Curley's automobile at each corner or square, just out of reach of the open tonneau, hissing whispered obscenities for Curley's ears alone. At the third or fourth stop it was getting on Curley's nerves. Members of his bodyguard inched through the dense crowds, unable to identify and remove the disturber. At one stop, he pointed his finger in the direction of his heckler.

"Would you like to ask a question, sir?" he said.

This was the heckler's big moment. He had stopped the master, and he had a question prepared. "Sure, I've got a question," he whispered. He seemed to have laryngitis.

The bodyguards moved closer, but it was still difficult to identify him in the crowd.

"Fine, my good man," Curley said. "Just a moment. Before you state your question; there are ladies present. Would you please remove your hat?"

The heckler took off his hard, protecting derby, exposing a round bald head. A guard near by swung a sockful of BB shot upon it, and then with a couple of bystanders carried

him through the crowd. Curley went on with his speech
as though nothing had happened.

It became clear that Curley would go in on a local landslide. Kenny talked about the tax rate. Curley promised them
work, more playgrounds, more schools. He talked about the
new generation in a promised land of plenty, sandy beaches,
parks, gymnasiums and clubrooms, and drew such fascinating
word pictures that even as they listened they were swimming,
watching ball games, or playing pinochle in the cozy municipal building clubrooms that he described. He talked of better
streets, highways, a new Boston in which the Yankees were
tolerated for sentimental reasons and the Irish had all the
money, a glowing, glittering dreamworld that unfolded night
after night like a continued serial story—and he never repeated
himself.

Kenny scoffed and said "Tut, tut," and was looked upon
already as a relic of yesterday. He talked of amortizing loans,
pay-as-you-go, the cost of borrowing money in anticipation of
taxes. The voters listened and could not understand. During
the last week of the campaign Curley was patronizing and
condescending toward him. Kenny was finally irritated. He
attacked Curley, but his choice of epithets was mild—"A
charlatan, a vender of magic municipal remedies, a pretender.
Where was Curley during the Spanish American War?" he
asked.

Curley clipped this attack upon him from a newspaper,
and his ridicule of it was devastating. He read the full text
of what Kenny had said about him to his audiences that
night, paused for a long time, looking down at them, smiling
as they contemplated it. Then he held up his hand and shook
his finger, as though reproving a child, and said simply.

"Naughty, naughty! Tommy."

Heckling was well organized one night in Flood Square,
South Boston, the heart of enemy territory, Kenny's home

ward, when a group of Fitzgerald followers infiltrated a big audience and taunted him. He interrupted a smooth, well-modulated flow of words, a pause that became an exclamation point, looked them over slowly and deliberately, turning up his nose and lips in scorn, and snarled from the corner of his mouth in language they understood. "You're nothing but a pack of second-story workers, milk-bottle robbers and doormat thieves. I'll be elected mayor of Boston, and you don't like it. Here I am. Does any one of you bums want to step up here and make anything of it?"

The South Boston Irish were tough, and a challenge like that would ordinarily incite them to riot, and yet he faced them, standing on a cushion like jelly beneath his feet, in the tonneau of an open automobile, glaring. He was an easy, inviting target, and they took it silently with narrowed, hateful eyes, as though they were hypnotized, rooted to the spot, spellbound by his eyes and voice. There may have been other factors involved. Flood Square toughs offered lame alibis. They said the hecklers were "ringers," Curley men planted there and that this was a planned and surprising piece of Curley showmanship. The explanation was tortured, a face saver. Flood Square corner gangsters knew when they were being insulted, and it was not like them to let anybody get away with it. They never had done so before. A more plausible explanation is that they were stunned by the unexpected. Curley created the situation, mastered it, made the most of it and passed over it before they could decide to do something about it. After he had resumed his oratory, the right moment was gone and reprisal was out of place. He carried that ward on election day.

On the night before, both candidates made whirlwind tours of the city, visiting all wards and precincts. Curley's open car rolled up to a prepared platform near Saint Augustine's Church, South Boston. Police broke a lane through the crowd from his car to the platform and the crowd cheered as he

walked swiftly through it. They stood enthralled as he dramatized the final chapter in this new Boston. He paused in his
peroration to sympathize with and comfort Kenny, and answered his attacks very simply.

"Here in the shadow of the spires of Saint Augustine's,"
he said, "I am reminded by Brother Kenny of those beautiful
words in that beautiful prayer 'Give us this day our daily
bread, and forgive us our trespasses . . .' "

He paused at he caught sight of a bum clambering into his
open car at the outskirts of the crowd, turned almost imper-
ceptibly to a bodyguard saying in an undertone, "Get that son
of a bitch heisting my fur coat from my car," and went on
after what was, to them, merely a slight pause for silent
emphasis . . . " 'as we forgive those who trespass against us.
Lead us not into temptation, but deliver us from evil,' Amen."
The fur coat was safe and in a few moments the car was
beside the platform and he was stepping into it to go to the
next stop. He ended his campaign that midnight in Mechanic's Building, the biggest arena in town, where the crowd was
so great that police had to pull him through it and he entered
the hall over a ladder and through a side window.

The outcome was no surprise. Next day, Curley polled
43,000 votes against Kenny's 37,500. He announced immediately that he would cut expenses, clean out City Hall, give
an efficient and businesslike administration, fire all loafers,
goldbricks and payroll patriots, and insist upon a full day's
work for a day's pay from all city employees. He warned them
that he would be tough and ruthless. Boston Bankers, the
Chamber of Commerce, Good Government Association, Retail Trade Board, Real Estate Board and the city's businessmen rubbed their hands in anticipation; but the warning had
an ominous ring to city employees, Fitzgerald supporters and
the contractors who did business with the city. Meanwhile,
Curley was aloof, distant and independent. He would see
none of them until after he had taken office.

He began breaking precedents right away. It had been the custom for an incoming mayor to go to City Hall before the inauguration ceremony to meet the outgoing mayor. The two mayors would lead a march of all department heads, executives, dignitaries and invited guests, to the aldermanic chamber where the oath of office would be administered. Curley changed that. He didn't like the idea; said he didn't want to enter City Hall except as mayor, and to suit his wishes, the ceremony was held in Tremont Temple, not far from City Hall, before twenty-five hundred spectators, a large number of them members of the Tammany Club.

His inaugural address was a biting arraignment of the outgoing Mayor John F. Fitzgerald, sitting on the platform, for leaving him with an empty treasury. He excoriated him as a bad administrator and expressed his opinion of his appointees. When it was over, police pulled Curley through a big overflow crowd outside the Temple, walked him through a lane of spectators from the Temple to City Hall. Standish Willcox followed not far behind. Curley signed the oath book, called for the city clerk and dictated a letter to him, firing the building commissioner.

The new broom swept clean. It was a grim day for six hundred city employees and their families. They were bounced around and reshuffled. Men who had soft desk jobs were assigned to pick-and-shovel gangs. Employees who worked at the aquarium and in the birdhouse at the zoo, where the temperature was 80 degrees, were equipping themselves with woolen underwear and heavy clothing to work at the pumping station where the temperature was zero. It was no coincidence that most of those so transferred had voted for Thomas A. Kenny. Curley made that plain. "Mr. Fitzgerald," he said, "has left in office a number of men who are hostile to me, and as I have no desire to be ambushed in my own camp, I am removing them. Every time I drop a friend of his from the payroll, I substitute an equally competent citizen, who has the additional advantage of being a friend of mine."

Next he dropped all Fitzgerald contractors, and a company of new ones filed into his office. He outlined his terms and conditions and made it clear that as long as contractors lived up to them, they would continue to do business with the city. He told newspapermen that he would have a press conference every morning at eleven to report on what he was doing, tell them what was going on, and to answer questions, and said that he would always see them together, and never one privately. He would give no exclusive interviews. The fine hand of Standish Willcox was discernible in that directive.

He put in such a long day that newspapers had to rearrange their schedules for covering City Hall. It required a part-time and a full-time shift for two men. He got to the office at ten in the morning and was likely to be there at ten at night. As he was leaving one night soon after he took office, scrubwomen already were at work. He watched them for a minute. Next day he ordered scrubbing brushes with long handles so the women could stand up and work and made it a rule that no scrubwoman was to get down on her knees in City Hall.

He made it impossible for newspapermen to get on friendly terms with him. He discouraged any approach that might lead to familiarity. He had no close associates, no intimates outside his family, except Willcox. He had thousands of political friends, but few personal friends. He did not play poker. It is doubtful that he knew one card from another. He did not gamble or play the horses. He drank sparingly and temperately at public functions. He had no club, no hangout. When the day's work was done, he went home. He was a solitary, lonely man. Any portrait of Curley as a boisterous, genial, rollicking companion is a caricature, a mythical person who never existed. He asked no one for advice and would not accept it when it was volunteered.

People who enjoyed the campaign show, laughing and grinning at his biting wit, discovered that they had been watching an actor play a part. In City Hall, he was an entirely different person. On a public platform he could win friends with his charm and voice. Behind a desk, he was serious, thoughtful, able to divine the aims and designs of those who came before him. He was disconcerting, uncomfortably direct and revealed an unerring knack for antagonizing nine out of ten men who came to do business with him. He looked through them, pinned them down to specifications and agreements; and yet he could turn the charm on like a faucet for the unbusiness-like, the voters in the anteroom.

Throughout the campaign, wherever he appeared, he invited everyone to come to City Hall and see him personally. As mayor he repeated and emphasized the invitation. No mayor of Boston had ever done that. Ward leaders had no power over him and no influence. They had no patronage, could not provide jobs, promotions, welfare assistance or satisfy even trifling needs among their followers. Voters wondered whether Curley meant what he said. They were doubtful, skeptical. It had not been common political practice for ordinary voters, not sponsored and supported by local political influence, to drop into City Hall casually and ask for jobs or talk things over face to face with the mayor. The local ward leader had always done that. Few voters ever got close to a mayor, except to shake his hand at a rally. A handful of men in various wards tried it, came to City Hall, asked to see the mayor and were channeled quickly from one secretary to another until each stood for a minute or two by the mayor's desk, shook hands with him, looking at him, speechless and fascinated as a secretary read crisply from a card the supplicant's name, address, position in society, political and fraternal affiliations, place (if any) on the city payroll, salary or other enlightening financial statistics, and the request he was making of the mayor. Curley listened, sizing up the voter, thought it over and decided immediately.

"Okay, you've got it," he told the visitor, gave the secretary precise instructions, shook hands with the voter again and he was on his way, utterly satisfied and almost unbelieving. He got his job, promotion, welfare aid or whatever he asked for on the spot; or was assured that it would transpire before a definite deadline, and it did. There could be no disappointments, no failures. If a request could not be granted, a reason and explanation were given. The supplicant never was permitted to remain in doubt. He knew where he stood. His card went into the file as a Curley voter.

The first handful brought the news back to their wards and it spread like wildfire. Before many weeks the anterooms, corridors and staircases were crowded. The Boston *Transcript*, traditional old lady of Boston journalism and voice of the Back Bay Brahmins, shuddered and turned its eyes away from the painful scene. It was characterized as the "spectacle of the corridors." Curley was never concerned over the opinion of the *Transcript*. He said that City Hall was not a place for stuffy decorum. It was a city workshop and it was about time it was put to the purpose for which it was designed. The spectacle of the corridors grew. Extra police were added to the detail, and extra secretaries were put to work under the general direction of Standish Willcox.

So was born the Curley machine and what came to be known as "Curleyism," a new departure in Boston politics. Curley wiped out ward leaders by destroying their power, took it away from all but Martin Lomasney, still too strong to be overcome, and centralized it in himself. Voters in the city's twenty-five districts abandoned their ward bosses and looked toward Curley as the bigger boss of the city. Ward boundary lines never again would mean anything, except in local contests among local candidates for state senator, representative and minor city offices.

Eight · First Administration: A Legend Is Born

THE CURLEY legend and a new kind of city boss were twins born early in this administration. The city was ready for him. Curley owed his election to nobody. He had labeled the Democratic city committee "a collection of chowderheads" and "eggshells." No ward boss ever was invited to City Hall. Even those who sincerely wanted to be friendly were rebuffed. He lived, worked and operated within a shell. It could not be penetrated. Boston ward bosses, with one exception, were starved to death and under the Curley system none could ever arise again to take their places.

They had served their purpose. There was no longer any political, social or economic need for them. They had germinated in Boston in a day when most Irish immigrants had been illiterate and needed leaders whose thinking and direction they could take on faith. Sixty years and successive generations had changed the character of the voting herd. The votes of Irish immigrants were not nearly as important as the votes of their sons and grandsons. They were literate, grounded in the habits and customs of the city. They were inclined to depart occasionally, temporarily or permanently from the leadership of a ward boss. They did not depend entirely upon him for jobs. They were able to get work for themselves. They did their own thinking. Some were unusually successful in business and their wealth made them the equal of the ward boss. Grandsons of the original immigrants were far better educated and much further removed from the Irish tradition. They were inclined to scoff at the ward boss, to be contemptuous of him, and irritated at their elders for being so subservient to him.

Second-generation Irish did not need to be told how and where to vote. They resented it. Sample: "You'll vote for George Holden Tinkham for Congress," Mrs. O'Donnell told her son about to go to the polls for the first time, "or you'll never darken my door again. He put your brother Bill in the customs service and no son of mine will be blackguard enough to run out on him." She was angrily demanding that he vote for a Yankee blueblood with red whiskers. Twenty years earlier the question would never have been raised; now it was raised. How he voted, she never knew. These new voters were too well informed. They could not be herded around and the ward bosses lost them.

Martin Lomasney survived and was able to keep his ward intact because he had a large block of recent Italian immigrant illiterates and a lesser group of Negroes. His services were necessary to them and he found out how to get along with them. He picked the most intelligent among them, trained them and made them sectional leaders. He was adaptable. He was just as foresighted in his treatment of the deserting first- and second-generation Irish. He improved his clubroom, made it an attractive hangout. A good salesman, he coaxed and persuaded the younger generations to come into the club, to use pool and card tables free of charge. He listened to them, mingled with them and permitted them to educate him in their ways. He flattered them by taking their advice, looked for ways to do favors for them, even paid tuitions to college to place them under obligation to him, but he trained no one to follow in his footsteps, although he tried hard. The new material could not be molded in that fashion. It was clear even then that his ward would disintegrate when he died.

Even among his annual crop of new voters were a large number of skeptics who asked embarrassing questions. Young voters in all wards disdained doorbell pulling, house-to-house canvassing and political yeomanry because they thought they were above it. Worse than that, each one who developed an interest in politics wanted to be captain. They wanted to start at the top, not at the bottom. After casting their first votes (and some even before) they took out nomination papers to become candidates to the new city council, circulated them, got the necessary signatures and filed them. Candidates blossomed like weeds. Some even took running jumps up the political escalator and, without experience or political training, tried first for the legislature. A few were elected.

As a by-product, the ballot and the ballot box became sacred once again. No longer could precinct workers mark all blank ballots for a machine candidate at the end of a day's voting; nor could they make erasures or tamper with ballots already cast. The eyes of too many novice candidates were always upon them, and these novices were too quick to blow a whistle and yell "Cop!" When the ward boss lost control of the election machinery, he lost control of the ward. Another by-product was an earache that would plague Boston for the next half century. Curley's oratory and success spawned more imitators than impersonators of stage celebrities and these pseudo-Curley voices either made the voters laugh—or cry. Out of this kind of uncertain, undependable and elusive material, Curley built a city-wide machine. Where the average ward boss had to remember only a few hundred names and faces, Curley learned to remember thousands.

Curley's design for future political success was to talk to every voter in the city of Boston if only for a handshake and an exchange of a few words. He would have talked to everybody in the Boston directory, if it could have been arranged. Such a system required a strong man. Even the physical labor entailed was monumental. He talked to at least two hundred persons a day, a thousand persons a week, fifty thousand persons a year. There were repeaters, of course, but in a four-year term he talked to as many persons as there were votes cast.

As he got settled in the job, the tempo increased. He shifted department heads, fired some, reprimanded others, sometimes in tones loud enough to be heard in the anterooms and corridors. He behaved as though he had had his eyes on Boston's mayors for fifteen years, knew what was wrong with the office and would correct it by reorganizing the whole governmental structure to suit his personal taste.

Newspaper editorials praised him. The Good Government Association, bankers and business groups cheered him. This, at last, was something like it. Quite suddenly the cheers froze on their lips and praise stuck in their throats. Curley upped the valuations of bank, business and newspaper properties. He said the city needed the money. Department stores cried in anguish. Bankers implied that this wasn't cricket and suggested discreetly that Curley reverse direction and wipe out the increase right away. Instead, he vilified the banks publicly for conspiring to milk the city by submitting almost identical bids for loans in anticipation of taxes. He characterized the bids as window dressing and said he saw no reason why the city should not shop around for a better deal among banks in other cities. Within three months after his election, he had offended almost every organized group that had approved of his election and a number of prominent state Democratic leaders who might have been of use to him in future elections. All told, he created an impressive bloc of enemies. Some of them would hate him for life.

His administration had become one of highly efficient and effective confusion with two exasperated groups, a Good Government Association and the Finance Commission, carefully watching and examining every move that he made, constantly frustrated by a sleight of hand that they could not follow or explain to the people. Money appeared as if by magic and disappeared the same way. It took the Finance Commission three or four months to investigate a single purchase or contract award, and while they were investigating that he was piling up others to investigate so fast that it was impossible to keep track of them.

Few cities have ever witnessed such a spending spree or such feverish destruction and reconstruction. The topography of the city began to change. Streets were ripped up and buildings torn down, tunnels and transit systems were extended. Almost every jobless person in the city went to work on one of a score of projects. The city payroll climbed to unheard-of heights. Doctors and nurses were hired in scores for City Hospital. New and bigger buildings began to rise there. Tenements in the slums were knocked down to make way for playgrounds. Bathing beaches were rebuilt and miles of Strandway appeared along the South Boston shore.

To do all these things he appeared to be ignoring all kinds of laws and regulations, cutting corners, spending money with a lavish hand. He emptied the treasury, spent money on the city's credit and went before the legislature to borrow money against the future to pay the city's debts and finance further improvements he had planned. The legislature was determined not to give it to him, but he talked them into it.

Contractors were rolling in money, turning up on jobs with liveried chauffeurs at the wheels of latest model cars. Their foremen seemed to be almost as well off, and at this point it would have taken a battalion of auditors and investigators to determine the facts on thousands of transactions involved. The Finance Commission was so far behind him that it was now charging "waste, extravagance, or worse" in the award of contracts for a germicidal wash for the floors of school buildings during the first week of his administration. At the rate they were going it would take them twenty years to establish what happened, financially, during the first two years of his administration.

Curley seemed to know what he was doing, and he was alone in that. City Hall reporters tried desperately to explain and interpret. They asked Curley from day to day how these things were financed and how they would be paid for, as ultimately they must. What he said to them was made crystal clear and made sense, until it appeared in print, when financial experts shrieked fallacies over telephones and in person to editors. Curley's explanations were always much more convincing in speech than in print. In the meantime, the Chamber of Commerce, the Retail Trade Board, the Real Estate Board and Boston business generally recovered from shocks long enough to try to count the cost. There were protests and indignation meetings, and threats to oust him from office, but Curley told them, in effect, to "shut up" or he would raise their valuations and taxes even higher.

Midway in his term, Curley began building a house. Any politician who does that usually commits an outrageous, tactless, foolhardy political blunder. The new house was to be a surprise for Mrs. Curley. It was much more than a surprise to the people of Boston. It was a shock. They were to discover that Curley would be unorthodox in many ways.

He knew that the house would concentrate attention upon him, but he wanted the house and was determined to have it. He did not know what kind of house he wanted until he read in the newspapers that the beautiful summer home of Standard Oil's Henry H. Rogers in Fairhaven was to be sold at auction. He went there with Standish Willcox to look it over. The winding staircase captivated him. A romanticist at heart, he could vision Mrs. Curley walking down that staircase in a white evening gown, his children in stunning frocks and formal dress. Before the auction ended, Standish Willcox bid nine hundred dollars and became the owner of a spiral staircase. Standish bought, too, assorted hunks of the house that attracted Curley's eye, including a huge crystal chandelier, marble fireplace, mantels, columns, balustrades and the entire finish of the showplace dining room.

The new mayor looked around for an exactly appropriate landscape for a house with such a staircase and picked a site high on a hill facing Jamaica Pond. As one of the most exclusive residential areas of the city, it had been the first retreat of the Brahmins, crowded off and pressed back from Beacon Hill as Irish immigrant invaders and their progeny crept up its west side toward the State House. It was a place of big estates and rolling lawns sloping toward a pond, outlined by a beautiful park road. It satisfied his artistic eye. He managed to buy enough land there and hired experts to build the right kind of house around the staircase.

As it began to take shape, the indignation of property owners there began to rise. Architecturally, it was perfectly in keeping with its surroundings until white shutters were affixed. Upon each was a cut-out shamrock that seemed to symbolize thumbs to multiple noses with fingers extending in all directions. Curley's opinion of Boston bluebloods had been well advertised.

A number of groups, organizations and personalities developed an intense interest in the Curley house. Chief among these was the Boston Finance Commission, a curious body, distinctive of Boston, whose function originally had been to keep alert and watchful eyes on city expenditures. It had been brought into being, not by the people of the city, but by the

Governor Roosevelt
d Mayor Curley at
olonel House's es-
te, 1931.

Victory, 1932: Mayor Curley presenting James Roosevelt with a picture of the
sident-elect. Left to right: Mayor Curley, Mrs. James Roosevelt, Mary, James
osevelt, State Treasurer Charles F. Hurley.

Former Governor E
shakes hands with h
successor at the latter
inauguration, Januar
1935.

The new governor at work.

legislators of the whole state. The Watch and Ward Society was devised to police Boston's morals. The Finance Committee was the inspiration of a majority of Republicans from rural areas to police politics and prevent ambitious mayors from enriching themselves while administering the city's affairs. The cost of maintaining and operating the capital city conceivably might be levied in part upon them, and they didn't want that.

Even before the Irish conquered Boston, Yankee Brahmins had not been entirely unskilled in channeling part of the city's revenue into their own pockets and bank accounts. Curley did not devise the spoils system. He inherited it; and he inherited the Finance Commission. He added his own ingenious improvements to the system and found many novel ways to defeat the Finance Commission. Well-educated, college-bred, first-generation Irish and Brahmin Yankees whose interests now dovetailed had been appointed by Governor David I. Walsh to serve on it. One of Curley's first acts as mayor was to appoint its chairman, John A. Sullivan, his own corporation counsel. John R. Murphy, who hated Curley, was promptly named by the governor chairman of the Finance Commission.

The first thing the commission turned up was that although Curley paid a tax on personal property valued at only $1,000, received a salary of only $7,500 as a congressman, and was getting only $10,000 a year as mayor, the land for his house was assessed on the books for $15,600, and the commission valued the house, exclusive of the land, at $35,000, a total of $50,600—and wanted to know how he did it. The mayor's answer was quick and complete. He itemized his personal income, taxes, his mortgage arrangement with the bank, and the amount of money that he got for the sale of his half interest and silent partnership in the Daly Plumbing Company, which nobody knew he owned until then, adding for good measure that he did not think the lot upon which he had built his house was quite big enough and that he had purchased the adjoining lot, too, for $4,500, something the Finance Commission did not know; and he invited them to investigate that. He went further. He challenged the Finance Committee to debate his personal honesty with him in Mechanic's Building, the biggest hall in the city. The Finance Committee could prove nothing and decided to forget the whole thing.

Curley had been in office scarcely six months when World War I began. Its impact upon him and the people of the city at first was not great. It was merely another European war, too far away to have any effect upon the city. Curley was far more interested in creating a Board of Port Development to spend $82,000 contributed by Boston businessmen for that purpose. Six months later the war had a different aspect and Curley and the people of Boston discovered that the war was not so far away, that it was having a tragic effect upon Boston business. He ordered all schoolhouses, the ferry headhouses and the state pier thrown open to 4,200 able-bodied unemployed, set up cots and toilet facilities and opened soup kitchens there. The city was experiencing a local business depression.

The war that caused it also cured it. Within a year city mills, machine shops and factories were working overtime on two and three shifts. Almost every passenger ship that docked in Boston carried European diplomats or companies of them, arriving on "good will" missions, an extended interlude of "Welcome to the city; here comes the parade." Between 1914 and 1917, when the United States declared war, every nation in the world had at least one delegation in Boston at some time. Whether they came from England, France or Germany, Curley maintained the city's neutrality. Perhaps it was for this that lucky curiosity, years earlier, had schooled Standish Willcox in protocol.

There were banquets, parties and balls in what seemed like endless succession. The Allies wanted America in the war. Their treasuries were becoming bankrupt and they wanted money. Power politics and city politics were becoming snarled, and since there were no votes for a Boston mayor in London, Berlin or Rome, Curley could not easily be persuaded to declare war.

When Marshal Joseph Jacques Césaire Joffre, hero of the Marne, and René Viviani, the French statesman, arrived in Boston with Admiral Cochepret of the French navy, Curley suspended a war with the railroads over a three cents per one hundred pounds differential rate to entertain them. Bands played, champagne glasses tinkled. There were cheers and confetti, and the small French population was thrilled. Willcox worked overtime preparing speeches for Curley, helping himself to the best of Descartes, Voltaire, Rousseau and the translated works of French statesmen. Curley had a special gold medal made and at a pretty ceremony pinned it on Marshal Joffre's chest and was kissed on each cheek. When it was over, the secretary to René Viviani murmured a complaint to Curley that the statesman deserved a like honor. Curley had another gold medal struck off, scheduled another celebration and demonstration, but it could not be held. Somebody stole the statesman's gold medal from Curley's desk in City Hall, and the event was called off. The delegation left Boston with fond recollections, moral support, but with no money.

The Easter Week uprising in Ireland excited and mobilized the Boston Irish in a cause that touched them deeper than the war. Irish societies held emergency meetings. Fund raising was begun. All other delegations were brushed off quickly to make way for Irish heroes who came to Boston, an Irish capital in America. They were greeted with wild excitement. Receptions and banquets topped anything that had been staged for representatives of warring nations. When they left, the budget appropriation for receptions and celebrations was wiped out and well-to-do Bostonians of Irish descent were footing the bills. The visitors left with their hands full.

Ambassador Ishii of Japan could not have picked a worse time to come to Boston to be received. His visit was of importance chiefly because Japan was still a neutral and both the Allies and the Central Powers were exerting pressure to force Japan to make a choice. Dr. Morton Prince, for whom Curley had a good deal of admiration and respect, had been trailing the ambassador for a year. Boston was now tired of its long-sustained diet of banquets and celebrations; and the city was broke.

"How about it?" Prince asked Curley. "Will you stage a big banquet, get Ishii up on his feet for a speech and see if you can persuade him to say something that will commit him as being sympathetic to Britain and France?"

"Let's try a small celebration," Curley suggested. "It will be less expensive."

The city honored Ishii at a luncheon in the Copley Plaza. Ishii was introduced to a select Boston audience by Curley who implied that Japan would soon be in the war fighting on the side of France and England, but when Ishii got up to speak he delivered an eloquent panegyric on New England in the autumn.

"Will you try again?" Dr. Prince persuaded. "Give him a bigger reception, a dinner this time." Curley did, and this time Ishii eulogized the Forbes family of Boston, whose seafaring ancestor, Captain Forbes, had done so much to open Japan to the outside world.

"Try again," Dr. Prince insisted.

Curley shook his head. "There isn't any money left in any appropriation for that purpose," he said.

"I'll pay the bill," Dr. Prince agreed.

The third reception was like a Hollywood production in the ballroom of the Copley Plaza. Everybody who was anybody in Boston was present. This time, Curley, who had no regard for the niceties and subtleties of striped-pants diplomacy, took no chances. Before the banquet he backed Ambassador Ishii into a corner and made perfectly clear and plain what was expected of him that night; whether Curley turned the trick or other factors made the time ripe for his announcement, Ambassador Ishii made the statement that led newspapers around the world next morning, and Dr. Prince paid a hotel bill of $1,500.

"Was that your money?" Curley asked Prince sometime later.

"No," Prince answered.

"Where did you get it?" Curley wanted to know.

Prince grinned. "From Sir Edward Grey."

Nine · The Last Chair of Charles I

CURLEY HAD been a professional politician continuously employed for eighteen years. During the last year of his term, the United States was at war. Business was booming. The number of unemployed and on public welfare was lower than ever in the city's history. Curley was a candidate for re-election and there was not much that he could offer. Most of the city's voters were making more money than they ever had in their lives. It was not a time for expansion or construction. Even if materials were available at reasonable prices, the city would have to compete with war industries for labor. There were no issues that he could throw into a fire, heat up and hammer out on his anvil.

For the first time Curley faced the prospect of being unemployed himself, although that did not frighten him. He was sure he could make a living. He had enough votes to ensure his election. The octopuslike city machine he had created, with tentacles reaching into every ward, guaranteed a majority vote if he could hold it together. There were a number of groups determined to break it up. The ward bosses whom he had snubbed and ignored were broke and politically hungry. They wanted their own controlled candidate in City Hall again. They hated Curley cordially and were thirsting for vengeance. The bankers and financiers, whom he had characterized as "insolent, arrogant sharpies, swindling the city of all they could get away with, while at the same time prating about the high cost of government," were bitter and smarting. They wanted any candidate but Curley, and preferably one who could answer the description "a good, honest man." Department-store owners, big real-estate holders, businessmen and industrialists, who had been pinched when he increased the valuations of their properties, wanted no more of Curley and were willing to contribute fancy sums to any group who came up with a candidate and a recipe to defeat him.

The ward bosses found a way. It was very simple. They persuaded Andrew J. Peters, a Republican of unquestioned integrity, to become a candidate against him (a rare anomaly; twelve Democratic leaders plotting to elect a trustworthy Republican). Then they persuaded two of the city's best-known Irish congressmen, James A. Gallivan and Peter Tague, one popular in South Boston and the other in Charlestown, to become candidates for mayor.

One of Boston's fabulous eccentrics was Mrs. Jack Gardner, one of the few persons in Boston who could call Curley "Jim." Throughout her life Mrs. Jack did whatever suited her fancy, and what the neighbors said never bothered her. She was a member of Beacon Hill society and hated everybody in the Social Register. Most of them feared her, and very often it delighted her to make them quiver and quake. Mr. and Mrs. Curley were frequent visitors at her palace. She loved them because they were outspoken and forthright, while most people were so awed by her that they choked up and were speechless.

She came to Boston an unknown outlander from New York. She had married Jack Gardner, Boston's richest man. Until she snared him he had been the city's most eligible bachelor. It was a bitter disappointment to Boston's dowagers when they were married. Society snubbed her then, and for a half century she made Boston society pay through the nose. She was a redhead, a rebel who lost all respect for convention after a short association with socialites of the eighties and summed up her opinion of them when she was asked for a donation to the Boston Charitable Eye and Ear Infirmary by saying, "I don't believe that there is a charitable eye or ear in Boston."

Boston society still prefers to forget Mrs. Jack. When society matrons were airing diminutive dogs on leashes, Mrs. Jack ridiculed the fad by ambling down Beacon Hill with a lion on leash. When wealth was subtly indicated at social functions by the width of ropes of pearls around the neck, Mrs. Jack assembled thousands of the most exquisite pearls from all over the world and wore them in a band a foot wide around her waist. Sargent painted her portrait that way. When she missed a train for a coaching party on the North Shore, she hired a locomotive from the railroad and arrived coated with soot at the throttle, tooting the whistle. If she heard a musician or singer at a recital and liked the performer except for one little thing that irritated her eardrums, she sent the person abroad for three or four years and paid all expenses to have the error remedied, so that he could come back to her three or four years later and do it right. She did the same thing with painters and sculptors whose work she did not like.

She built a palace in the Fenway. She didn't like the architecture of most palaces she had seen in England, France, Germany, Switzerland and Italy, and was determined that this one suit her taste. She had accumulated a vast number of art treasures and wanted to display them. When one of the workmen complained to her that the windows in the palace were not all the same size, Mrs. Jack turned on him and snorted: "They certainly are not, and you ought to get down on your knees and thank God for it."

She watched every detail of construction and when a workman did something she did not like, she took his tools away from him and showed him how she wanted it done. The workmen complained that she didn't belong to the union, so she joined the union of every craft involved in building the palace. Her voice wasn't strong enough to be heard by the workmen when she called them. She remembered a musician named Bolgi who played, she said, "the most tactful cornet I ever heard." She brought him halfway around the world and paid him more money than he would get for a concert tour just to signal the workmen: one toot for a mason, two for a steamfitter, three for a carpenter and so on. Mrs. Jack had the world's most sensitive ears. She was afraid of nothing but darkness. She always carried a flashlight.

Curley met her through her eighty-two-year-old uncle George, who came to him for a list of Boston charities to include in his will. She was about seventy-eight years old then, still the whipcracking mistress of Boston society. Her razor-sharp tongue deflated egos, ridiculing socialites pictured in newspapers. She told a secretary she wanted to know all about Curley, and before the day's end she had a complete biography and dossier. She invited the Curleys to have dinner with her at the palace.

She looked Curley over. "You're as tough as I am, aren't you?" she said.

"Right," Curley nodded.

"I've always been the most gossiped-about woman in Boston," she went on, "but I've never cared a hoot about what people said about me. You're the most gossiped-about man in Boston. How do you feel about what people say?"

"I don't care what they say about me," Curley told her. "It's how they vote that interests me."

"I've always got everything that I ever wanted—everything that I went after."

"So have I," Curley said, "and I plan to keep right on getting everything I want and everything I go after."

"Good," Mrs. Jack nodded. "You and I are going to be friends."

A few nights before election, Mrs. Jack Gardner had the Curleys to dinner. She had been talking to them about the campaign and had been following it in newspapers and through her own personal sources. She had arrived at the conclusion that Curley would be defeated. She had a grisly sense of humor. After dinner they were walking about the palace. She pointed out a chair.

"Here's a chair with a curious history," she told Curley. "I'd like you to sit in it."

Curley sat down.

"Feel comfortable?" she asked.

He nodded.

"Head feel quite secure in it?"

"Quite," he agreed.

"That's the last chair Charles the First sat in," she said, "before they chopped his head off."

Curley grinned and got up.

For four years newspapers had been filled with scandals, Finance Commission reports of its findings in the construction of roads, schools and other buildings. At first Curley had answered and after a while did not trouble to do so. The campaign was bitter and spectacular, but money spoke louder than Curley. The ward bosses proved they had the right answer. When the votes were counted, Peters got 37,900, accounting for little more than the total Republican vote of the city, Curley 28,000, Gallivan, 19,400 and Tague 1,700. The total Democratic vote added up to a majority, and as the law provided no runoff primary, Peters became a minority mayor.

When Curley walked down the steps of City Hall on a cold, brisk day in January, 1919, he was entering private life, not returning to it. He had known nothing but public life since he became old enough to vote. He had to find a job. There was nothing he could do now to make a living politically. When he wiped out the ward bosses as political entities, he had erased himself as one of them. He had gone further. He had ripped up his roots in Ward Seventeen and established himself in another. The Tammany Club was still his, but he could do nothing for its members, he had no influence in City Hall, and none among the public utilities he had offended as mayor. Nevertheless, the Tammany Club was loyal to him. Its members were sure that he would be back again one day in the driver's seat.

He knew a good deal about public business, but he was a rank babe in the woods in private business. Various jobs had been offered him and he elected to go into business with William Grueby as a partner in the Grueby and Faince Tile Company. It was probably the worst choice he could have made. Grueby was a delightful person, an artist who painted well and loved stained-glass windows and designs in tile. He had an artist's contempt for business practices, conformists and the demands of what he called a crassly materialistic world. He was a devoted Curley apostle. He was sure that Curley would take charge and with his administrative genius make a couple of million dollars without boring him with the stark and deadly details.

When Curley showed up at the plant, he found eight hundred medallions dedicated to and memorializing Mary Baker Eddy, founder of Christian Science.

"What are these for?" he asked a bookkeeper.

"It's just an idea Grueby had. He thought the Christian

Scientists would grab them up. They did for a while. We sold a couple of handfuls, but they haven't been buying them lately."

"Why not?" Curley wanted to know.

The bookkeeper couldn't answer. Curley reached for the telephone and got one of the trustees of the Mother Church on the line. "What's the matter with these medallions?" he asked.

"They look too much like Mary Pickford," the trustee said. "The woman on the medallion has a curl hanging over one shoulder and she's wearing drop earrings. Mary Baker Eddy wasn't like that. Who is this?" the trustee asked.

"My name is James Michael Curley," he answered. "I'm one of the partners in the concern."

There was a long pause. Finally the trustee said hoarsely: "Goodbye."

The sale of Mary Baker Eddy medallions dropped dead.

Six months later, the Grueby and Faince Company was making money, and Curley was going so hot as a salesman that he wound up by selling the company itself to the Pardee Tile Company of New Jersey. He sold Grueby into a gross income of $40,000 a year, and in doing so he sold himself out of a job. All the stockholders got 300 per cent. Two years later, Grueby was dead. Prosperity killed him.

Curley got what he needed from the experience—confidence in himself. He decided that private business was a push-over, looked around for another enterprise and met a man who owned an oil well. A genius at administration and a past master of the art of mystifying finance, he turned out to be a sucker for a confidence man. He could have used the money he invested in the oil well to keep him going for the next three and a half years while he was out of office. When this transaction ended, Curley felt as if he had been through a washing machine. He had been cleaned.

Next, the board of directors of the Hibernia National Bank hired him as president, a smart move that paid off profitably for both. Curley got a salary and was forced to live within it, and the Hibernia National Bank got widespread advertising and a flock of new depositors. Wherever he went after that, he sold the bank to depositors as one that had never foreclosed a mortgage in its history. Curiously, as a banker, he had now joined the fraternity he had criticized so scathingly as mayor, but the presidents of other city banks did not come around, slap him on the back and welcome him into their society.

He sat in an office and looked wistfully across a narrow alley at City Hall. He knew what was going on there. He had served with Peters in the common council. He knew him as an amiable, affable and high-principled Yankee. He knew that Peters could not be openly controlled by the ward bosses who had helped to elect him, that he would not accept dictation, and that his back would straighten and he would resist any hint of it.

On the other hand he knew that Peters would be controlled, that the powers of administration would be taken from him subtly, stealthily and almost without his knowledge. Peters was interested in the "honor" of being mayor, and not in the tedious chores that administration entailed. He could not stand the confinement and hard work necessary to do a good job of running the city. He liked golf and the outdoors. His face was always well tanned. He liked yachts and boats, parties, gaiety, congenial friends and a good time.

He had been grateful to those of the Boston Irish who had supported him and worked hard for his election. He was not reluctant to listen to a suggestion from a Democratic ward leader, if it lightened his burden somewhat. His secretariat was loaded with men appointed as a result of such suggestions. A number of lush appointments had gone to Boston Irish.

The work of his office seemed to run smoothly. There was no friction. Life was pleasant again for city employees. Their ratings were not changed, but their salaries were increased. Peters vetoed all further city improvements. The city would take a breather from Curleyism. The result was that nothing was being done. The expense of government was climbing to a higher peak than under Curley, and that inevitably would be revealed.

Peters' staff was only too happy to relieve him of all the work and responsibility they could shoulder, including such matters as rebating the high taxes Curley had imposed, cutting valuations of their properties back to previous size—and quite naturally, Peters' subordinates, who were running the city, got fancy fees for their services. Nevertheless, businessmen liked Peters. His administration, they thought, was saving them money. Peters' lieutenants were so skillful that it took a little longer than it had under Curley to discover that the city treasury was being systematically raided and that although the cost of government remained about the same, the city's revenue was shrinking. Taxes were much lower. The fees the new City Hall gang charged were making them independently wealthy.

Peters initiated no construction. He had his hands full completing what Curley started and had not been able to finish, including a new six-million-dollar high-pressure water system for downtown Boston to minimize the conflagration hazard and reduce fire-insurance rates. He appointed as fire commissioner John R. Murphy, sixty-three-year-old party wheelhorse who had been editor of a weekly newspaper, merchant and advertising agent. Murphy demonstrated the new high-pressure system with showers and curtains of water, a spectacular show, but fire-insurance rates never came down.

Peters was one of the most trusting souls ever placed in a job that required the quick eyes, ears and instincts of an honest poker player among cardsharps. He believed implicitly everything he was told. He signed his name to documents without reading them, and even repeated into a telephone acknowledgments and commitments which his secretariat called to him, an innocent dupe for a conscienceless corps of bandits. He was an utterly honest mayor—just what Boston wanted. He had an independent income, and that presumably made him immune to graft. He never took a wrong nickel while in office, and a time came when he looked around blinking, bewildered and uncomprehending, not knowing what had happened. He never did figure it out.

In a room adjoining his office there was a "bagman" who would deal, dicker or negotiate for almost anything. For an agreed price a play would not be banned. Burlesque shows at the Old Howard or the Gaiety were seldom disturbed. Jobs and promotions had price tickets on them. Political affiliation meant nothing. Anybody could buy almost anything at the bargain counter. All that was needed was the price. With a half dozen reporters covering City Hall every day, this could not go on quietly and secretly. They exposed it, but nothing happened. Newspaper readers showed little interest, and prosecutors less. It was exposed again and again, but the people of the city appeared to be so conditioned to crime and corruption that they were indifferent. Even Peters poohpoohed these exposés and dismissed them with a wave of his hand as "newspaper sensationalism."

The war was over. The world was at peace. Prohibition was the law of the land. Calvin Coolidge, governor of Massachusetts, had settled the Boston police strike and became famous for his pronouncement, "There can be no strike against the public service," with no premonition of how wrong history would prove him to be. Speakeasies were commonplace in Boston. Eight men murdered and their ship scuttled on Rum Row off the Massachusetts coast, eleven Chinese frozen to death while being smuggled across the Canadian border in a railroad boxcar to Boston at $350 a head made no dent upon public conscience. Life was cheap. Crime was casual. Irregularities, embezzlement and theft in City Hall were trivial.

Ten · Second Administration: Reform and Royalty

CURLEY at the age of forty-eight took to the hustings, again as a "reform" candidate. He exposed and dramatized what was going on in City Hall, citing case after case in an arraignment that might have sent scores of office holders to jail had the matter been presented in a court. He did what newspapers had been unable to do: focused public attention upon it. "Throw the rascals out" was his theme everywhere. He counted and tallied the cost to prove that a do-nothing administration was far more expensive than his do-something system.

The anti-Curley block did not want another Peters administration, and they did not want Curley's either. The best candidate they could find to pit against him was sixty-six-year-old John R. Murphy. He was the ideal public speaker to condense the history of Ireland after dinner before the Charitable Irish Society on the seventeenth of March, but never the candidate to mix it up with Curley in rough and tumble debate.

Curley followed him upon a municipal building platform

where Murphy had been reminiscing with his audience about his long and active life and his venerable age. Curley stepped up to the dais, impersonated Murphy in voice and action, an unmistakable caricature, squinted his eyes, searching the audience and wheezed: "I don't see anybody here that I welcomed back from the Civil War."

The ward bosses did not want Curley. He was pointing an accusing finger at them from every street corner and public square. The bankers did not want him. He was characterizing them as arrogant, insolent, and accusing them of exploiting the city. Businessmen wanted no part of him. Those whose taxes had been rebated knew that they would be doubly squeezed, while those who were too ethical to arrange rebates knew that their valuations would be pushed even higher. At the same time bankers and businessmen wanted no traffic with the city's ward bosses, and found themselves in bed with them. Curley labeled it an unholy alliance to defeat him and defraud the people of the city of good government. The voters were impressed. Curley antedated Roosevelt by many years in acquiring the dubious "that man" distinction. He became "That Man Curley" in 1922.

The "Stop Curley" groups were fairly confident. They would stop at nothing to keep him out of office. Nevertheless, they hedged their gamble against the future. Suppose Curley should be elected and, with the start that he had made during his first administration, build a city-wide machine that would perpetuate him in office until death, possibly in a far-distant future. The prospect was unthinkable. It made them shudder. The state legislature, traditionally and overwhelmingly Republican, had never been reluctant to intrude in Boston's business. A bill was introduced making it impossible for a mayor of Boston to succeed himself. It passed. Governor Coolidge signed it; and that took care of that.

Curley staged a spectacular show, but money spoke loudly and in some places made even sweeter music than his voice.

On the night before election, the odds against him were two and a half to one. He ended his campaign at a mass meeting hard by Calvary Cemetery, pointed toward it dramatically and with the proper oratorical pauses and flourishes reminded the huge crowd that his father and mother were buried there. "We'll bury you there tomorrow," a heckler called. "Wait until the returns come in."

The vote was close, but Curley won: 74,200 to 71,800. Heaviest losers to the gambling bookmakers of Boston were the ward bosses. Three of the best known among them had pooled $128,000 against $60,000 on Murphy.

Two months later, Andrew Peters left the office, his head bowed by other, more painful misfortunes than a reputation for ineptitude as mayor; but be it emphasized for the record —he was an honest man. Curley took the oath of office in Mechanic's Building and delivered his inaugural address before twelve thousand cheering and applauding spectators. He demanded that the Finance Commission hire a staff of expert accountants at once to examine the books and find out what had happened during Peters' administration, and the warning was implied that the Finance Commission would need them for the number of future investigations he was planning for them. He took the legislature apart for interfering with Boston's affairs. The idea of preventing a mayor from succeeding himself meant endless changes in administrations, he said, and gave any mayor little time to complete the work that he started.

He wanted a bigger city-planning board with wider powers and made it clear that he intended to change the topography of the city a good deal more. He was going to wipe out another large section of city slums, build more roads, granolithic sidewalks for all of the city's parks, widen a bridge and several more miles of congested streets, add a couple of hundred acres of playground and acquire a huge hospital, abandoned by the federal government, for a home for the aged.

He wanted more money for child welfare and for soldiers' and sailors' relief.

He warned all city employees that he expected a full day's work for a full day's pay. If they didn't like that, they could turn their resignations in immediately; and he warned his own city contractors that if they violated their contracts and agreements, or deviated in any way from architects' or engineers' specifications, he'd fire them, too. He had enlarged and expanded City Hospital under his first administration. He'd enlarge it and expand it more; and if he couldn't complete the job during this administration, he'd come back again in a future administration and finish it then.

Boston bankers, businessmen and real-estate owners read his speech with sinking stomachs and prepared for the worst. They knew that he meant what he said, and they knew they would have to pay for it. There was no way to make peace with him. They would have been glad to make up a pool and pay him personally whatever he might have made by prosecuting his program of razing, building, construction and reconstruction, but he wouldn't listen to the proposal. He wanted to build. He liked it. He got more fun out of that than he did out of the money he made. He was not interested in who paid the bills. Sometimes he was not even interested in whether the bills were paid in the current generation, the next, or two generations hence.

Curley left Mechanic's Building for City Hall. His office was banked with flowers. He received all day, champing at the bit. There was work to be done. Within a week he had settled into the routine of the office. His new staff was well organized and he was ready to go.

Francis Daley, the treasurer of his campaign committee, came into the office with the ward leader of East Boston, Thomas Giblin. Giblin had been a professional fighter. He was about six feet tall, weighed around 240 pounds, and was known to be very quick and handy with his fists. Curley was signing city bonds. He looked up at Giblin as Daley said: "I'll leave Tom here. He wants to talk to you," and Daley left.

"I know what it is to be on the outside looking in, Tom," Curley told him. "If there's anything I can do for you, I'll be glad to."

Giblin glared. "I should think you would be glad to. If it hadn't been for the likes of me, you wouldn't be in that chair." His voice boomed through the corridors. The tone indicated that there was a fight brewing.

"What do you mean"—Curley's temper was rising—"if it hadn't been for the likes of you I wouldn't be elected?"

"Just what I said," Giblin answered. Both were standing up now. "If you didn't have guys like me out in the wards to fight, you would have been licked and you know it."

"You mean that by opposing me, you helped to elect me?"

"Right!"

"If I depended upon the likes of you, I'd never be elected to any office."

Curley and Giblin were squaring off, each measuring the other, when cultured, refined, Edward J. Slattery, a minor secretary who wore a white vest in winter and summer, frock coat, glasses with ribbon attached, stepped between them.

"My, my, Mister Mayor," he said, shaking his finger reprovingly in Curley's face. "You musn't strike that man. There's a dignity that goes with the office of mayor! And you must respect it."

Curley looked at Slattery, blinking, trying hard to comprehend. "Thank you, Mister Slattery," he said, turning back to his desk. "Call in the guard."

The guard was made up of four police officers, all in their seventies, too old for street duty. Two of them, Patrolmen McHugh and Gately, responded.

"Throw him out," Curley ordered.

Five seconds later both officers were stretched out on the floor.

"Call the reserves," Curley told Slattery.

The other two officers came in and forthwith joined their companions on the floor. Giblin looked down at his handiwork, astonished.

"Get out," Curley told him.

Giblin left. Curley turned to his dignified secretary. "Thank you very much, Mister Slattery," he said. "That was the most profitable observation you ever made in your life. From this moment your salary is increased five hundred dollars a year."

Curley's second administration did not have the same slow, moderate start as his first, gathering momentum as the months passed. It opened with a rush as the wheels of his machine meshed immediately in high gear and raced with dizzying speed. Contracts were awarded so fast that Good Government Association and Finance Commission were far outdistanced the first week. Streets were opened almost before residents knew what was happening. He widened the approach to City Hall immediately, bought property or took it by right of eminent domain. The two mayoral policing organizations scarcely had time to find out how recently these properties had changed hands and how much the city had paid for them before Curley was floating a three-million-dollar bond issue to enlarge City Hospital (he enlarged it in each administration), four million dollars to extend the East Boston Rapid Transit Tunnel, twelve million dollars to extend the transit system, and five million dollars for a tunnel far out into Back Bay.

He accounted for twenty-four million dollars in these projects alone, talked fast and convincingly about amortization, while the businessmen of the city began to scream and cry bankruptcy. Valuations and the tax rate were jumped to new highs. An avalanche of investigations was begun. So many contracts were awarded so fast that investigators could pry into almost any one of them at random, break it down and find irregularities that made them choke. It would take years to prepare a single case for a court and jury, and there were hundreds of them—and there was no one to prosecute him anyway. Neither district attorney nor attorney general wanted to tangle with Curley, and even if they did, they were not up to it. The size of such an investigation was in itself discouraging. It got so that nobody knew what was going on but Curley, and he didn't explain. Bankers, financiers, the legislature and the people had to take him on faith. Most of them kept their fingers crossed and hoped everything would turn out all right.

Once again, though, everyone was working. Welfare rolls were pared down to the bone. People who had been collecting without trouble were swinging picks and shovels. Trucks rumbled day and night over city streets. Brilliant floodlights at night made daylight over tunnel excavations, work going on night and day. Girders and stringers went high into the air. A new maternity hospital grew as an addition to City Hospital. It was followed by a new administration building, pediatric, pathological and laundry buildings. There was scarcely a doctor, surgeon, nurse or medical employee who would not have voted for Curley. He gave them a home. The hospital was becoming a model that visiting doctors looked upon with outright envy.

Businessmen, building owners, department stores were screaming in anguish, and the more they screamed, the more he milked them. He needed plenty of money and was ruthless in raising it. Everybody knew there wasn't a contract awarded that did not carry with it a cut for Curley, but perhaps that was a useful counterirritant: they were so indignant at what they estimated he got that their attention was diverted from the millions being spent in improving the city.

Inevitably the city treasury got so low that there wasn't money enough to pay city employees. Curley had to borrow money against future taxes. He put the proposition up to the president of one of the city's biggest banks, casually, on the telephone. The banker said "No!"

"Listen!" Curley said. "There's a water main with flood-gates right under your building. If you don't know where it is, your architect can tell you. You'd better get that money up by three o'clock this afternoon, or those gates will be opened, pouring thousands of gallons of water right into your vaults."

At three o'clock that afternoon, the bank had the money on the line in City Hall.

With so much city building and construction going on, the treasury was drained again. Curley decided to replenish it by upping taxes a little more. He was a full decade ahead of the New Deal in the application of the theory of tax and spend and tax and spend for public improvement. There wasn't enough money on hand to pay the city employees. They could not very well wait until he collected the new taxes. Once again he proposed to pledge the uncollected taxes as security to the bank if it would lend him the money. Once again the bank put its foot down and said no. It was opposed to the idea of raising further taxes on business properties. What affected the profits of business affected the profits of the bank. It was opposed to Curley and to everything he planned to do with the money.

"You'd better get the money up," Curley said. "That water gate is still there, but before I come to that I have a better idea. I'll have six hundred city employees lined up outside your bank tomorrow with checks for their salaries. That will make a line about a mile long; and I'll advise all of the city contractors who have accounts in your bank to be in that line, too, with any of their employees who have money on deposit to transfer their accounts to other banks. You don't want a run on your bank, do you?"

He got the money.

The third time he ran into that kind of difficulty, he told the bank president: "I have a nice picture of you, and I have a good picture of that beautiful estate you have in the country. If I don't get the money to meet the payroll, I am going to print those pictures. Under your picture, I'll have a caption: 'This is the man who is responsible for payless pay-days for city employees'; and under the picture of your beau-tiful house will be the caption: 'This is where he lives.' When a man gets hungry, he's likely to do something desperate. I'd keep away from that house if I were you."

There were no payless paydays during his administration. The bankers characterized him as a bandit, a gangster, a foot-pad and a thug. He had given them plenty of reason to do so, but he did not seem to mind.

Meantime, he was carrying on a continuous and running fight with the Finance Commission. The Finance Com-mission made suggestions for improvements that it felt could be made with no expense. Curley snorted; said he could get far better suggestions from the people of the city and had a suggestion box placed in City Hall where he invited the people to drop in their ideas. He argued that the Commission showed an absolute lack of knowledge of municipal require-ments and a total disregard of the public weal. He said that it had wasted a million dollars of the city's funds investigating him and the government, and had got nowhere.

Mayor Peters had had an abiding respect for the Finance Commission. Curley considered it a nuisance. During the depression of 1921, Peters had asked the Finance Commission if it would approve hiring five additional social workers for the Department of Public Welfare. Peters could have hired them without asking. The Commission's function is entirely advisory in such matters. The reply to Peters' request came to the mayor's office two years later to Curley. The Commission approved hiring the workers.

Curley held this up in the newspapers and on the radio as a glaring example of the Commission's ignorance of what was going on. The depression was over. Employment figures were at peak. The number of persons on public welfare was lower than it had been in ten years. Because of that the department was now overstaffed and had no use for five additional social workers. Curley told the Commission to wake up and find out what was going on in the world and in the city.

The Commission replied by moving seventeen auditors into City Hall to go over all the books. Curley surprised everybody, including the Finance Commission, by instructing all department heads to give the auditors full co-operation and to let them have access to all books and records. When astonished reporters asked him why, he explained that although his opinion of the Finance Commission was low, he had an idea that the seventeen auditors at least must know their business. He thought it would be a check on his own city auditors and bookkeepers. He would be as interested as the Finance Commission in their findings, and might find out something about the condition of the city that he did not know.

Within a couple of months each of the seventeen auditors was lost in a separate labyrinth of figures. Curley had a total of $10,000,000 in construction projects either under way or in the works at that time. When the auditors came up with complaints that city councilors had spent $6,000 on illegal trips investigating hospitals and $28,841 for parades and celebrations of such events as the Battle of Bunker Hill and Evacuation Day (March 17), he lost patience. Mayor Fitzgerald, ten years earlier, he pointed out, had spent $122,653 on the same kind of celebrations. With all the books, records and contracts open to them, the auditors were spending their time on trifles. He wanted to throw them out of City Hall and asked the legislature to abolish the Finance Commission and divert the city's money, allotted to them under statute, to him for further city improvements.

The legislature refused. Curley lumped them all together as "pious humbugs and hypocrites."

The cold war between Curley and the Finance Commission

was resumed. A few days later it notified Curley that it would publicly disapprove of any expenditure of money for a visit of the mayor and council to attend the opening of a new Statler Hotel in Buffalo. Curley snapped that the Commission still was ignorant of its own function, that its jurisdiction was city government; he rebuked the members for their stupidity and told them that if they had only paid attention to teacher and learned to read while in school, they would have discovered in the newspapers that the mayor and council were guests of the Statler Corporation, which was paying all expenses.

Contracts for hundreds of thousands of dollars in land takings for bridge and street widenings were still being awarded, or remained to be awarded. The Commission probably would reach them long after Curley was out of office. The Commission was made up of Curley's enemies and bitter critics, and yet it was inept and becoming absurd. It had fallen in prestige and public confidence. In any exchange Curley made it look silly, and the people of the city were beginning to look upon it as a joke.

While all this was going on, Curley still was lavishly entertaining visiting celebrities, some genuine, others international charlatans, impostors and fakers. Lord and Lady Aberdeen arrived to collect money for the Irish cause. She was large and capable. He was small and whiskery. The American Association for the Recognition of the Irish Republic was at its peak. Its president, in Boston, curiously enough, was of Italian descent, John Sawtelle. He later became a member of the governor's council. It was an era of high wages, when professional Irishmen roamed from city to city visiting Irish societies, raising money for which there was seldom an accounting. The Boston Irish took Lord and Lady Aberdeen to their hearts.

Lord and Lady Carleton arrived hard upon them. They

were received in the same style. They were wined, dined, entertained, whirled through the city in automobile parades with motorcycle outriders. On one occasion they wanted a Boston Irish cop fired for being insolent. Curley sent for the policeman. Next day, Standish Willcox channeled the royal couple quietly out of town. A month later they were picked up for jumping a hotel bill. Curley asked the police commissioner to raise the cop one rank and it was done.

Decorations were being showered upon Curley by foreign governments. The Japanese made him a Third Degree Knight of the Rising Sun. The French gave him the Medal of Recognition; the Serbs, the Medal of the Knight of St. Savior; Italy made him a Commander of the Order of the Royal Crown. He had a trophy room built in the basement of the house on Jamaicaway and placed in it the loving cups, medals, plaques, illuminated testimonials and extraneous junk that had come his way up to now including the medals and decorations from foreign governments. Some of the stuff could be hocked in time of stress.

Calvin Coolidge had gone from the State House to the vice-presidency to become president when Warren G. Harding died. He was succeeded by Republican Governor Channing Cox. E. H. Armstrong, Premier of Nova Scotia, arrived in Boston. Cox gave a banquet in his honor. Curley was present and the governor talked about reciprocity with Canada, at that time a prominent national issue. Everything was swimming along smoothly until Curley got up to speak. Perhaps he was bored by the monotony of successive receptions and banquets. Perhaps he was surfeited with royalty and visiting celebrities. Perhaps he was disappointed at such a complete lack of excitement and interest. Perhaps he thought of the trophy room and the foreign medals and decorations, or perhaps he was annoyed by the dull, placid, expressionless masks of the well-fed, successful businessmen before him; or it could be that he was inspired to engage in a venture in international political mischief. Wherever he went he made news. That's why the guideline "new lead—Curley" was the most overworked in every newspaper office in Boston.

When unsuspecting Governor Cox called upon Curley, he stood up. Premier Armstrong looked up with casual interest and very soon head table and guest were sitting straight up in their chairs. Curley shot away the underpinning of reciprocity and for the next twenty minutes went on to develop the theme that it was time now for Canada to ask for the admission of all of her provinces as states in the United States of America to make one great Democratic North American continent.

Nothing of Armstrong's prepared speech, delivered nonetheless, ever reached print. All that was reported is that Armstrong said that the time and the place were not appropriate for a discussion of Mayor Curley's suggestion.

Eleven · The Mayor at Home

JAMES MICHAEL CURLEY, mayor of Boston, and James Michael Curley, husband and father, were two persons. Politics was his business—a business that involved a good deal of acting and fakery, sleight of hand and a more entertaining, diverting or bewildering accompanying patter than that of any magician. It required props, an extensive wardrobe, an ability to maintain an appropriate facial expression, to simulate intense interest where none existed, sympathy, indifference or indignation.

When in public, he was on stage, and he never permitted himself to forget the fact, but once he crossed the threshold of the house on Jamaicaway he was a husband who lost himself completely in his family: kind, thoughtful, considerate. He never forgot a birthday or anniversary, and he was easily managed by the women of his household.

He was completely in love with his wife. She could control him, contain him and change his mind when none else could. He loved to please her, and she worshiped him. He was a congenital monogamist. He could not be otherwise. He shied away from other women, kept his distance. He could be pleasing and charming for about ten minutes, but after introductory pleasantries and the state of the weather, he could not stay on common ground with them.

Mary Emilda Curley knew she had married a strange genius with a rare talent. He was an adult problem child, but she understood him. Balancing his impulsiveness with restraint, hers was sometimes the heavier burden. She was wife, mother and manager. Curley could not be a hypocrite before her. When he knew a scandal was about to break in the newspapers, he warned and prepared her. If he felt that it was the result of bad judgment or a mistake on his part, he acknowledged the fact, and they tried to chart a way out.

She had a keener perception than he of many things. She could, and did, make and break rising young politicians, but the quickest and shortest way to political oblivion was to try to persuade her to use her influence with her husband. Politics, to her, was her husband's profession, more exacting than medicine, engineering or law, though lacking their dignity and constancy. Her husband attended to his profession. She looked after her household and her children, a full-time task. She never discussed her husband's business with anybody. Her close and intimate friends knew better than to try to wheedle from her any hint of what he planned to do. Her household was constantly being up-ended, but she became accustomed to that. Dignified businessmen and panhandlers were always at the door. The telephone was always ringing even though its number was unlisted and frequently changed. Many a Boston housewife envied her, but her life was no bed of roses, entirely because of the nature of her husband's calling.

She never appeared in print. Only once did she allow herself to be photographed, and then with her husband and children surrounding her. She had her own group of intimate women friends, and they were nonpolitical. Curley and his family were kept separate in the public mind. His enemies attacked him, but never his family. She would not be her husband's public partner in politics. She was his consultant and adviser and as such a silent partner, but she disdained the parties, banquets and balls. Sometimes, however, common courtesy, good manners and good taste required her to be present, and for her husband's comfort and peace of mind, she attended.

Jurists, financiers, brokers, lawyers, the men with whom he did business or traded, had the Curleys to dinner when polit-ico-business deals were cooking, but Curley and his wife learned that the wives of the men who invited them, par-ticularly those in the Social Register, had a sly way of changing the purpose of a dinner. An invitation list was enlarged. The dinner became a feature production in which the buffoon mayor of Boston and his wife would be placed on exhibition to make fools of themselves before a select group. As soon as the Curleys stepped across a threshold they could sense this kind of dinner in the studied glances and suppressed sneers of women and the discomfort of the men there who knew Curley.

When this happened the Curleys became meticulously courteous and careful and the mayor became the charming and cultured raconteur with an inexhaustible fund of stories. These experiences were not uncommon, and whatever the design of the women, Curley could master the situation or top it with his tongue, choosing with uncanny instinct the right verbal drug or weapon. He could tell which to use merely by watching the expression on Mrs. Curley's face.

The Curley family lived on a roller-coaster. When in office, his income skyrocketed. When out of office, it shrank to a trickle or stopped entirely. When in office, household ex-penses were prodigious. Curley bought anything that attracted his eye. He didn't care what Mrs. Curley or the children spent, or for what they spent it. He bought works of art that the family knew, in lean years, might wind up in hockshops.

He lavished gifts upon his wife and his children. Nothing was too good for them. He spent money like a profligate, contracted outrageous debts that would have to be paid, commitments and installments that would have to be met while he was out of office; and out of that capricious stream of money, Mrs. Curley would have to dam up or channel into a reserve enough to last through drought and famine; and she could never know how much of it would be drained away.

A professional politician's household is almost impossible to budget. Perhaps it can be done, and has been done in some cases, but if the politician is a big operator it would require the services of an expert accountant, and the things the accountant would find out would very easily give him a blackmailer's life of ease. There were times when nobody in the Curley family knew how much was on deposit or on hand. Money came quickly, and often Curley stuffed it into his pockets without counting it.

In office, her husband was a great administrator. Out of office, he was certain to be a get-rich-quick lamb, ripe for shearing, and all her counsel, remonstrance and advice could not stop him; a pushover for hairbrained inventions, trick investment trusts, oil gushers, mines or sea-water gold. In his reading, he was as impressed with the fortunes made by lucky inventions and discoveries as he was by Gibbon's *Decline and Fall of the Roman Empire*. He was certain that one day he would meet the promoter with the right gadget or the right hole in the ground. Boss Tom Pendergast was a glutton for horse races, and at least got a run for his money. Curley never did.

Curley's wife and children never could see him as a Doctor Jekyll and Mister Hyde. Any portrait of him as a ruthless boss who would drive soft, flabby men out into below-zero cold seemed a caricature. To them he was amusing, entertaining, a husband and father who knew all the answers, words, definitions, a walking encyclopedia who made the preparation of term papers easy.

He could lose his temper completely in business, but at home he was quiet and gentle, a husband who would walk the floor at any hour of night with a baby in his arms and worry about whooping cough or measles. He seldom raised his voice. He indulged every whim of his children: James, Jr., Mary, Dorothea, Leo, Paul, George and Francis. Because he had been denied everything as a child, whatever they wanted they could have. He played with them, counseled them, studied their report cards and catechised them.

His office set them apart from other children in private and public schools. The son or daughter of a mayor was handled carefully and gingerly by instructors and teachers, and classmates divided themselves into small-fry sycophants, hero worshipers and the shy and embarrassed, who would like to be the friends of the Curley kids, but were afraid of being misunderstood and classified with the first. The brave among the jealous and envious, and the sons and daughters of Curley haters, called them names and repeated sarcasms they had heard from parents, tempting and provoking the Curley children to fight.

They became accustomed to that kind of isolation early in life and herded together or with the children of the friends of their parents. The Curley boys, although they were good football material, could not play the game until they got into the different atmosphere of college. High-school coaches hesitated to treat them like other students, and students in practice were inclined to be too gentle with them. In college, they were tossed around indifferently. Frozen out of high-school sports, the Curley children played football on the Jamaicaway lawn, where Mary played center or quarterback and often wound up with black eyes and a bloody nose.

Of the children, Mary resembled her father and seemed to have the same instinctive understanding of him as her mother. In school she became fiery and indignant and furiously angry when classmates said insulting things about him. As a girl growing up, she sat on the arm of his chair in the study listening to him. She soaked up his problems and became concerned about them. She inherited his love for books and added to it a love for music. They were always very close in thought, taste and understanding. Fiercely loyal to him, she had some qualities he lacked. She was blunt and bold, forthright and utterly honest. She wanted to know, in high school, why some classmates hated her father and she learned how to defend him. She learned a good deal of politics even as a child.

He built an extensive library and was critically selective in his choice of books. He had first read *Pilgrim's Progress* while in Charles Street Jail, perhaps because it was written while John Bunyan was in jail, and it became the cornerstone of his collection. His speeches were fashioned here, not by writing them out in longhand, but by closing his eyes, framing the sentences in his mind and committing them to memory, phrasing beginning, body and ending as he thought it through. For important speeches that divided themselves into parts, he wrote not more than five or six cue lines—and thirty years later he could deliver any one of them almost word for word.

Reference works were within easy reach, and he knew the thousands of volumes, biographies, histories and classics so intimately that it was never necessary to index them. He could go unerringly to the right shelf and section and pick out what he wanted. Library trustees who gathered there for conferences occasionally knew far less about the books in their custody than he did, a shortcoming for which he chided them often.

He had a sort of personal revolving museum, a collection of canvases, carved ivory, gems, oriental art, rare pearls, painted medallions and miniatures that were priceless. These were displayed carelessly in odd corners. Typed or printed legends were not attached. Only Curley knew their histories and value. He memorized them and was sometimes distressed that other members of the family hadn't. He was such an expert on jade that collectors came to him for opinions. He liked rare china and pottery and glassware, gold and silver craftsmanship—all because of his phenomenal memory.

When he bought the first string of pearls for Mrs. Curley, he read all that he could find in libraries about them. He read about precious stones and precious metals, discussed them with dealers and gemologists, and remembered what they told him. He made sharp trades and developed a genuine appreciation of all art, except painting and sculpture. Beautiful canvases and statuary left him cold. He could recite their fine points, paraphrasing critics with an authentic ring in his voice, but he would sit silently for an hour examining a finely carved piece of ivory and his silence was the greater appreciation.

He couldn't work with his hands. They were soft and sensitive. He couldn't paint. It's doubtful that he could even whittle a piece of wood. Sports bored him. His boxes at National and American League parks were usually occupied by his children or his friends. He went to football games when he could not avoid them, waved the right flag or pennant, but actually he enjoyed the spectacle of crowds and color in the stands more than the game, and he could estimate within a few dollars either way the size of the gate.

Underneath his hardboiled surface, Curley was a sentimentalist, easily moved and genuinely charitable, but he could never solve the problem of being honestly charitable without an awkward result. If he took off his overcoat and gave it to a shivering bum, he had to be sure that no one saw him; and he could not mention it to anyone except the members of his immediate family. He knew that if he were observed, the inevitable comment would be that he was playing to the gallery.

Once a year he disappeared on Christmas Eve for several hours. Neither Standish Willcox, his secretariat nor his family knew where he went. It was a mystery for years until a reporter followed him to find that he had slipped away quietly, hired a cab, loaded it with six of the biggest and most expensive baskets he could buy and made a lone pilgrimage to the rookery on Fellows Court where he was born.

Seldom did the same family live in this slum two years in succession, and he knew that anybody who lived there must be poor. Hat down over his eyes, coat collar up, he delivered the baskets as though he were a messenger, saying merely: "I have a basket for you." When the reporter asked for a picture, Curley was genuinely disappointed. "Don't print it," he pleaded. "Don't do that to me. I can't explain it, and I don't want to, but I wish you'd forget it."

It was perhaps the only time in his life that he asked to have something kept out of a paper. Sometimes he threatened, when he knew something critical of him was to be printed, and sometimes he sued for libel. In this case he asked, and the request was honored.

Twelve · A New Force in State Politics

FROM THE various viewpoints of Curley's family, Standish Willcox, his secretariat and the multiplying number of persons who looked to him for contracts, jobs or livelihoods, it was the better part of wisdom to keep him in public office and out of private business, and Curley needed no encouragement in that program. Since he could not succeed himself as mayor, he looked around for an interim office and decided to be a candidate for governor. Aside from the fact that he could make much more money in the bigger job, it had other attractive aspects. He could not very well be prohibited by law from succeeding himself there, and he could alternate between the State House and City Hall if circumstances made it advisable. This would give him a neatly ordered political life and might even lead to retirement to the men's club of the United States Senate.

Lieutenant Governor Alvan T. Fuller, the Republican candidate, had been both a successful businessman and a politician. From a small start in a Greater Boston suburban bicycle repair shop, he had worked his way onward and upward in both fields to become the owner of the largest Packard agency in New England and a progressive liberal in the Republican party. He married a Catholic girl, which fact did not hurt him at all with the Boston Irish. He was one of Boston's wealthiest men. The state was Republican, but Curley thought he had a chance. Here is why:

There are three Bostons. The city proper, as it is usually designated, is corporate Boston, made up of Proper Bostonians and Improper Bostonians around its periphery. The Boston Metropolitan District is made up of Boston Proper and a number of cities and towns adjacent to it. A district commission, appointed by the governor, has jurisdiction over the water supplies, sewerage and the scenic parks and parkways that overlap Boston and the cities and towns surrounding it, the banks of the Charles and Mystic rivers, the Blue Hills and state reservations. The commission has its own extensive police force to patrol these roads and ways, and it polices the rivers around Boston, but not the harbor. It's a silly arrangement made necessary by jealousies among the towns and by an always-present fear that Boston will euchre them out of their autonomous governments.

The third division is Greater Boston, made up of the whole thirty-nine cities and towns within fifteen miles of the State House. Boston Proper has a population of only 750,000, but Greater Boston has a population of more than 2,000,000. In all elections Greater Boston is the tail that wags the dog. It outvotes the rural areas of the state, which are Republican; therefore a Republican candidate might come down to the Boston line on election night with a whopping plurality and see it wiped out by the votes of Greater Boston.

Curley had no trouble financing a campaign. The prosperity boom of the roaring twenties was rising. Everybody was playing the stock market. Curley looked like a good gamble.

He needed an issue. The New York *World* had been exposing the Ku Klux Klan. Its spectacular series of stories had been reprinted in Boston. Most of the people of Massachusetts had never heard of the rejuvenated Klan. Until then it had been an episode in history books. The exposé backfired in Massachusetts and created a weak and faintly discernible imitation of the original. It put the Klan idea into the minds of the moron prejudiced, provided an excuse for the organization of another secret order for those who were attracted by white hoods, regalia and trick titles. Two meetings, one in Stowe and another in Needham, not far from Boston, had been looked upon as novel and transient curios and were thoroughly covered and pictured in Boston newspapers with close-ups of the burning crosses.

Curley seized upon the event and made it a red-hot political issue. His attacks incited and stimulated the organizations of incipient Klaverns. He toured the state from the Berkshires to Cape Cod, visiting every city and town, usually followed by a motor caravan of followers. Inevitably a fiery cross appeared on a hillside facing him wherever he spoke at a rally, and inevitably, his voice ringing with emotion, he pointed to it, saying: "There it burns, the cross of hatred upon which Our Lord, Jesus Christ, was crucified—the cross of human avarice, and not the cross of love and Christian charity. . . ."

Police were alerted everywhere to prevent the cross from being burned, but in spite of them, the crosses appeared as if by magic. They appeared with such regularity that Alvan Fuller charged Curley with touching them off himself. There is no doubt that they made dramatic stage props, but Fuller was not entirely correct. A few of them were genuine. Some were touched off by local practical jokers, and when neither of these appeared, it is probable that they were touched off by Curley followers, who wanted to be sure that Curley had the needed inspiration. He taxed them with the fact several times and was glad when they protested innocence. A legitimate fiery cross on a hillside kept the fire in his voice. Nevertheless, the end of the campaign marked the end of the Klan.

The Klan as an issue was not enough, and Massachusetts was not yet ready for Curley. Republican Fuller came down to the Boston line with a heavy majority. When the first Boston wards came in, it was clear that Curley would not make it. A coming event, though, already was casting its shadow. Fuller got 650,000 votes; Curley polled 490,000 in his first state-wide campaign, a figure of such size that it surprised the politically wise.

One of the least important factors in his defeat was a feud with Frederick W. Enwright, publisher of the Boston *Telegram*. During the campaign Enwright revived the story of Curley's jail term, reprinted it with elaborations and used a cartoon showing Curley in a striped suit in a cell, wearing a ball and chain. The caption beneath it was libelous and Enwright made one unpardonable mistake. He made a snide reference to Curley's family. Curley met Enwright accidentally on State Street. Their conversation was short, quick, fiery and ended when Curley's fist landed on Enwright's chin and knocked him out cold, ironically enough within the cobblestone ring that marked the site of the first Boston massacre. Before he was through, he went much further than that. He put Enwright in jail for criminal libel, closed up his newspaper plant and put him out of business.

Curley returned to City Hall, raised the salaries of scrubwomen again, from ten dollars to twenty-two dollars a week. He never forgot that his mother had been one. He doubled the salaries of city laborers in the lower brackets. He established a retirement fund to provide pensions for all city employees, and built up the city's reserve fund to $22,000,000. The reserve fund was his ace in the hole whenever he got tough with bankers. He threatened to borrow from it.

He decided to build seven health units, one in each of the

city's congested areas, but couldn't get the money. The legislature had established a statutory limit to the city's borrowing,
knowing full well that Curley would spend all he could get
his hands on. He asked the legislature to raise the limit, but
the legislators said no in an emphatic majority.

Curley sent for the city assessors and their tax records. He
found that the biggest taxpayer in Boston was George Robert
White, who owned $5,500,000 worth of real estate. Curley
called him on the telephone, tried to make an appointment,
but White would not see him. Curley assigned his office
sleuths to find out all about White, learned that he had
luncheon every day at the Copley Plaza, and went there forthwith to corner him. A head waiter pointed him out. Curley
went to the table, pulled up a chair and went to work on him.

"I want you to give me the money to finance those health
units," he said.

"Why should I?" White, an undemonstrative Yankee, was
astonished.

"As outright philanthropy," Curley said. "You've got more
money now than you know what to do with. You can't take
it with you. Wouldn't you like to be remembered as a man
who did something spectacular for the health of the people
of the city? I'll chisel your name in granite all over them.
I'll see to it that as long as you live, you'll never be sorry you
gave me the money."

White was not impressed.

Curley laid siege to him. He followed him around, button-
holed him wherever he went and applied the heat about seven
health units that the city needed badly. White listened, but
gave him no encouragement and Curley gave it up as a
bad job.

He died while Curley was in office and left his $5,500,000
to the city. He specified in his will that the fund be administered by the mayor, the city auditor, the president of the

Bar Association and the president of the Boston Chamber of Commerce. The health units were built. George Robert White's name is chiseled in granite or marble upon them and upon a number of other improvements in the city of Boston. Within five years, the fund had doubled. It is still being used.

Louis K. Liggett, manufacturer of patent medicines, owner of a chain of drugstores bearing his name, a man who knew Coolidge, was chairman of the Republican State Committee, but everybody knew that this was an honorary title. The man who really distributed Republican patronage, appointed postmasters, collectors of port, federal judges and such was Charles Innes. Curley and Innes still got along very well together.

There was no upcoming interim election in which Curley could be a candidate, except for governor, and he would not try that again until there was better assurance of success. His recent attempt had been expensive for him and his contributors. He looked forward to an enforced retirement of four years. His opposition was powerful, its financial resources unlimited. It was now well organized and pugnaciously determined that when he left the office this time it would be forever. A good businesslike mayor, preferably a trustworthy Irishman, would do the trick. Being politically forehanded, Curley wanted to be sure that would not happen; and he dropped around to see his old friend, Innes.

When the same group had defeated Curley in 1917 by putting three Irishmen into the fight, they had given him the cure for just such a situation. Without Democratic help a Republican would have no chance of being elected mayor of Boston. The first candidate to emerge was Malcolm E. Nichols, a well-born, innocuous accountant. Innes had persuaded President Coolidge to name him Collector of Internal Revenue. Nichols was followed by a procession of Irish candi-

dates. Nine of them filed enough valid, properly certified signatures to have their names on the ballot. The Boston Irish
vote was so hopelessly divided that Nichols walked right in.

Nichols' inaugural ceremonies were pallid compared to the
monster farewell for Curley. Nichols had a mild and perfunctory ball in the armory. Curley had the larger crowd at
a banquet in the Copley Plaza where he suggested, as a trial
balloon, that he might become a candidate for the United
States Senate. Boston newspapers headlined the story. Curley
found out quickly what he wanted to know, and did not
become a candidate for the Senate.

Nichols' administration became one of complete confusion.
Only Innes and Curley seemed to know what was going on in
City Hall. Nichols, it appeared, could not make any decision
without seeing Innes or calling him on the phone, and sometimes the answers to questions he asked Innes came to him
from Curley. An examination of the record seemed to establish that about half the Curley contractors continued to do
business with Nichols and half were newcomers who had
never done business with the city before. About half of his
appointees were Curley holdovers, or Curley supporters. The
rest were either Democrats or Republicans known to be
friendly to Innes. City Hall reporters designated Innes as the
day mayor, and Nichols as the nightmare.

Curley retired to his whilom job as president of the Hibernia Savings Bank. Inevitably he met a man who had a
secret formula for processing metal, turning it, as if by magic,
into stainless steel, Monel metal or chromium. There is little
doubt that he had enough money to tide him over until the
next election, but he became a heavy stockholder in a metal-
lurgical research corporation and very soon he was broke.

In the meantime, a dramatic national figure had captivated
the Boston Irish. Politically, the city was dripping wet, crying
for repeal of prohibition. Alfred E. Smith was forthright in
demanding it, and in everything else, as well, he was the kind

of champion they gladly would have adopted as their own. They liked what he did. They liked what he said. All the state's industrial cities and towns felt the same way about him. The campaign to make him the presidential nominee of the Democratic party was growing fast. He became Boston's ideal Irishman, a symbol of all they held to be good in the race. As the months passed, his name worked political magic. His influence bridged the boundary line in the Berkshires separating the two states and became such that even a mildly approving word from him could elect a candidate.

Curley sensed quickly what was going on, as did another of the state's most painful problem children, Senator David I. Walsh, and in time every vote seeker down to those aspiring for the least important minor offices, the eager-beavers who clutter up every political scene, were all but trampling each other down in the rush to climb on Smith's bandwagon. Lacking Al Smith's personal endorsement, the next best thing was to be connected in some way with promoting his nomination and election. It followed that Curley, Walsh and all Democrats of reputation in the state would be identified prominently with him, and smart Republicans in Massachusetts would be wisely discreet, even though Calvin Coolidge "did not choose to run" and later died heartbroken because he had not been compelled to do so.

While all this was taking place, Curley was a fire horse in pasture when bells were ringing. Joseph Buell Ely, a western Massachusetts Yankee lawyer and sincere Smith disciple, a second-time candidate for governor, was making his first important impression upon Boston Democrats. He had been brushed off once by the Boston Irish because of an almost unbelievable mistake. Named as a candidate for lieutenant governor, he was shamefully defeated in a primary by an unknown bus starter who was working his way through law school. His name was Dooley. He had a sense of humor and got enough signatures to get on the ballot as a practical joke.

Many Boston Irish voted for him under the misapprehension that he was "Mister Dooley," the sage and witty statesman created by Finley Peter Dunne.

Curley had offended almost every political leader in the state. He was universally feared and hated by them. They relished any chance to speed him to political oblivion. He was frozen out, denied any part in this crusade, one that might have been shaped expressly for him. It had everything he needed, and more: multiple causes, repeal, racial discrimination, the sidewalks of New York, and the religious issue was so prominent that it needed no stage properties like fiery crosses. Altogether, it was a natural for Curley's oratory; but he was compelled to stand on the sidelines, biting his fingernails.

After Al Smith was nominated, Curley turned the tables. He hired an abandoned hotel, twenty feet from City Hall, called it "The Bull Pen," plastered it with Smith signs, and had loudspeaker horns outside to attract crowds from the busy adjacent streets, presenting a continuous talkathon, including music and entertainment. Anybody who had anything to say about Al Smith could come there any time and sound off. For weeks, spectators crowded the place to listen with rapt attention to the same things said in the same or different ways.

As election day neared, the Bull Pen was jammed so tightly that an ambulance was always on hand to carry away men and women who were overcome. Special police details were assigned. Denied participation in the national convention, Curley could not be deprived of his city-wide spectacle. He created it. When Smith came to Boston it galled all politicians to see Curley and David I. Walsh riding in the same automobile with Al Smith from the railroad station in a shower of confetti and ticker tape through streets crowded as Boston had never seen them before. When the votes were counted,

Al Smith, who did not carry his own state, carried Massachusetts. His majority in Boston alone was around 100,000. His majority in the state was only 17,000. Metropolitan Boston had given him the state, and even Curley's enemies had to concede that he did it.

Thirteen · Third Administration: Deaths and Disaster

THE BOSTON IRISH were now beginning to split into factions. In seventy years they had completed a cycle in much the same manner as the Yankee Brahmins before them. Both original Irish immigrants and Brahmins were dwindling to thin, unimportant strains in the population. First- and second-generation American-born Irish were now as reactionary as the Brahmins, and in some cases more so. Some out-Puritaned the Puritans. Brahmins had been whipping boys and scapegoats for so long that a growing number of second- and most third-generation Boston Irish were bored by the spectacle as a monotonously recurring political stratagem. There were hardly enough Brahmins to count and they were now being stuffed with straw, held up by tiresome common scolds as horrible examples and as the cause of most of Boston's troubles. A growing minority of Boston Irish were coming to the conclusion that the Boston Irish themselves were the cause.

His Eminence William Cardinal O'Connell disapproved of James Michael Curley. He made that clear. None of his flock could quarrel with him as a churchman. He was a far-sighted and efficient religious administrator. Politically he scarcely could be classed as a progressive. He was suspected at times of voting Republican. His influence in state government was extensive. His influence in city government was never as important as it had been represented. He did not tell Catholics how to vote, nor would he permit his priests to do so from their pulpits. Although he really meant his flock to understand it that way, he never said: "Don't vote for Curley," and he could not bring himself to imply "positively." His approach was always oblique. He talked of electing only "men of good character" to public office. The intelligent and progressive among the Boston Irish knew what he meant.

He and James Michael Curley were of the same generation. Their backgrounds were very similar. Cardinal O'Connell's parents had come from Ireland to settle in the mill town of Lowell. His father and mother had worked at the looms before he studied for the priesthood. He had a brilliant mind, and soon after his ordination was dispatched by his predecessor, Archbishop Williams, to the North American College in Rome. The cardinal, too, was an orator of distinction, a composer and musician. He had a charm of personality that could have made him a statesman in secular life. Instead he became a statesman within the organization of the church.

From the same kind of beginnings as Curley's, Cardinal O'Connell became an aristocrat, passionately proud of Ireland and the Irish; and the growing reputation of Curley, the manner in which he got his money, the public portrait of him as he was known outside of Boston, made him cringe. The cardinal could exert influence in the State House and in the legislature with rectitude and respectability, but he knew that he never could cross swords with Curley in city politics and maintain his dignity, and there were many reasons why he would have liked to do so. For example: His diocesan jurisdiction overlapped Curley's political jurisdiction. He maintained an extensive parochial school system. There were Catholic churches, rectories, convents and hospitals throughout the city. Next to the city itself, the church owned the most land and buildings. There was a minimum of co-operation between them. Curley never turned to him for advice, nor could he be influenced in his public life by the cardinal's obvious but silent disapproval.

Frederick W. Mansfield, a conservative labor-union lawyer, was Cardinal O'Connell's personal friend and represented him occasionally as legislative agent before committees in the State House. As the 1929 election was drawing near, Mansfield announced that he would be a candidate against Curley. There was a good deal of eyebrow lifting. This was taken to mean that the cardinal had finally decided to stamp out Curley and Curleyism. If Mansfield had been able to say so, the effect in Boston, and the repercussions elsewhere, would have been interesting. There is little doubt that the cardinal wanted it that way, but he would not degrade the church or endanger the eminence of his office by saying so. Had Mansfield been able to claim even an implied endorsement, it might have had a devastating effect on Curley's vote. Mansfield, it appeared, had been given the heavy artillery, but was forbidden to use it. He was expected to win on his known public association with the cardinal and his ability as a campaigner.

The Finance Commission, muckraking Curley constantly for fifteen years, had accomplished the impossible. Tiers of filing cabinets were filled with investigations of transactions down to the minutest details. It had unearthed so much that the dirt thrown up became an impressive mountain of waste that could not of itself destroy him. Somewhere in that slag pile may have been buried the explosive cases, complete with detonating caps, to blast him out of office, but each case either was considered not good enough or was discarded for something better. Nobody could decide whether to convict Nero

of putting martyrs to death, burning Rome or being a lousy
fiddler. The Good Government Association had disappeared,
asphyxiated, perhaps, under the pile, or worried to death trying to make the decision.

The campaign was dull and prosy. Mansfield was tall, gaunt,
bespectacled, a methodical lawyer, past president of the Bar
Association. He had removed an erring district attorney from
office. He was not a finished public speaker. He appeared to
have reached into the Finance Commission dossiers and to
have come out with the wrong material—charges against Curley in previous administrations that had long since been forgotten. So it was too late for those. Curley was still putting
on his customary show. He gave it a new twist halfway
through the campaign by announcing that Mansfield had
already been defeated. Curley conducted himself henceforth
as though he had already been elected, telegraphed invitations
all over the country to conventions to come to Boston the
following year during his administration and read the replies
at rallies.

He proved to be right. Odds against Mansfield were quoted
at ten to three. When the votes were counted, Curley had
defeated Mansfield 117,000 to 96,000.

Mansfield was not the usual adversary, though. He joined
the extensive group dedicated to getting Curley out of office
forever and became the most formidable in it. Both as a
labor lawyer and as head of the Bar Association, he had been
slow-moving, deliberate, surefooted. He became sleuth and
bloodhound, untiring, unrelenting, unhurried, determined to
drive Curley from public life. He became the bane of Curley's
life, caused him more discomfort, inconvenience and exasperation than all others put together, but even he could not do it.

He began by demanding a recount, in spite of his overwhelming defeat, but it was his practice to examine everything, even the obvious. The recount established that all
ballots were in order, properly marked, properly checked and

the count accurate. There was nothing wrong. Mansfield set himself a long task. The Finance Commission would change its tactics; but Mansfield would be back in Curley's life from time to time to give him bad moments and bad years, and that would be the extent of his success.

When Curley took office in 1930, Boston business braced itself for the shock. Within a few months, bulldozers were knocking down buildings; heavy-tonnage trucks were rumbling through narrow streets. Curley was closing off Dorchester Bay, adding seven more miles of sandy beaches, building solaria for mothers and their children and hiking up tax valuations, particularly upon the properties of those who disapproved of these public improvements, including the Boston *Herald*. He took acres of land by right of eminent domain in the North End to make a Prado and appropriately landscaped surroundings to shrine the Old North Church, wiping out two blocks of the city's worst slums in the process, doing away with a bottleneck to make a wide approach to a vehicular tunnel under Boston Harbor, improvements badly needed and long overdue. Ordinarily it would take ten years to condition Boston for them; Curley did it in ten minutes. The legal fight over it occupied the next ten years.

The Finance Commission surprisingly dropped everything to investigate these land takings immediately. Witnesses were called. Questions were asked and statements signed while memories were fresh. The Commission was trying to find who owned the properties before Curley took them, how recently title to them had changed hands, how much they were actually worth, how much the owners were awarded and who got the money—but there were a lot of land takings to examine. It took time.

Curley's city treasurer, Edmund L. Dolan, a short, squat, cherubic bond salesman, had been trained for fourteen years in Boston banks and bond houses. He was Curley's intimate friend and next-door neighbor. Curley's yacht, the *Maicaway*, was owned by him. The Finance Commission found reason to believe that he was also head of the Mohawk Packing Company, a corporation organized to buy meat and sell it to city hospitals and institutions at prices ranging from 25 to 30 per cent higher than the state or private individuals paid for beef. The Commission learned that the Legal Securities Corporation had been organized in a suite of offices that had been Dolan's before he became city treasurer.

The affairs of the city treasurer and of these two corporations alone led through such a fairyland jungle of finance that the few who tried to find their way through it were confounded and befuddled. The record, the evidence and the testimony added up to a Disney cartoon. One trail led back through the years to Benjamin Franklin, who left the town of Boston a thousand pounds English sterling in 1790, so that Dolan could invest part of it with accumulated interest in bonds to build water systems for Dallas, Texas, and Paterson, New Jersey, in 1930. Another led back two and a half centuries to 1674 when Christopher Gibson left a modest bequest for the maintenance of the schools of Dorchester, not then a part of Boston, and wound up with accumulated interest in a blind alley somewhere on State Street. The Legal Securities Corporation itself was traced back, in court, by Dolan to five thousand dollars that a trusted employee found in a black box under his bed one night, and it paid off in one year fifty thousand dollars in dividends.

Dolan turned out to be one of Curley's greatest mistakes. Curley could do a daring thing without troubling to tell the people of Boston about it until after it was done—and get away with it. Dolan did daring things without troubling to tell Curley until they were done—but he couldn't get away with it because not even Curley could explain Dolan to the people of Boston. Newspapers printed the details, but their readers paid little attention. As usual, when Curley was in office, the city was a continuous three-ring circus, dominated by Curley as the central ringmaster, and the people were too fascinated by the shows he contrived to be diverted by the Finance Commission and newspapers on the side lines hawking what they thought was a better show in what was happening to the money in the box office. The Prado, the land takings, the Mohawk Packing Company and the Legal Securities Corporation were shaping up into major scandals. Curley seemed to have the right answers to questions and to charges concerning the Prado and the land takings, while he looked on at the exposés of Dolan as interested and astonished as anyone in the city.

These investigations disturbed him very little. He wanted to be governor of Massachusetts and he thought that the time was becoming ripe. The state was nearly ready for him. The political complexion of Greater Boston and of most of the thirty-nine cities of the state had been changing steadily, although the Republican vote of its 316 towns had remained almost static. The Democrats of the cities now could easily outvote the towns. A governor was to be elected during the first year of his term in City Hall. It was certain to be a Democratic year. The state was ready for Curley, but he was not ready. It was inconvenient for him. He preferred to stay in City Hall for three more years and then become governor.

Democratic leaders of the state suggested Ely, but Curley never agreed with other leaders, and it would serve his purposes better to have a Republican remain in office for two more terms. Al Smith liked Ely. That was enough for the Boston Irish. Ely was their boy, and as he was a Yankee, he could count upon heavy Yankee Democratic and Republican support. His election was a cinch.

Curley wanted no part of him. He could become the core of a state-wide machine that would bedevil or defeat Curley when he was ready to become governor. Curley forthwith made his peace with his ancient enemy John F. Fitzgerald, who announced himself as a candidate for nomination in opposition to Ely. A Republican could not beat Ely in the election, but a Republican could beat Fitzgerald, particularly if Curley men turned against Fitzgerald just before election.

Both sides bought radio time extravagantly and took to the air with language and epithets that have since been barred under a later-day radio code. Chief radio hatchet man opposing Curley was Daniel H. Coakley, once his close friend and legal counsel, disbarred as a result of a shakedown racket, using women to lure wealthy men into hotel rooms, signals, discovery and blackmail. As a result, one trusting district attorney died heart broken and another in an adjoining county was disbarred and faded into obscurity. The feud got so venomous that after one attack upon him, Curley knocked out the chairman of the Democratic State Committee in a fist fight in a radio studio, and then felled Gael, the son of Daniel Coakley. Later, before a radio engineer could pull a switch, Coakley barked: "Bully, bravo, coward, thug, blackleg and jailbird."

John F. could not take it and withdrew, but Curley continued the fight demanding that Boston nominate him anyway. Ely was nominated. Curley lost.

After Massachusetts Democrats have torn each other apart in occasional assaults and mayhem, it has been customary for them to get together, shake hands, kiss and make up. This time the inevitable harmony meeting was held in Worcester, in the heart of the state. Curley and Ely appeared before five thousand campaign workers and spectators on the same platform. They shook hands. The crowd cheered, applauded, threw hats in the air. Curley quieted them.

"The party has spoken," he said, smiling. "It has selected Joseph B. Ely as its nominee. I accept that; and as a token of my willingness to support Joe for election, I am presenting him with a check for one thousand dollars to help defray the expenses of the campaign."

He handed the check over. Ely smilingly accepted it. The crowd roared its enthusiasm. When Ely looked at the check sometime later that night, after the meeting had adjourned, he found that it was made out to the Boston Democratic Committee, which Curley now controlled. Curley would spend it—not Ely. Ely was elected.

All Finance Commission investigations up to this time, Curley had been able to dismiss, ridicule or shrug off. Their investigation of Dolan disturbed him. He could not do for Dolan what he did so easily for himself. Curley was sure of himself. He always stayed within the law. The Finance Commission could prove nothing against him. Dolan was his close friend. He assumed that Dolan, even though he strayed into the shadowland or twilight zone between the legal and the strictly illegal, was smart enough to keep within bounds where nothing could be proved against him. He was wrong.

Misfortunes piled upon Curley. For two years he had known that his wife was going to die. During that time he had spent not more than ten or twelve evenings away from her. She died, and six months later their son James Michael Junior followed her, the third death in the family; the fifth, counting the infant twins. His daughter Dorothea had died six years earlier. For a while he was dazed and listless. His son had mirrored him in many ways and had been the apple of his eye. He had been training James Michael Junior in politics and in the science of government since the day he was graduated from Boston College, and the son had been serving an apprenticeship on his father's secretariat. When Curley had oriented himself to life without them, he took the rest of his children on a tour of Europe and brought Dolan along to get him out of the clutches of the Finance Commission and keep him out of further trouble.

Fourteen · The Grand Tour

STANDISH WILLCOX had a fine and sensitive appreciation of the ruling class everywhere in the world and from his point of view James Michael Curley had become a member of it on the very first day he took office in 1914. Standish recognized only two divisions of society, the ruler and the ruled, the aristocracy and the common people. He respected both, but never confused the two. He felt that the ruling class everywhere should be friendly. It eliminated friction and misunderstanding and made life much more pleasant and agreeable, particularly for the ruling class. From that day forward, Standish was punctiliously careful in observing all courtesies and thoughtful little amenities on behalf of James Michael Curley, Mayor of Boston.

If a king, shah, sheik, sirdar, sultan, mogul, maharajah or potentate lost a wife or married one, became a father or grandfather, fell ill or was thrown from a horse, won an obscure war or diplomatic battle, added a couple of colonies or lost the crown jewels at Monte Carlo, Standish would write the precisely proper sentiment, cable it or have it translated, prepared, engraved or illuminated on parchment and lay it before Curley, if necessary, for his signature. Standish usually briefed Curley. Sometimes Curley paid attention; sometimes he did not. This was a personal department Standish had created, and Curley let it go at that. It made Standish happy, and it was harmless.

Usually, Standish beat the State Department to this expression of solicitude, cabling the equivalent of "I'm sorry for your trouble" to kings and emperors who were grieved by deaths in the family, and over a period of fifteen years there had grown up an impressive number of burghers and lord mayors who might be excused for assuming that Curley ruled America. For the most part, this was no play for the support of local racial groups. There weren't any from many countries. Boston's political head-hunters and Hottentot vote was distinctly of domestic origin.

When Curley went abroad, Standish notified everybody at all foreign ports and European way stations. When Curley arrived aboard ship, all passengers knew immediately that the mayor of Boston was on hand. It was an honor for the captain to eat at the mayor's table. Standish did a thorough job. He had written ahead or cabled instructions for the mayor's reception, even including, in some cases, the names of those who he felt should be included on reception committees and on guest lists. Standish thought of everything, except, perhaps, a twenty-one-gun salute.

Curley toured Ireland so fast that people in some places learned that he had been there only after he had gone. He covered six hundred miles in three days, paid a flying visit to the home of his ancestors in County Galway, was entertained at dinner by the president and ministers of the Irish Free State, conferred with the lord mayor and harbor commissioners of Cork about establishing a direct steamship line to Boston, looked over the River Shannon power station. He cornered the market on blackthorn sticks and shillalahs, picking up seventy-nine decorative ones and eleven war cudgels. He detached one such club to carry around with him in Europe, had the rest shipped back to Boston and commissioned a local scout to buy up all he could find in Ireland. Being forehanded, Curley wanted to hand them out to the first three or four hundred persons who could do him the most political good when he got back home.

He sped off to the Blarney stone with his party. His children were lowered down to kiss it, but not Curley. In Boston, where thousands of words of cable news about his trip were being printed every day, an editorial wag observed that the Blarney stone probably leaped up and kissed Curley. He toured the Parliament Building, looked over Trinity College, established a new record for sightseeing Ireland in such a short time, left breathless dignitaries behind him and hopped off for London and another whirlwind sightseeing tour. He was the guest of Ambassador Charles G. Dawes, looked over the Houses of Parliament, Saint Paul's Cathedral, had luncheon in the Old Cheshire Inn, toured the slum districts, Limehouse and Cheapside.

Next day the Curleys went on to Boston, England, where the town really turned out for them. They were guests of Mayor Reuben Salter, who had been Curley's guest in Boston, Massachusetts, a year earlier. A holiday had been declared. Mayor Salter had picked up a number of tricks as Curley's guest. Curley was received by a band and headed a parade. Two miles of spectators, among them a large number of schoolchildren, cheered him, waving Union Jacks and American flags. Later he spoke to a gathering of twenty thousand from the balcony of Guild Hall, where Cotton Mather, who carved a niche for himself in the history of Boston, Massachusetts, once preached. Curley visited the cathedral of Saint Botolph. The celebration went on until midnight.

Next day he hopped off for Paris to be the guest of General Pershing and Charles G. Dawes at the French Colonial Exposition, and after these official functions were over, he went strolling through the Louvre, wearing a beret and swinging a shillalah. He stopped long enough to cable his scout in Dublin to inquire how he was getting along on the shillalah project, paid a visit to Longchamps, placed an eight-dollar bet on a horse's nose and won seventy-five dollars.

He went on to Rome, where Standish Willcox had been conducting, by remote control, a good-will building campaign for twelve years. When the consort of King Victor Emmanuel died, Standish had seen to it that Curley sent flowers and condolences. When an Italian mission, led by Prince Udine, successor to the throne in Italy with the title of Duke of Genoa, arrived in Boston in 1917, Curley entertained the mission with a parade and banquet. When Benito Mussolini made his march on Rome, Curley sent him a silk flag of the city of Boston with a gold shield attached to the staff, proclaiming: "Presented to the Savior of Christian Civilization, Benito Mussolini, by the City of Boston, James M. Curley, Mayor." Mussolini had been proud enough of the flag to display it in his office and to show it to visitors. Before he arrived in Rome, Standish had cabled the King, Mussolini, the Duke of Genoa, and Monsignor Francis J. Spellman in the office of the Papal Secretary of State. Spellman knew Curley. Born in Whitman, Massachusetts, he had been a priest in the archdiocese of Boston and editor of the *Pilot*, a Boston Catholic weekly newspaper.

Spellman met Curley at the train as soon as he arrived and warned him to take the next train out on the grounds that there was at that moment too much friction between the State Department and Mussolini, and that Rome could become a very dangerous place for an American very quickly.

That was the wrong approach. Any kind of public dispute was Curley's meat. He had been reading the newspapers, but had not realized how serious the conflict had become. Mussolini, determined to build and train a big army, was then trying to drive all available young men into military service. He had ordered the disbanding of Catholic Boy

Scouts and Catholic Action groups. He had ordered playgrounds established by the Knights of Columbus during World War I to close. He was threatening to close convents and monasteries.

Curley did not believe that things were as bad as that, and even so, a fight was too attractive. "Rome isn't a dangerous place for me," he assured Spellman. "Mussolini is a friend of mine; so is the King, so is the Duke of Genoa. We've exchanged friendly letters. They know I'm here. They'll see me. I'd like to talk this thing out with them."

Spellman protested that it was impossible. An American had taken a potshot at Mussolini the day before. There was a drumhead court-martial and he was sentenced to death. Mussolini then made it a rule to see only Italian subjects, or persons who had lived in the city for six weeks.

While they were discussing the matter further, a stranger looked over Curley's party. "Are you Mayor James Michael Curley of Boston?" he asked.

Curley nodded.

"The Duke of Genoa commands your presence," he said. "May I escort you to a car?"

Curley nodded. He turned to Spellman and said, "This is it." He followed his escort, was driven to the palace, ushered into the main hall and down two flights of stairs to a small room with a bare table and three chairs. He shook hands with the duke, visited for fifteen minutes and was driven to his hotel. Monsignor Spellman was waiting there to suggest that Curley discuss any proposal he might have in mind for settling the problem with Secretary of State Pacelli at the Vatican.

Curley was agreeable. He talked the matter over with Cardinal Pacelli and was given an unusually long audience of an hour and a half with Pope Pius XI. He returned to the hotel and met Count Cecini, representing Premier Mussolini. Standish Willcox cablegrams were working. The count told

Curley that Mussolini wanted to see him at Gigi Palace. Still wearing his beret and carrying the blackthorn stick, Curley went to see the premier.

He was ushered first, he said, into a small chamber hung with paintings of the sixteenth and seventeenth century. He was examining them when two guards frisked him.

"I have no weapons," said Curley, ignoring the blackthorn stick.

After that, according to Curley, he was led into a succession of three small rooms before entering the main palace hall, a place he estimated to be about 125 feet long, 40 feet wide and 30 feet high, bare of furnishings except tapestries and a desk in the far corner of the room. Behind it sat Mussolini.

Curley walked the length of the room, whacked his blackthorn stick smartly upon Mussolini's desk and said: "I come to present you with the chief weapon of my ancestors and the traditional symbol of their authority."

Mussolini, Curley said, looked up narrow-eyed, puzzled and blinking, trying to comprehend. Curley decided he had no sense of humor.

He had been allotted ten minutes. An hour and ten minutes later he was still talking to Mussolini. They had covered a good deal of ground. Curley thought that Mussolini seemed to be far better informed about what was going on in the United States than anybody else he had met in Europe. Finally, Curley, never in his life known to balk at an indelicate question, asked Mussolini bluntly: "How do you plan to adjust this dispute with the Vatican over Catholic Boy Scouts and Catholic Action?"

Mussolini stood up. The interview was over.

"Wait a minute—just a minute," Curley went on. "Ever since I've been in Rome, the Associated Press, United Press and all the American newspaper correspondents have been asking you for an interview on this question. That's what they're going to be asking me about when I get out of here, and I want to be able to answer. I'd like to say something like this: 'When, by his masterly courage and supreme statesmanship, Mussolini was responsible for stopping the mad march of communism in 1922, he won the good will and the esteem of Catholics of the world as well as the hatred of the communists of the world. When Mussolini settled the dispute between Italy and the Vatican and released the Pope from his imprisonment, he performed an act of exalted virtue which won for him the respect of all right-thinking people the world over.' " He paused a moment. "So far, am I right?" he asked Mussolini.

The premier nodded.

Curley waited for him to take it from there, but Mussolini remained silent.

"Has it ever occurred to you," Curley asked Mussolini, "that in the performance of those two great acts—one, superior statesmanship, and two, exalted virtue—you have erected a pedestal, consciously or unconsciously—a pedestal so chaste that there is no way you could justify a failure to settle the question of putting the youth of Italy in the army against the wishes of the Vatican and the right-thinking people of the world?"

Mussolini did not answer.

"Am I right?" Curley persisted.

Mussolini nodded.

"Take my arm and we'll walk out together," Curley suggested. Mussolini did and they walked out together.

Next day, Curley received an invitation to talk to the king of Italy for five minutes. He discussed many things with the king: a comparison of the economy of the United States with that of Italy; reminded him that a Eucharistic Congress was to be held in Dublin the following year, and felt that Italy could garner at least 20 per cent of an estimated 500,000 who would attend it as tourists, if the country used modern advertising techniques, promoted tours to the Eternal City and could arrange for mass audiences with the Pope.

Ordinarily it is the king who concludes an interview, but when the five minutes had stretched into an hour, Curley remembered that he still had sightseeing and other things to do. "Your Excellency," he said. "You have other duties, and with your kind permission I'll take my leave."

"Please don't go," Curley quoted the king. "I'm very lonely here. The only people I have an opportunity to talk to are theoretical economists. You've had practical experience."

At the end of another half hour Curley asked the king: "How do you feel about putting Catholic young men into the army and breaking up Catholic Action groups?"

"Have you any idea of how the premier feels about it?" the king asked.

"I talked with him yesterday," Curley said, "and I got the impression that he is inclined to be favorable to excluding them."

"If that's true," the king said, "it will make me happy. I shall talk to him tomorrow."

Curley was given a reception by the governor of Rome. The band played the Star-Spangled Banner. Reading in the newspapers the cabled news Curley was making, Standish must have been sending cablegrams by the score to Italy. So many events were scheduled that they overlapped the time of Curley's departure. He returned with his children on the *Leviathan*. Newspapermen, newsreel men and photographers met the liner at Quarantine. Curley told his story for Pathé News, and when he got ashore called Jack Conway, vice-president of Pathé, and asked him to send duplicate clips of the reel to Mussolini and the Vatican.

The following November, when Monsignor Spellman came home to spend the Christmas holidays at the home of his father, he dropped in to see Curley at City Hall and, according to Curley's report, told him that a provident thing had happened after the film was shown in Gigi Palace and at the Vatican. Mussolini notified the Vatican that he was ready to negotiate a settlement of the dispute.

Fifteen · The Roosevelt Band Wagon

On a train from New York to Boston on his return from Europe, Curley learned that Governor Franklin D. Roosevelt was aboard. He sent his card to Roosevelt's drawing room and was invited to come in. They had met in 1924. Each knew much about the other. Roosevelt had not yet announced that he would be a candidate for president. Roosevelt told Curley he was on his way to Magnolia, Massachusetts, to visit Colonel E. M. House, wartime adviser to Woodrow Wilson. Roosevelt asked for Curley's analysis of Massachusetts and Curley gave it to him honestly. He told him that the state was overwhelmingly for Al Smith and that if Roosevelt were contemplating running, he doubted that it could be turned over to him. Curley agreed that the 1928 election had established that a time had not yet come when a Catholic could be elected president of the United States, but he told Roosevelt that nevertheless it was his opinion that any Irish Catholic in Massachusetts who promoted the candidacy of Roosevelt as against Smith would be committing

178

political suicide. He explained how the Metropolitan District dominated the state of Massachusetts.

They talked for the remainder of the trip to Providence and Curley found the same charm working on him that Curley himself had worked on others. Roosevelt not only wanted Massachusetts, but he also wanted an Irish Catholic with Curley's persuasive voice to help sell him to the country, at least as a partial offset to the absence of Al Smith among his active supporters. He suggested that Curley join him.

It was not an easy decision. Curley knew that he would have to cut himself adrift, that he would become the most unpopular man in Massachusetts, although he acknowledged that because of the stock-market crash and the growing depression, Roosevelt might win. It was by no means a sure thing or a foregone conclusion at that time. Roosevelt told Curley that he never would have cause to regret his decision and implied that he would take good care of him if he won. Still the practical politician, Curley wanted to know how, and Roosevelt told him he would have a place in his cabinet or an appointment of almost equal rank if Massachusetts voted for Roosevelt. Curley had already dismissed Roosevelt's chances of getting a pledged delegation to the convention from Massachusetts.

"I'd like to get away from city politics, from investigations and the things a man has to do to stay on top in a city like Boston. My name has been pretty well blackened in some quarters because of the things I've had to do. I'd like to be a member of the cabinet. I'd like to be secretary of the navy," he said.

According to Curley, Roosevelt told him he knew of no reason why he couldn't have the post.

"It's a deal." Curley shook hands. "I think you know what this means to me in Boston. I'm sure that Al Smith never can be president of the United States. I think that you can be. You won't be nominated by the Democratic party in

Massachusetts. There is no miracle man who can do that for you; but if you're nominated by the convention, I'll do my best to put Massachusetts on the line for you in November."

Roosevelt asked again whether there was a chance of his getting any of the votes of the Massachusetts delegation in the convention.

Curley shook his head. "Not even mine," he said, "because if I abandon Al Smith, I won't even be elected to that convention. That's how strong Smith feeling is in Metropolitan Boston. When I announce myself for you, I'll be branded as a deserter, a hypocrite, a traitor to my own people. They'll run out of adjectives; but if you're nominated, the tide will turn and I'll be able to do my work then. In the meantime, I'll be taking a lot of punishment."

The above is the substance of the conversation as Curley remembers it. At any rate he apparently believed he had got a commitment from Roosevelt. On the other hand, James Roosevelt, who was particularly concerned with his father's affairs in Massachusetts at this time, says that his father never considered Curley even a possibility for appointment to the cabinet.

The conference ended when the train reached Providence. Two hundred persons were on the platform, not to greet Roosevelt (they didn't even know he was on the train, and it is doubtful that they would have been very much impressed at that point in Roosevelt's career, even if they had) but to cheer Curley, who left the train, without too much persuasion, to address a delegation of the Providence British Empire Club. From Providence to Boston, three army planes were a spectacular escort, sometimes buzzing it from two hundred feet above, a prelude to the welcome that was awaiting him.

Two bands were playing, five thousand persons were cheering and Back Bay Station was bathed in brilliant red fire when Curley stepped off the train. Another disappointed thousand was at the South Station, mistakenly supposing that he would arrive there. He stepped into an area of brilliant white light for movie cameras and told how glad he was to be home. Police pulled and tugged for half an hour to get him through the mob to his car. The car whisked away, escorted by motorcycle outriders with sirens screaming, and was followed by a cavalcade of twenty cars. Another thousand had gathered outside Curley's house, bathed in another glow of red fire. Inside there were more than two hundred waiting to see him. It was the first of a long series of identical spectacles whenever Curley returned home after an absence. If they had known the decision he made on the train, both stations, the area outside his house and the house itself would have been deserted.

Next day he was back at his desk in City Hall, catching up on what had happened during his absence. Standish Willcox was briefing him. While he had been touring Europe, the Finance Commission had had greater freedom and had made much more progress than during any of his administrations. The sun had been shining for his subordinates, and they had been making hay. Some were not as careful of things as they might have been if Curley had been around.

Curley's name had not been on the list of guests invited to Colonel House's place at Manchester-by-the-sea. An invitation was delivered by messenger on that busy morning and Curley left his office hurriedly.

Newspapermen, newsreel and sound men and photographers had gathered outside the House estate. They were unexpected and unwelcome. Gathered on the porch of the old rambling mansion were Colonel House; his son-in-law Randolph Tucker; William H. Coolidge, a railroad attorney; Ellery Sedgwick, editor of the *Atlantic Monthly*; Bob Washburn, political columnist of the Boston *Transcript*, friend of

Theodore Roosevelt and the Roosevelt family; United States Senators from Massachusetts Marcus Coolidge and David I. Walsh; and Franklin D. Roosevelt. Curley was sped up the drive to the house to join them, as newsmen looked on, wondering what it was all about. It was all very hush-hush. They had gathered like conspirators and had everything but masks and aliases.

It was the first important Roosevelt-for-President meeting outside of New York and it was talked over in undertones. House suggested an innocuous, meaningless statement for reporters and the newsreels. When the meeting ended, they were invited in. Newsreel men focused their cameras, set the scene and asked for statements. Senator Walsh spoke of the beauty and majesty of the sea that lapped the strand below and pointed to it. Curley looked directly into the lens and said: "Ladies and gentlemen: We have been making history here today. Franklin Delano Roosevelt is the hope of the nation. His splendid administration of the affairs of the Empire State make him outstanding as the man to nominate for the presidency."

The elation of Colonel House and Franklin Roosevelt and the consternation of the rest of the group were apparent a few days later on every screen in the country. Boston newspapers banner-headlined Curley's announcement that afternoon.

The Boston Irish hardly could believe their eyes and ears when they read and heard the news. The switchboard at City Hall was clogged with calls. Three telephone lines into his Jamaicaway house were inadequate. The Jamaica telephone exchange was swamped. The news was repeated and confirmed on the air and by nightfall the Boston Irish were seething. Within twenty-four hours Curley dived from a pinnacle of popularity to the depths of degradation. They heaped scorn and contempt upon his head, characterized him as a traitor, a betrayer of his people, a renegade and a double-crosser. A chorus of I-told-you-so's echoed wherever people gathered. Throughout the city his name was mud. He had not exaggerated when he foretold that this would happen.

Even his children were disappointed. They had not been warned. Curley had not foreseen that he would make the announcement so soon. He had had no chance to prepare them or to give advance notice to any of his associates who should have been told. Many of these thought he had been temporarily bereft of his senses. He had no engagements that night and went home to explain himself, and to do some thinking and planning.

He was pilloried at meetings of divisions of the Ancient Order of Hibernians, condemned by men who had been proud to couple his name with that of Al Smith; men who had all but worshiped Curley for a quarter of a century; men who wept as they passed resolutions of censure. Telephone calls that he answered, telegrams and personally dispatched messengers who came to his house with hand-written notes that night ended long friendships that he had valued and enjoyed. Curley was all alone in a sea of Smith sentiment.

Next day the newspapers exploited the news. His critics decided that he had at last taken enough political rope to hang himself and they were happy to wave him on to oblivion. Roosevelt was merely the governor of New York then. His political friends in Boston were but a small handful, and they were not the kind of people who ever would approve of Curley, what he had been and what he was. They were sure that his announcement was a mistake; that it would do more harm than good.

Curley was grim and determined when he showed up at City Hall next day. For the first time in his three terms as mayor, the corridors were empty. He was shunned, snubbed, ignored. City employees glared at him. Contractors who had to see him did their business quickly and left.

Standish Willcox looked down at his boss. "Are you sure you know what you're doing?" he asked.

"I know what I'm doing, all right. Roosevelt is going to be the next president of the United States and from here out I'm with him."

"That's a bit of long-range crystal gazing, isn't it?" Standish suggested. "The convention is still a year and the election is almost a year and a half away. I hope you'll excuse me. I can guess what you've been going through since last night, but quite frankly, I never heard of Roosevelt as a possible candidate. Smith was nominated once, and in view of what has happened since the stock-market crash, Smith can be . . ."

"That will be enough about Smith," Curley interrupted. "You can depend upon it, Smith will never again be the choice of a Democratic convention. He lost once and he's a Catholic. That's two strikes against him. I talked to Roosevelt the day before yesterday and again yesterday. I'm sure he can be the candidate, and I'm going to do all I can to bring that about. Don't you like that?"

Standish shrugged his shoulders. "I'm indifferent."

"If he's nominated and elected, you and I are going to leave all this. We'll be gentlemen. Would you like that?"

"I think that would be top-hole," Standish agreed. "Stop looking at me and talking to me as though I were a complete stranger. I wouldn't run out on you, anyway. Whither thou goest, I do and so forth. I'm only trying to reorient myself. What do I do now?"

"Find out all you can about Roosevelt. Study his record. Dig out all the stuff you can that will make good campaign material. Get an artist to design a campaign button. Let me see some sketches. Order a couple of hundred thousand and let's get rolling."

Campaign buttons were made, but this was a bad mistake, and they never were distributed. Portraits of Curley and

Roosevelt were linked. An inference might be drawn that Curley fancied himself as a candidate for vice-president, and the temper of the Irish in Boston was such that they might throw them in his face.

Meanwhile, Curley had become a John the Baptist, crying the name of Roosevelt in a wilderness of backs turned toward him. Roosevelt's son James, married to Betsy Cushing, daughter of the famous brain surgeon, and living in Framingham, became his constant companion and appeared with him on public platforms, but in the Metropolitan District, Curley talked to empty chairs. James was a partner in a Boston insurance firm and divided his time between his office and City Hall.

Wherever Curley went he was ridiculed, heckled and insulted. Democratic state and city committees ostracized him. He became stubborn and lantern-jawed, carrying on a one-man campaign, fighting harder than he had ever fought to put himself into office. He talked wherever he could assemble two or more persons to listen. He had no volunteers, no background of music and no show. The followers who performed these duties for him in every campaign had deserted him. He made no headway. The harder he worked for Roosevelt, the more popular Smith became.

Nevertheless, he could not be swerved. He bought time on the air and tried to jam his pleas and arguments into the ears of the Boston Irish and of the voters of the state.

Smith Democrats, led by Governor Ely, were a solid front, thoroughly organized and well financed. Curley could not make a dent. Every well-known Irish name in the state was on their roster. Whatever the Smith faction did was news and good publicity. Curley's meetings were not even covered. After nine months of this kind of campaigning, the Smith Democrats were whooping it up. A slate of delegates pledged to Smith was announced for the Democratic primary and Roosevelt called Curley to Albany to discuss the matter.

"How about putting up a slate pledged to me?" Roosevelt asked.

Curley shook his head. "It wouldn't do any good. I warned you on the train that it would be hopeless. It's impossible to beat Smith in Massachusetts. There aren't any important vote-getting names that I can get as delegates."

"I think it ought to be done," Roosevelt insisted.

"I don't agree with you, but if you want it that way, it will be done."

The Roosevelt slate was snowed under in a preferential primary. Smith-pledged convention delegates swept the state. Newspapers and the Smith faction made the most of that, too. It looked as if Curley's hoarse campaign for Roosevelt had been wasted. His power, the Boston Irish were told, and honestly believed, was now ended. He was politically dead.

The Smith delegation left for Chicago in high jubilation, serenaded at the South Station by bands. Some thirty thousand spectators were on hand to see them off. They were certain that Smith would be nominated. The name of Curley had been erased as a factor in state politics. He was weary and tired. He had suffered the worst defeat in his history. He did not even have the credentials, as far as they knew, to get into the convention hall.

Sixteen · Jaime Miguel Curleo

He was counted dead a little bit too soon. The Smith delegation arrived in Chicago on the morning of June 26 and went quietly to the Hotel Stevens. Curley arrived with his children that afternoon, detrained with a Roosevelt delegation from Maine, and was given a noisy reception. James Roosevelt was there to meet them, with Colonel Gaw, Chicago's official greeter, and they were escorted in one of the city's white guest cars by a fleet of screaming motorcycles to the Congress Hotel. The Massachusetts delegation knew right away that Curley was in town and wondered why.

The Puerto Rican delegation was seated directly behind Massachusetts in the convention hall arrangement. Curley dropped around to see F. Val Spinosa and Mrs. Jean Whittemore, chairman and vice-chairman of that delegation. Puerto Rico could use a little advertising on coast-to-coast networks carrying the convention. Curley made Spinosa a proposition. Mayor Anton Cermak of Chicago came into the room, too. Gentle pressure was enough. Spinosa took a trip to Baltimore and Curley left the room, now acting chairman of the Puerto Rican delegation, with Spinosa's blessing and by unanimous vote of his delegates. As soon as that became known, a complaint was registered with the credentials committee. Curley won the contest and was accredited.

When the roll call of states began on that hot last night in June and Puerto Rico was reached, Alcalde Jaime Miguel Curleo, recognized by the clerk as James Michael Curley, delivered the vote of that possession, and even the bitterest of the Boston Irish at their radios could not restrain a grin. Listening to the convention proceedings, the analyses of commentators and reading newspapers on the fight developing in Chicago, a good many of the Boston Irish already were entertaining second thoughts. If Smith were the nominee of the convention, was the tenor of their thinking, he had been beaten once and he could be beaten again. New England had been the last section of the country to feel the depression, and in 1932 the Boston Irish were really feeling it in hardship. If Smith were nominated and beaten in the election, it would mean four more years of Hoover. That was a frightening prospect.

When Curley's familiar voice came over the air, they shook their heads in admiration. There he was again, unconquerable and irrepressible, and many of them began to speculate that perhaps Curley might have been smarter than they were. When the chips were down after that first roll call, listening to their radios, they sensed, as did the convention delegates, that Smith never would make it. If they could not have Smith, Roosevelt was their next choice, and for the first time they developed an intense interest in the stop-Roosevelt combinations in the convention.

Commentators and newscasters describing the scene, furnishing background information, fact, rumor and gossip, had explained that Smith must win on the first or second ballot; that favorite sons, including Jack Garner of Texas, would be dropped on the third ballot. The band wagon would start when William Gibbs McAdoo, whose California delegation was pledged to Garner, abandoned him for Roosevelt on that ballot.

When Smith did not make it on the second ballot and running explanations of what was happening poured into their ears, the Boston Irish gave up hope for Smith. The battle shaping up to stop Roosevelt by switching to another candidate was outlined. The band wagon did not start rolling on the third ballot. Something had happened, the radio audience was told, and nobody knew that better than Roosevelt's manager, Jim Farley, darting around the convention floor. Neither McAdoo nor Texas had abandoned Garner, as expected. A deal was suspected to build up Garner to defeat Roosevelt. The convention was adjourned.

A few hours later, Roosevelt's top strategists, James A. Farley and Louis McHenry Howe, Roosevelt's personal secretary, were huddled in conference in Room 1502 of the Congress Hotel. Both were in shirtsleeves. They were opposites in appearance—Farley big, heavy, florid; Howe short, slender, weighing about a hundred pounds. Curley rapped at the door and was admitted. The problem to be solved was this:

William Randolph Hearst wanted first to stop Al Smith. He had never forgotten that Smith snubbed him when he was a resident of New York and wanted to run for the United States Senate on a ticket with Smith as a candidate for governor. Having accomplished—or helped to accomplish—that, he wanted next to have John Nance Garner nominated for president. He liked Garner. His newspaper chain had been supporting him. McAdoo campaigned for Garner in California and the Hearst papers supported McAdoo for the United States Senate. All the Hearst papers had already published Garner's life story in anticipation of his nomination.

Hearst was key man. Garner's vote was not yet impressive. Curley and Hearst were friendly, an original outgrowth of Standish Willcox's proclivity for writing letters to famous men.

As an ex-Hearst man, whenever his former chief wrote an editorial, or did something Standish approved of, he commended
and complimented him in a letter that he placed on Curley's
desk to sign. An interesting correspondence had developed
between Curley and Hearst. Curley had dropped around to
see Hearst and visit him when he was in New York and later
in San Francisco. They got along well together and the relationship ripened into a friendship. Hearst's Boston newspapers never attacked Curley. When they could not find a way
to praise him, they said nothing.

"I'd like to talk to Hearst," Curley suggested. "I'd like to
call him long distance, tell him how I size up the situation
here and ask him to persuade McAdoo and Garner to release
the California and Texas delegations on the next ballot."

Farley and Howe vetoed the idea. "We don't like the idea
of any personal contact between Roosevelt and Hearst," he
was told. "We don't like the idea of being supplicants at
Hearst's door, and we don't like to be under the obligation
that any solicitation of that kind might imply."

"Maybe so," Curley agreed, "but the nomination of Roosevelt happens to be too important to me to pass up anything.
It's too important to sacrifice on an altar of things left un-
done."

They were finally persuaded, reluctantly, to let him do it.
He put through a call to Hearst at his California ranch.

"Garner can't possibly be nominated for the presidency,"
Curley told Hearst, "but if you'll throw your support to
Roosevelt, I can guarantee that Garner will be nominated
vice-president. In fact, I'm ready to lead the fight for him."

Curley had nothing to back up that guarantee. He talked
to Hearst for ten minutes and was told that he would discuss
the matter with McAdoo. That afternoon, Hearst's *Chicago
American* softened considerably in its attitude toward Roosevelt, a switch that did not escape the delegates.

Soon after nine o'clock that night, the fourth roll call of

the states began. California was reached at 9:20. William Gibbs McAdoo addressed the chair and asked permission to make a statement. A buzz began in the convention hall as he took his place on the platform before the battery of blinding lights for the motion-picture cameras.

"California came here tonight . . . " he began.

There were cries of "Louder!" from the audience.

McAdoo paused. "I'll make it loud enough," he said. "California came here to nominate a president of the United States. She did not come here to deadlock this convention or engage in another devastating contest like that of 1924. . . . When a man comes into a convention with almost seven hundred votes . . . "

That's as far as he got. The convention sensed what he was about to say and broke into a roar like herds of seals. The aisles were crowded. Roosevelt parades began. The hall was in complete confusion. It was a half hour before he could resume to end with "California, 44 votes for Roosevelt!" It was another half hour before the convention could be brought to order.

The band wagon had started. Chairman Alcalde Jaime Miguel Curleo, in the Puerto Rico delegation, grabbed the standard of the island and plunged into the maelstrom of the aisles, shouting himself hoarse.

The Massachusetts delegation sat glum and steadfast. Grimly and until the final curtain, when the roll call was resumed, Governor Ely announced the vote of Massachusetts for Alfred E. Smith, but the tide had receded and left his delegation high and dry.

Next day as "a delegate from beautiful Puerto Rico," Curley seconded Garner's nomination for vice-president in a five-minute speech devoted almost entirely to "the forgotten man."

Back in Boston, like an airplane rising from the bottom of a steep dive, Curley's popularity had zoomed to heights he had never before experienced, an overnight transformation in the attitude of the mercurial Boston Irish that was fantastic; a sudden mass abandonment of Al Smith and a fervently enthusiastic adoption of Franklin D. Roosevelt. No doubt Roosevelt's voice on the air, like Curley's with which they were so familiar, had worked some of the magic; but there were other factors. The Boston Irish love a fighter. Curley had been beaten unmercifully. He came back to win, and they liked to be with a winner.

Curley was due to return on the night of July fourth. Spontaneously throughout the city groups got together and organized to give him a reception that would dwarf in size and magnificence anything he had ever seen. Two groups returned home from the convention that night. Police estimated that more than 250,000 persons turned out to meet Curley. He arrived on the Minute Man at the North Station. The crowd on the concourse was so dense that a hundred police reserves were sent in to clear some semblance of a path for him. All streets in the area were jammed with automobiles.

There were twenty-one bands inside the Station. Firecrackers and torpedoes were exploding. Ambulances were clanging. Spectators were being overcome. A big sign proclaimed: "We love you, Jim, but what the hell! We're all for Roosevelt." The Minute Man arrived at seven-thirty. Spectators broke through police lines into the train shed to swarm around and all over it. Curley stepped off the train, his seven-year-old son Francis in his arms. Police formed a flying wedge and saved Francis from being crushed. Curley was hauled through the crowd by a battalion of sweating policemen.

The scene outside was worse. The streets were lined with spectators all the way to Parkman Bandstand on Boston Common. James Roosevelt and his wife, who had arrived on another train at South Station, across the city, were now in a car at the North Station surrounded by motorcycle police. Curley was shouldered and lifted into the tonneau of an open automobile. Somebody put an Indian headdress on him under the mistaken belief that this was a characteristic costume in Puerto Rico. He wore it for a half mile before he could get rid of it.

At Parkman Bandstand he faced another 150,000 that had spread over Boston Common and mushroomed into the streets surrounding it. Amplifiers had been set up. He looked down upon the prominently displayed signs and flags of organizations that had so recently condemned him, waving vigorously as if to say: "Honest to God, Jim! We didn't mean it." Societies that had read him off their rosters in disgrace were trampling each other down in their haste to make amends. Seated behind him were sheepish contractors, politicians and office holders who had snubbed him, only too happy now to eat crow, if he so directed.

"Señores and señoritas," Curley addressed them and broke them up in laughter, "as the delegate from Puerto Rico . . ." But they continued laughing so that he could not go on. "I can't claim residence in Puerto Rico, but my ancestors, the Irish, have always boasted Spanish blood." And then he went into a ringing speech of praise for Roosevelt and the Democratic party.

The Irish were happy that night. They had kissed and made up with Curley: a procedure that was becoming something of a routine.

Next day he turned up in City Hall and planted the standard of Puerto Rico that he had carried back from the convention hall between the city and state flags behind his desk. He was no longer interested in city administration. He was remembering a conversation with Roosevelt on a train coming from New York, and his mind was on a wider horizon. His office was an auxiliary campaign headquarters. He needed money and he would set about immediately acquiring a fund. He called in his secretaries and staff and began delegating work to them. He ordered the Bull Pen reopened in Young's

Hotel. Amplifiers and horns were installed. Day after day Roosevelt was given the same treatment Smith had received four years earlier.

He became immersed in the campaign. His subordinates ran the city. The most the National Committee could contribute to the campaign in Massachusetts was five thousand dollars. Curley mortgaged his house (not an unusual procedure for him when he needed money) for $25,000 and raised $85,000 more among his friends and those with whom he did business. More than that was spent in Massachusetts, but it was difficult to keep itemized accounts.

Farley asked a group of Democrats across the country to present speeches that could be used generally during the campaign, and he invited Curley to make a movie short in Warner Brothers' Brooklyn studio, giving his views. Curley outlined and dictated speeches to Standish Willcox for a couple of days, and then left to make the movie short. When he arrived at the studios, he discovered that he had forgotten his script and stepped before cameras and microphones to make it extemporaneously. The director shook his head. Curley insisted that he could do a better job without the script than he could with it, a claim that few Bostonians who had ever heard him would doubt. The director shrugged his shoulders and Curley delivered his speech. He talked about "the Forgotten Man." It was reviewed a few days later by a select group of critics at Hyde Park. They concurred in the opinion that it was one of the best pieces of political propaganda they had ever heard. It was later shown to twenty-five million persons in every city and state visited by Roosevelt.

During the remainder of July and August he divided his time between the Bull Pen and a tour of all major New England cities.

The American Legion had invited all mayors of cities that had entertained conventions to be its guests at the annual convention in Portland, Oregon, in mid-September. Both

Roosevelt and Farley advised Curley not to go. They were opposed to intruding politics into the convention, but Curley was sometimes hard to handle, thought otherwise and could not be persuaded. It was finally agreed that Curley would make a swing around the country, in advance of Roosevelt, including the northwest coast, all the principal cities of California and across the country back to Boston.

He left Boston on September 1 and was given the customary send-off—bands, entertainers, automobile parade and crowds along the streets and at the South Station. His farewell to Boston was a vitriolic radio attack upon Herbert Hoover and the Republican party. His first stop was South Bend, Indiana, where five thousand paid an admission fee to hear him; next Milwaukee, where seventy-five hundred paid admission. Selected by President William Green of the American Federation of Labor to give the Labor Day Address on Soldier Field, Chicago, he spoke to seventy-five thousand there and was on a national network.

He went on to the American Legion convention, and after receiving a medallion from National Commander Louis A. Johnson for his courtesies to the Legion when in convention in Boston, he was invited to speak. He attacked Herbert Hoover for ordering the bonus marchers out of Washington and blamed him because some were shot down. He brought the veterans out of their seats, cheering and whistling, and left the convention in an uproar; and yet he did not mention politics or the Presidential campaign, although his parting shot could not be misunderstood: "I am not fearful of the future. The old law of compensation never fails; right is always rewarded, wrong always punished."

Curley carried along in his caravan his own personal staff, trained in his rally technique. Tall, giant-sized Joseph Conry, his traffic commissioner; William Saxe, his publicity director; and his son Leo, both square-shouldered athletes. They knew exactly what to do under any set of circumstances.

They arrived at the Palace Hotel in San Francisco, for example, at the precise hour that a luncheon was being given in honor of William Gibbs McAdoo, Mary Roberts Rinehart and George Creel were the speakers. Curley learned about it after he had been in the hotel about five minutes. He had not been invited to the luncheon. Nobody asked him to speak. He walked into the hall, went immediately to the head table, sat down and began eating. Conry, Saxe and Leo walked in, found empty chairs at tables in the rear—right, left and center —and they, too, had luncheon.

After the two distinguished writers got through saying nice things about McAdoo and the chairman indicated that the meeting was about to adjourn, there came a chorus of booming voices from the three tables: "We want Curley!"

Curley needed no further introduction. He got up, wiped his lips with his napkin and went right into a speech about Roosevelt. The crowd sat back wide-eyed. The head table looked at him in surprise or consternation. Twenty minutes later, two-thirds of the audience crowded around him.

"Just like Bourke Corcoran," one old soul told him.

Curley shook his head in appreciation. "I've always admired old Bourke," he said. "He had the eyes of an old Gaelic sorcerer and a voice like an incantation. I can't be that good."

McAdoo didn't like it.

In Los Angeles, Curley addressed a veterans' association. The meeting was supposed to be nonpolitical. As he began to speak, somebody passed up a card. It read: "Lay off Hoover. Two-thirds of the crowd here are for him."

Curley read it aloud and then went on. "Ever since I started this swing-around, I've been looking for a real Hoover crowd. I saw one once in a psychopathic hospital in Chicago. There were forty men in the ward and all arose and cheered his name."

When he got to Salt Lake City, he looked up a Catholic priest who had been asking him for five years to go there and address his coreligionists. "They have an inferiority complex," the priest had written. "The Mormons have them buffaloed."

Curley delivered an eloquent eulogy on the Mormons. Elder Smoot characterized it as the finest tribute to his people ever delivered by "a stranger within our gates."

Next day, in Curley's honor, there was a special gathering at the Mormon Temple. As he went in, the organist was playing "Believe Me If All Those Endearing Young Charms," and he followed with "The Wearing of the Green." Curley met the organist afterward. He was from South Boston. Curley described him as a poor Mormon but a wonderful organist.

He went on to Omaha, Nebraska, to debate Edwin P. Morrow, former United States Senator from Kentucky, a spokesman for Hoover. Curley described Morrow as a fine Kentucky gentleman whose speech that night was remarkable for lack of logic and the presence of platitudes, bromides and half-truths. Morrow appealed so heavily to the patriotism of the audience that at one point Curley leaned over and interjected: "Careful, Senator. If you wrap the American flag around you any more snugly, you'll strangle yourself."

Morrow became livid. Later, in his peroration, Morrow offered an eloquent testimonial to good old corn whisky. It was almost like an ode. When he finished, Curley walked over to him, put his arm around his shoulder and comforted: "Don't cry, Senator. Roosevelt will be elected and whisky will be legal again."

His tour was man-killing and record-breaking. He delivered 140 speeches in 41 days, traveled 10,000 miles by plane, train and automobile, covering 23 Western and Midwestern states. It cost national and state Democratic committees nothing. He paid his own expenses.

Seventeen · Almost Secretary of the Navy

ROOSEVELT arrived in Boston on his campaign tour on November 1, 1932. He was moved, in his wheelchair, down a ramp at the railroad yards, placed in an automobile with Curley, Governor Ely and Senator Walsh and was given a Curley reception that outstripped all others up to that time—bands, cheers, crowded streets and confetti. He spoke that night in Boston Arena before fifteen thousand, the capacity of the place, presented in two introductions, one by Curley and the other by Ely. It was not easy for Ely, but he was a good sport about it. Roosevelt talked about unemployment relief.

Massachusetts went for Roosevelt in a landslide on election day. Curley was cheered on packed Newspaper Row where thousands had turned out for the returns. He was kingpin wherever he went, and already his friends and the Boston Irish were speculating upon what he would get. It had become known that he wanted to be secretary of the navy. Curley was tired, worn out. He rested for two weeks and then, upon the invitation of the president-elect, went to Warm Springs, with Mary, to visit him.

Curley missed his wife. He would have appreciated her advice at a time like this. His daughter Mary had taken her place to some extent. A young girl of twenty-four, Mary was now the city's first lady, playing hostess for her father to politicians, contractors, celebrities who visited the city—the endless procession that marched into the mayor's house. Dinners were often catered now, with strange servants in the house, hired for the occasion. Curley turned to Mary, though not quite as he had to her mother. He did not take her as completely into his confidence and she had to guess at much; nor was he inclined to take her advice as easily. She did not address him as "Father" or "Pa." Her affectionate nickname for him was "Fid."

On a plane, flying from New York to Washington, Mary sat by the window looking down upon the clouds and the ground below. They were on their way to White Sulphur Springs, where they were to be picked up by William Gaston, son of a former Massachusetts Senator, in his private plane. Curley sat beside his daughter, a copy of the New Yorker on his knee. There was a good deal of white space on the cover. He had sketched a battleship on it and was roughing out his idea of an admiral's hat above it. Mary looked down and saw what he was doing. She put her hand over his and stopped him.

"Don't do that, Fid," she said.

He looked at her surprised. "Why not?"

"You're not secretary of the navy yet," she reminded him. "You may never be secretary of the navy. You're too sure of it. You may be counting your chickens before they're hatched."

He patted her hand. "You're a lot like your mother," he said. "Stop worrying about this, Mary. It's all settled. Roose-

velt knows what I want. He's known it all along. He agreed
to it and a deal is a deal."

"I hope you're right," she said.

"You'll see," he assured her. "I'm going to be secretary of
the navy, and you and I are going around the world on a
battleship with the fleet. We're going to see the world from
the bridge of an admiral's flagship. We're going to see it as
few people have had a chance to see it. We're going to sail
into the harbor of Yokohama with all flags flying. How many
guns does a secretary of the navy get as a salute?"

"Let's stop kidding ourselves," Mary said. "You've been
reading the newspapers, and so have I. It isn't going to be
easy for Roosevelt to appoint you secretary of the navy."

Curley's eyes narrowed and his jaw stiffened. "He's got to,"
he said. "I went the full distance for him, and now he's got
to go the full distance for me. He owes it to me."

"Maybe," she agreed, "but if what the newspapers are saying is true, the pressure against you is building up. There
are a lot of people around him now who are not our kind of
people. To them, you're that hateful man Curley, the boss of
Boston, leader of the Boston Irish. They don't understand
you, and they don't want to. To them you're the horrible example of the worst in politics. They're not practical politicians."

"*He* is," Curley said.

"You wait and see," she said.

They met the president in the study of "The Little White
House" in Warm Springs. Missy LeHand, his secretary, Mrs.
Anna Roosevelt Boettiger and Roosevelt's personal physician
Admiral Grayson were with him.

Roosevelt was smiling, cheerful, genuinely glad to see
Curley. He inquired about their trip down and put them at
ease, and they got down to business.

"I suggested a long time ago," Curley reminded him, "that

I'd like to be secretary of the navy, and I haven't changed my mind. I think it has come to be something of a Massachusetts prerogative. Charles Francis Adams, the present secretary, is a Massachusetts man."

Roosevelt agreed at once. He turned to Admiral Grayson and invited him to shake hands with the new secretary of the navy.

Mrs. Boettiger, the only witness still living besides Mary and Curley himself, says that she remembers the Curleys' visit but has no recollection whatsoever of the conversation Curley says took place.

Curley hugged his daughter when they left. "I told you," he said, confidently, "that it was in the bag."

On the way home in the plane, he talked about what they would do with the house. Jamaicaway would always be home. He would not sell it. The place would have to be moth-proofed. Some things would have to be stored. He needed a caretaker to look in occasionally. He'd hire a place in Washington or near-by Alexandria.

Mary listened, staring pensively into blue space. "It can't be true," she said. "I don't believe it. I heard him say it, but I still don't believe it."

The Curleys were home for the Christmas holidays. The mayor was busy planning. He wanted to leave the city with a clean break, without any aftermath of investigation or scandal to embarrass him or the administration, and that, he knew, was not going to be easy. He had been too preoccupied and too busy helping to elect Roosevelt to pay much attention to city affairs. He had left everything in the hands of subordinates. For them it had been a prolonged field day. Finance Commission investigations were piling up, and a new staff under new direction had been sinking their teeth into several luscious morsels.

He returned to his office on January 2, prepared to settle affairs, and next day received a jolt that shook him badly. Standish Willcox, a diabetic for many years in an era when the insulin treatment had not yet reached its later stage of perfection, died. Curley was stunned. Standish had been almost as close to him as the members of his own family. He had been planning to take him to Washington.

He gave Standish the kind of funeral that he knew he would have approved, except for one detail. Standish was a high-church Episcopalian. Curley arranged to have him buried from swank Trinity Episcopal Church. He was able to persuade Reverend Arthur Lee Kinsolving, the rector, to permit a string quartette in the choir loft and a vocalist to sing "Danny Boy," one of the few tunes to which Standish knew the words. He loved it. But the rector of Trinity put his foot down on 'Hail, Hail, the Gang's All Here," which Curley knew Standish would want in view of the character of the mourners and their stations in politics and society.

Everybody who was anybody was present at the funeral, not entirely because they knew Curley would expect them to be there, but because they were sincerely fond of Standish. He had always been friendly, helpful, witty, with eyes that crinkled at the corners and sparkled when he engineered quiet practical jokes at public functions. A satirist, he once seated a fruit peddler at a head table and introduced him with a straight face as an ambassador. He had been a good public speaker and often substituted for Curley.

The church was filled. Curley was meticulous about protocol. He knew Standish would want it that way and spent hours figuring out the seating arrangements. Ex-governors, ex-mayors, judges, jurists, commissioners and ex-commissioners, police detail, guards, pallbearers were properly placed inside and outside Trinity. It was a striped-pants, full-dress affair, with a eulogy that would have done Standish proud had he written it himself.

When it was over, Curley returned to his City Hall office downhearted and disconsolate. He was seated at his desk. His son Leo, now acting as his secretary, ushered a woman in mourning to his desk.

"She wants to speak to you," Leo said.

Curley looked up. "Standish and I were all but engaged," the woman said, hesitantly. "He told me that if anything happened to him I was to see you."

"Sit down," Curley invited sympathetically. He told her how sorry he felt and what a really great man Standish was. "Did he suggest that you were to share in his estate?" he asked.

The woman nodded. He took her name and address. "How are you fixed for money?" Curley asked.

"I'm all right," she answered.

Curley reached into his pocket, handed her a hundred dollars. "You'd better take that," he said. "When the estate is probated, I'll attend to the legal details."

She left. Leo escorted another woman in black to the desk. "She wants to talk to you," he said. Curley looked up.

"Standish and I were practically engaged," the woman began. "He told me that if anything happened to him, I was to see you."

"Sit down," Curley invited. He looked at her suspiciously. "When did he tell you that?" he asked.

"Only a couple of weeks ago," she said. "I think he suspected he was near the end."

"How did he happen to make that suggestion? Do you know?"

She shook her head. "He just called me up and told me; that's all."

"Do you expect to share in his estate?" Curley asked.

"I don't know," she said.

Curley rubbed his chin, thoughtfully. "Let me take your name," he said.

She gave it to him and he wrote it on a pad. He put his hand in his pocket, gave her a hundred dollars and dismissed her. "We'll talk about the estate some other time."

She left. Leo returned with another woman in black. "She wants to talk to you," he said.

Curley looked up. "I presume you are Standish Willcox' fiancé," he said.

She nodded. He made a note of her name; gave her a hundred dollars. She left, and he rang for Leo.

"Is that the end of the procession?" he asked. His eyes were filled with tears and he blew his nose.

"There aren't any more women in black waiting," Leo said.

Curley looked up. "There will probably be more," he said. "That's Standish's last farewell, his final, unexpected practical joke. For twenty years I've been kidding him and ribbing him about his amours because I never knew him to go out with a girl. I guess I didn't know too much about Standish's private life. I can almost see him now, looking down at me, saying: 'Ah, Mister Mayor, my women may one day cost you a pretty penny.' He probably called up every woman in his address book and told her to see me."

Calvin Coolidge died that afternoon and Curley prepared to go to another funeral. As the mayor of the capital city he would be expected, and he liked Cal. He had always got along with him as well as any Democrat could be expected to.

After the services in Northampton, Curley talked with James Roosevelt, who was present with his mother. James said that, in his opinion, Curley's appointment as secretary of the navy was out of the question, that he had never been under serious consideration for the post. But, he said, an ambassadorship, perhaps to France or Italy, was a possibility if Curley was interested. They discussed the matter at some

length, and at last it was decided that Curley should com-
municate directly with the President-elect.

Curley told Mary about the conversation when he got
home. "I guess your hunch was right," he decided.

He got in touch with Roosevelt by telephone and told him
what James Roosevelt had said. He wanted an explanation
and an immediate appointment. Roosevelt explained that he
had discussed Curley's place in the administrative picture
with his son James. He said that the situation as far as secretary of the navy was concerned was awkward. A good deal of
pressure was being applied. He had overlooked some of the
claims of others when he talked to Curley at Warm Springs.
He had not yet made up his mind. Secretary of the navy was
still open, but in the event that Curley could not have it, he
wanted him to give some thought to the diplomatic posts
James Roosevelt had mentioned. He wanted Curley to be
satisfied and happy, and he was certain that when a final
decision was made, Curley would be both satisfied and happy.

Curley pressed him for an immediate appointment, but
Roosevelt protested that it would not do any good. He was
not ready to make a decision yet, and all his time until inauguration was now booked up. He was scheduled to make a
trip to Miami, and he would be in a better position after inauguration to settle that along with a number of pending
matters. He told Curley to see him early in March.

Curley and his daughter planed to California to visit William Randolph Hearst at San Simeon. Roosevelt followed a
tight schedule. He went to Miami, missed an assassin's bullet
that cut down Anton Cermak of Chicago. Curley and his
family attended the inauguration and he remained in Washington to talk to Roosevelt. He sent a note to him from the
Mayflower Hotel. An appointment was made. Mary and
her father taxied across town to the White House to see him.

"Hello, Mary; hello, Jim," he greeted them. "Glad to see

you. Did you have a pleasant trip down?" He came right to the point, said that secretary of the navy was out, that no amount of discussion about the reasons could make the appointment possible. Actually, Claude A. Swanson's appointment as secretary of the navy was already on its way to the Senate, though Curley was unaware of the fact.

After Curley had expressed his disappointment, Roosevelt suggested that he be ambassador to France.

Curley shook his head. "When I was in France two years ago, Ambassador Edge told me that it cost him $225,000 in excess of his salary the first year he conducted the embassy. I haven't got that kind of money. I can't take that."

Then Roosevelt suggested Rome, pointing out that Curley would be the first Catholic ever to be ambassador to Rome.

Curley looked at Mary. "I'd like to think that one over for a day," he said.

"All right. Come back tomorrow or next day," Roosevelt said.

Newspapermen were crowded around the door when he came out. "What was the purpose of your visit, Mr. Curley?" "What did you discuss with the president?"

He waved them away. "It was just a friendly, social call," he said, "no particular significance to it."

On the way to the Mayflower Hotel in a cab, Mary looked at her father and said: "What do you think now?"

He was silent for a moment. "I don't know just what to think yet," he said. "In spite of what Jimmy Roosevelt said, I still thought I might get it." He looked ahead at the road. "Perhaps he couldn't do it," he said. "He had his reasons. I won't go overboard on this one. Let's see what happens. If he's going to do it, he'll announce it. He'll tell the newspapermen why I was there today. It's not first prize," he admitted, "but it's a good second. I can almost see Cardinal O'Connell's face when he hears it. I'd like to go to Rome. How'd you like to go to Rome?"

"I'd like it," she said. "I think I'd like it better than seeing the world from the bridge of a battleship."

"Let's forget that," he said. "That's past history now. It was a short cruise. The flagship went down and the fleet was wrecked on uncharted reefs. We'll stay in Washington for a day or two and you can shop around for gowns and the things you'll need to wear in Italy. It ought to be an interesting interlude. We'll live a pleasant social life there for a few years—parties and banquets and balls, with a chance to read a lot, to write and relax, the country of Vesuvius and Pompeii, the opera, Italian art and sculpture, the Vatican, the center of our religion, audiences with the Pope." He nodded, thoughtfully. "Yes, I think I'll really like that better than being secretary of the navy. We'll learn to speak the Italian language. I loved it in Italy when I was there two years ago. What's the name of that pool in Rome? I threw a coin in it—and the legend is that if you throw a coin in you must come back. We'll go back—back to Italy."

"Not so fast, Fid," she checked him. "Let's take this one a little slower."

Mary went shopping. Curley sat down in his hotel room to do some deep thinking. An hour later he was in the office of Augusto Rosso, Ambassador from Italy to the United States. He knew Rosso. He had met him before.

"It has been suggested to me by President Roosevelt that I go to Italy as ambassador from the United States," he explained. "Would you be good enough to cable both Premier Mussolini and the King of Italy and inquire whether or not I would be acceptable as ambassador?"

Ambassador Rosso nodded, congratulated him and agreed to do so.

He left there to call upon Archbishop A. G. Cicognani, Apostolic Delegate to Washington, and asked him to cable His Holiness, the Pope, to ascertain whether or not he would be acceptable to him, and the Apostolic Delegate agreed.

Curley's procedure was highly irregular, but even Standish Willcox had not always been successful in getting him to observe strict protocol.

Next day he called at both embassies and received three cablegrams—one replying that he was acceptable to Mussolini, another that he was acceptable to the king and a third, from Cardinal Gasparri, Secretary of State of the Vatican, saying that he would be acceptable to Pope Pius.

The day after that, he was back at the White House again and was ushered in to see the president. Roosevelt was in his usual friendly, jovial mood.

"I've decided," Curley told him, "to accept the appointment as ambassador to Italy."

Roosevelt looked up in smiling, good-natured exasperation. "There's been some difficulty there, Jim. Objections have been raised."

Curley's blood came to a quick boil. "Who is it this time?" he demanded.

Roosevelt replied that the King of Italy objected.

Curley pulled a cablegram from his inside pocket. "When I left your office the other day," he said, "I had Ambassador Rosso cable the King. Here's a reply that says Curley would be acceptable."

Roosevelt shook his head, admitted he must be in error, and said it was Premier Mussolini.

"That's interesting," Curley said. "I also have a cablegram here from Premier Mussolini. He says I'm acceptable to him; and in the event you think the objection was raised by His Holiness, here's another cablegram. I'm acceptable to him."

Roosevelt clamped his teeth tightly around his cigarette holder for a moment and rubbed his forehead with his fingers. At last he said he had a cabinet meeting in about ten minutes and would talk to Cordell Hull and find out who raised the objection.

Curley left the president's office in an ugly frame of mind.

Once again correspondents crowded around him, asking for news. He brushed them aside with a curt "I have nothing to say," and strode directly across the street to the State Department. He knew Cordell Hull, had served in Congress with him, and he knew the under secretary, William Phillips. They were friendly. He was admitted immediately.

"What can I do for you, Jim?" Hull asked.

"I'd like to find out if Italy has raised any objections to my appointment as ambassador."

Hull shook his head. "Not that I know of," he said. He called in Phillips.

"Has there been any objection raised to Jim Curley as ambassador to Italy?" he asked.

Phillips shook his head. "None," he said. "There couldn't be any objection raised. His name has never been submitted."

Curley left the secretary's office blazing with anger and indignation and retraced his steps across the street to the White House. The correspondents were certain now that something was up. He stormed the offices of Marvin MacIntyre and Louis McHenry Howe. He wanted to see Roosevelt right away.

"You can't see him," he was told. "He's at a cabinet meeting. He can't be disturbed. Write him a letter."

He finally left the place, and next day he was back again, demanding to see the president. Once again he was told that the president was too busy. "Write him a letter."

He couldn't get by MacIntyre. He went back to the Mayflower and did as he was told. He wrote a letter. He set forth the facts as he knew them, averred that there must be some misunderstanding and went on to say that newspapermen were asking him about his possible appointment as ambassador to Italy, and that he thought it might be a good idea for him to compare notes with the president to avoid an embarrassing situation.

Next day he received an invitation in the mail to be at the

White House at three in the afternoon for an interview. He arrived on the dot and was admitted. Roosevelt disconcerted him by greeting him cheerfully, as though nothing but the friendliest relations had existed between them, and before Curley could speak, he said.

"Jim, I've been making a search of the whole country for a man to send as ambassador to Poland, and I've decided that you're the man who possesses the courage, the experience, the tact and ability to fill that post. Everything is now all settled and lovely. I want you to go as ambassador to Poland."

Curley swallowed hard. "Poland?" he said. "Poland? You want me to go to Poland! That's a job you ought to give to some Republican, or to some enemy you want to get rid of. I'm not your enemy. I'm your friend."

"You don't understand," Roosevelt said. "You're going to what will be one of the most interesting places in the world during the next five years."

"It certainly will be," Curley agreed, "with Russia on one side of me and Germany on the other. If Poland is such a goddam interesting place, why don't you resign the presidency and take it yourself? I don't want it." He turned his back on the president, walked out of the office and slammed the door viciously behind him.

Once again correspondents crowded about him. His lips were drawn in a thin, tight line. He was almost white with anger. "What did you discuss with the president?"

"Ask him," he snapped, and pushed his way through them. Some said he added an unforgivable name. Curley never remembered using the epithet.

So ended one phase of a beautiful friendship.

Eighteen · A Big Back Bay Bully

CURLEY returned to Boston bitter and disillusioned. He had spent a year and a half crusading for Roosevelt. He did not know how much he had spent. He had kept no track of it, but he estimated that it had been well over $100,000. He had worked, planned and schemed harder than he ever had for a chance to remit his sins, turn a new leaf and begin a new page that would retrieve his honor and reputation, only to find that with his time, his energy and his money he had bought another gold brick.

Back in City Hall there was a clenched hardness about his jaw. His eyes had become as cold as steel. Newspapers were beginning to ridicule him. One suggested that he might be made minister to the Irish Free State. A few days later Roosevelt added to his discomfiture and embarrassment by publicly offering him the appointment as ambassador to Poland. A Boston editorial wag averred that Curley probably would pave the Polish Corridor. It took him four days to devise an answer to the president, declining the post. Meantime, the Boston Irish launched a "Keep Curley at Home" movement, which grew to surprising proportions overnight. With all these circumstances in mind, Curley's published explanation was something of a classic. He said:

"President Roosevelt has seen fit to tender me the post of ambassador to Poland.

"This expression of friendship and the opportunity to serve America and the Polish people, which this generous tender epitomized, is an honor for which I shall be eternally grateful.

"The service rendered by me in the campaign was given unselfishly and was actuated by the conviction that is daily being borne out—that under the able, courageous and humane leadership of President Roosevelt, happiness through prosperity would be restored to the people of America.

"Until such time, however, as industrial conditions are materially improved, the clear call of duty to a citizenship which has honored me with public office, national, state and municipal, for a third of a century, cannot be disregarded.

"The opportunity for service even in a less exalted capacity, as evidenced by the demand of the public and the press that I remain in America, leaves no course open to me but to request regretfully that my name be withdrawn as ambassador to Poland."

Editorial praise in the country's leading newspapers, particularly that of the New York *Times*, rang in his ears for days.

The cumulative effect of all that had taken place had worked a change in Curley. He became purposeful, grim and determined. He was fifty-nine years old now. His one big chance to achieve national fame or recognition, above the level of political boss, had dissipated, but the popularity of Roosevelt was a magic carpet, and he decided to ride it politically wherever he wanted to go, to do things in the name of Roosevelt that would profit Curley, even though they might embarrass Roosevelt. Boston was now feeling the full force of the depression. Curley had seen the lengthening bread lines, the apple sellers, the discouraged and bewildered

unemployed in his tour through the West, and in spite of
the anguished cries of banks, Finance Commission and the
heavy taxpayers of Boston, he began planning extensive improvements, more tunnels, more road resurfacing, more buildings, and became hard-boiled about public welfare.

Unemployment, and what it was doing to the people of
Boston, challenged his administrative genius. He rolled up
his sleeves and went to work. Most of the people of the city
stopped worrying about whether he was getting his cut. It
was more important to them to keep working and collect a
week's pay. He held the welfare load down while the city's
debt began to climb, and he handed out to the City Hall
reporters a steady stream of letters and telegrams to Roosevelt
demanding millions for relief, assuring Boston that Roosevelt
would supply it. Washington administration officials tore out
their hair and made denials that Curley promptly shunted
aside in published explanations. In spite of denials, Curley
usually got what he asked for.

Roosevelt was in an awkward position. He couldn't say no.
He had brushed Curley off, and having shot his bolt, Curley
counted himself out. Never again would he go to Washington
or Hyde Park with his hat in his hand. Never again could he
ask a personal favor. There was an expression of contempt in
his eyes now, when he demanded and insisted that Roosevelt
take care of the Boston Irish whom he had put on the line.
"I'll still collect a dividend from you," he told Roosevelt,
while asking him for money at Hyde Park. "Because I worked
so hard to elect you, I'll be the next governor of Massachusetts. You won't like that, but there's nothing you can do
to stop it."

Scandals were brewing. At least two of them were dyna-
mite. The first was now well known to newspaper readers as
"The General Equipment Case." The Finance Commission
had investigated and the case got into the courts, something

that probably never would have happened if Curley had been paying attention to city business, instead of campaigning for Roosevelt. Briefly the facts are these:

Curley's contractors were building an extension to a subway under a wide square not far from the American and National League ballparks. The purpose was to eliminate the wide mouth of a tunnel in the very heart of big Kenmore Square, to move the tunnel mouth a mile farther away on Commonwealth Avenue, and to resurface the Square, leaving it open to traffic, wiping out one of the city's worst bottlenecks.

An excavating contractor, working in the tunnel, came too close to the foundation of a building, owned by the General Equipment Corporation, shattered a big, high-pressure, fire-service water pipe and flooded the basement of the building. The building owners were insured against water damage from any cause. The insurance company acquired the right to sue the city for the water damage done to the building. Whether the insurance company won or lost the case was of no concern to the building owners, the General Equipment Corporation. They got paid anyway.

The insurance company hired three lawyers, two of whom were prominent Democratic city politicians, to sue the city. The lawyers placed the damage to the building at $70,199.29. The case was tried before a Suffolk County grand jury. Suffolk County is Boston, and there is reason to believe that Suffolk County juries can be purchased reasonably. Jury fixing has been common in Boston.

The jurors brought in a verdict of $129,646 in damages. How they arrived at that figure was never explained. A judge, with far better wisdom than the twelve good men and true, set aside this verdict. He did not compute the damage, but he felt sure it was far less than the jury's figure.

It appeared that the insurance company was willing to settle for $20,000, but for a reason that was unexplained, the city settled for $85,000. Investigating the whole affair, the Finance Commission discovered that the insurance company got only $20,000, and wanted to know who got the other $65,000. It was an awkward and embarrassing question, and the Finance Commission wanted Curley to answer it in court.

Simultaneously, the Finance Commission had discovered the existence of a concern called "The Legal Securities Company," stock brokers doing business in Boston. Head of the Legal Securities Company was Edmund L. Dolan, who was also the Boston city treasurer. The Legal Securities Company bought bonds (some of which defaulted) from other brokers and sold them to the city. It also bought city bonds and sold them to other brokers. Dolan appeared to be buying bonds from himself and selling them to himself, collecting a commission on both ends. The Finance Commission wanted to know how and why he did it. This was not only disconcerting to Dolan, but he made it appear downright impertinent of the Finance Commission to pry into his personal affairs.

Revelations in both of these investigations were printed day after day in Boston newspapers. Apparently the people of the city read of them along with the comic strips and gave them about the same amount of attention. Headline writers had long since clipped Finance Commission to "Fin Com." Curley and the Fin Com had been paired together for years, like Mutt and Jeff or Amos and Andy. The only persons who appeared to be taking the matter seriously were the members of the Finance Commission (insufferable bores, continually yapping about things like these and unable to change the subject!). Curley classified them as public nuisances and implied that they were nothing less than a group of organized Peeping Toms who ought to be ashamed of themselves.

But Curley understood the Finance Commission. He knew that it was fashioning ammunition that could blow either him or his city treasurer out of office and into jail. Curley had never yet been trapped by members of the Finance Commission. He was still confident that he could lick them in any investigation; and he knew how to change the subject. He announced that he would be a candidate for governor to succeed Joseph B. Ely.

Ely readily made way for Curley. He had lost all interest in public life and was inclined to be contemptuous of it. A liberal, broad-minded Yankee Protestant, he had fought and worked as hard for Smith as Curley had for Roosevelt—a strange paradox, a Yankee Protestant championing an Irish Catholic and an Irish Catholic championing a Dutch-descendant blueblood. Ely had watched the spectacle of mass Boston Irish turning against Smith overnight. The attacks upon his motives as an ardent and fighting advocate of Smith had been wormwood and gall to him. He had turned up his nose at that kind of criticism, too principled to answer it. His own supporters pleaded with him to be a candidate for re-election, but he shook his head in bitter disappointment and disgust. "Al Smith took a walk out of the Democratic party and into private life," he said. "I'm going to follow him voluntarily. I'm fed up."

Gaspar Griswold Bacon was the Republican candidate. He was a progressive Republican, a good speaker and unusually popular throughout the state, a sensitive, thoughtful intellectual, whose collected speeches during the campaign, published under the title *Individual Rights and the Public Welfare*, were not only good reading but good literature. A fighting blueblood, he had come up through the ranks in the House of Representatives and the Senate to become president of the upper branch. For years, Curley had been his particular quarry. He had stalked him constantly.

Bacon might have beaten any Democrat in the state, save Ely or Curley. It was not his tough luck to be matched against Curley. He preferred it that way. For years he had been girding himself for a knockdown, drag-out fight with Curley. He had been making a long and painstaking study of him. He knew more about him, perhaps, than any Republican or Democrat in the state. The result of the election was important to Bacon. He wanted to be governor. But the fight was important to him, too. He wanted to meet Curley in the public arena and slug it out with him win, lose or draw. He was so well liked throughout the state that he had been elected Republican lieutenant governor when Ely had been elected Democratic governor. He got the biggest vote ever cast for any Republican in a state election up to that time.

In another day, it might not have been so easy for Curley, but in 1934, after an era of bank closings and unemployment, Gaspar Griswold Bacon was made to order for Curley. All Curley needed to do was to point out that Gaspar Bacon's father had been a member of the firm of J. P. Morgan & Company. "While many of the citizens of Massachusetts were on welfare lists," Curley told rally after rally, "Gaspar Bacon was on J. P. Morgan's preferred list. That was brought out in an investigation of the Senate Banking Committee of stock-market and Wall Street financiers—an investigation directed by Ferdinand Pecora."

This was enough. It made little difference that Bacon had profited little, if at all, by his father's connection with the firm. Bacon's father, a member of General Pershing's staff in the A.E.F., was dead. He had been connected with the House of Morgan in 1894. He had been secretary of state under Theodore Roosevelt. His son Gaspar had never been connected in any way with the House of Morgan, but he could not get that over and make it stick.

Curley's record in Boston was too good. Whatever else might be said of him, he kept people working. He was always in Roosevelt's hair, demanding money by mail, telegraph and telephone, and when it was denied him, he hopped off to Hyde Park, Washington or Warm Springs to barge in on the president in person. He embraced the Civil Works Administration, devised one project after another, even to laying curbstones in the public parks, reminded Boston and Massachusetts again what a really great man Roosevelt was, and asked him for more money. It was small wonder that Louis McHenry Howe, Marvin MacIntyre and a score of assorted bureau heads in Washington pulled at their hair and pleaded: "Can't something be done about this man Curley?" From their point of view, it would have been better if he, and not Breckenbridge Long, had been sent to Italy.

There was a disturbing catch in the political arrangement of city and state when Curley became a candidate for governor. His term as mayor expired in January, 1934. The state election would not take place until the following November. He could not succeed himself as mayor and then resign. It meant that he would be out of office for a year, and unless a mayor friendly to Curley were elected, the Finance Commission would have full access to all books and records in City Hall, and with the right kind of co-operation might build up an airtight case against him.

Fred Mansfield, defeated by Curley in 1929, became a candidate again, and this time there was not much doubt that the cardinal approved him. Mal Nichols, the Republican who had once succeeded Curley by prearrangement with Innes, opposed him. The Boston Irish Democratic vote was split four ways, and not through Curley's political design or strategy. He had no control over the personal ambitions of Boston politicos who wanted to succeed him. It served his purpose better. William J. Foley, for more than a decade a silent administrative district attorney who seldom appeared in a courtroom, filed for the office, as did Joseph F. O'Connell, whom Curley had defeated for Congress, and Judge Michael H. Sullivan of the lace-curtain set, who had been pursuing and investigating Curley as chairman of the Finance Commission. If the political picture had remained that way, there is no question that Nichols would have been elected and City Hall would have gone back to the control of Curley and Innes. Curley would have had nothing to fear from the Finance Commission.

He reckoned without Henry Parkman, Jr., the first Back Bay stevedore in eight or ten generations, hardheaded, hard punching, a blueblood who could come down from Beacon Hill and mingle with the Boston Irish without creating the impression that he was slumming. Except for his speech, his choice of words and his manners, he was just as tough as if he had been born in Boston's Kerry Village, the Cove, Brickbottom, or the Lower End. Politicians who had mistaken him for a sissy often awakened suddenly, blinking and wondering what struck them. His father had trained Charlie Innes.

Parkman had fought for the Irish and against them, depending upon whether he thought they were right. He had bludgeoned his way to the top by mixing it up with political bosses and it did not concern him much whether they were Republican or Democratic. He had fought, sniped at and attacked James Michael Curley until he became a thorn in his side. An infantry captain in World War I, he saw two years' overseas service. When he was mustered out he became a longshoreman on the Brooklyn docks for the Luckenbach Line, and after six months came to Boston to be a stevedore for the Western Steamship Company on the Boston water front. He was a bad man to tangle with.

He inherited a great name—a descendant of Francis Parkman, the historian. His cousin, George Francis, left everything he had, about five million dollars, to the city of Boston for parks and playgrounds, and his father, Henry, Sr., gave all he had to charities. All the Parkmans had a habit of giving their money away. Henry, Jr., went to Noble and Greenough School, entered Harvard in 1911, was paired off with another six-footer, Christian Herter, for a roommate. Members of his class thought he became prematurely bald brushing his head against ceilings and doorframes. He was graduated magna cum laude, got a Phi Beta Kappa key, earned a master's degree and went on to Harvard Law School.

He entered politics from Blueblood Ward Four, fought Innes' choice and was elected to the city council; fought him again and was elected to the House of Representatives, to the Senate, and finally bounced Innes out as a delegate to the Republican national convention, an honor the Brahmin ward leader had had for twenty-five years. He was currently in the process of wresting control of the ward entirely from Innes. He did not like the Curley-Innes combine. That was that. He set about breaking it up.

In politics, a man is known by the stir he creates, and it is significant that the big guns of both political parties had been trained constantly upon Parkman. He had been sticking his neck out and taking it on the chin regularly because of his independence and his impatience with political chicanery. Democratic ward organizations that fought him had christened him "Highpockets Parkman," and his enemies called him variously "the baldheaded Moses from the caviar belt"; "a longlegged torchbearer of civic purity"; "the great crusader of righteousness who stands six feet five inches tall, from the soles of his size-twelve shoes to the top of his simonized dome"; "a big Back Bay bully"; and "the heavyweight champion of Cream Puff Alley."

To beat the Curley-Innes combination, Parkman offered himself up on a sacrificial altar. He took out nomination papers, got the necessary signatures, filed them, had them certified and became a candidate for mayor. On the morning after election, when the votes were counted and the political debris was cleared away, it turned out that Parkman had not split the Republican vote as expected; he had hogged it. But that was not quite enough. If Nichols had not been a candidate, Parkman would have been elected mayor of Boston. Instead, he elected Mansfield, who got the largest segment of the divided Boston Irish Democratic vote.

The Finance Commission never got such co-operation. City Hall and its Curley records were laid bare for them. A battery of high-priced lawyers went to work. Their objective was to have Curley indicted, or at least to bring him before the courts of the state on a civil process before he could be elected governor. It became a race between them and Curley, with Curley carrying the handicap.

The Bull Pen came back in untenanted Young's Hotel, its amplifying horns drowning City Hall and the mayor's office in sound. During the summer and fall, Curley's buses and automobiles roared over Massachusetts highways, a cavalcade visiting every city and town in the state with loudspeakers shattering the silence of day and night. Curley was speaking five and six times a day, riding the Roosevelt magic carpet, whipping up the populace to support the New Deal, save Roosevelt and Democracy, promising work and wages for the unemployed. He said that he alone could get from this generous federal government the millions the state deserved. The voters looked at him and nodded agreement. He had already proved that he could do that. In spite of the fact that newspapers printed it, he never acknowledged a split with Roosevelt.

"When I'm governor," he said, "I am going to devote my time and influence to the abolition of the Governor's Council. It's a glorified pawnshop. It is an agency through which disgraceful deals are made, affecting judges, murderous convicts and the very foundations of popular government. It's an instrument through which State Street perpetuates Republican domination, even when Democrats occupy high elective office. Long ago, it forfeited its right to exist. It's an obsolete relic of royalist rule, kept alive by Republican tories and faithless Democrats.

"I shall enter office unafraid of either element. I shall go in without a promise, except to the voters of the state. All my life I have been a lone wolf in politics, refusing to take orders.

My campaigns have followed a certain pattern. I've had first
to defeat the bosses within my own party, then fight a combination of Republican overlords and disgruntled fugitives
from the Democratic camp."

He told them he wanted all grade crossings in the state
eliminated. It would save lives and provide work for men who
needed it. He wanted a State Planning Board and a program
to eliminate slums in all cities and towns of the state, and he
went on to say: "In some instances the insane in this state
are treated worse than wild beasts. Even animals in our forest
preserves are protected against fire. I want proper segregation
for the hopeless and enlightened treatment for the curables.
That's one reform that I am certain is coming. Even the most
stilted and pompous spokesman of the old regime will not
dare to obstruct it and I want to make sure that nobody in
the state starves."

While he was racing about the state making these speeches,
he was juggling five or six balls in the air all the time, attacking the Finance Commission, ridiculing Gaspar Bacon, attacking Mansfield, supplying ammunition to the Bull Pen, and
figuring out the moves that would let him beat the battery
of lawyers by reaching the State House before they arrived
at the courts.

Curley was swept into office on a floodtide of Democratic
votes. He had beaten the Finance Commission to the office.
With him came an entire panel of Democratic officers for
the first time in history—with one exception, Secretary of
State Frederic W. Cook, a Republican in a job where he must
at times be arbiter between the Democratic and Republican
parties, and trusted implicitly by both of them. He squeaked
through partly because of his reputation for honesty and fair-
ness, but of more importance in the result, because he was
opposed by the only Italian on the slate. All the rest were
Irish. The racial overturn in the government of a city within
a quarter of a century had now extended to the state.

Nineteen · Under the Gilded Dome

JAMES MICHAEL CURLEY's term as governor was a political aberration that he has never been able to explain satisfactorily, even to himself. It was fantastic, at times almost unbelievable, a hodgepodge of unforgivable mistakes and phenomenal successes, a daily seesaw of good and outrageously bad for two years. Only he could create and sustain such consistent confusion.

There were a number of contributing causes. He was tired, irritable, downcast by successive tragedies and disappointments. He missed the counsel of his wife and he had no one whom he could trust for sound administrative advice. He missed Standish Willcox, and realized fully now how much work Standish had spared him. He missed his son James Michael, Junior. Family troubles disturbed him. Dolan and others whom he had given free rein in City Hall had double-crossed him by involving him in scandals when his attention had been diverted. Their scandals had now become his scandals.

For twenty years he had been able to shrug off the Finance Commission, but he no longer could do so. Now he could feel its hot breath upon his neck. He knew that Mansfield, in City Hall, was out to get him, and he felt that Roosevelt was out to get him, too. The depression disturbed him, although he would not admit it publicly. Solving the unemployment problem would be a Herculean task and he knew that he would have to do that alone.

He had been a lone wolf in politics and had boasted about it year after year. He discovered now how lonely he really was. He had no competent, intelligent aides; no cabinet, no brain trust, no unselfish friends who would contribute the independent thinking and planning needed to run the state. He tried desperately to develop some quickly; invited newspaper editors, publishers, businessmen, his enemies to sit down at round-table discussions. All he wanted was sincere, honest suggestions and direction, but they looked at him coldly and suspiciously, trying to ferret out a plot.

From the day after election until the day of inauguration, he had no rest. Mail and telegrams stacked up. A parade of petitioners passed through his house every day. He divided his time between them and the telephone. Everybody wanted something—a job, an appointment, a raise, a contract. Some clung to him, determined not to let him out of their sight, fearful that they would not get the lush rewards they were angling for. Many who classified themselves as intimates were leeches and parasites. He was their meal ticket and their future.

When the time came for him to take office, he was worn down to a fine edge, restless and impatient to be installed. He got up that morning to discover that the Senate was snarled in deadlock, unable to elect a president. He fumed and sputtered indignantly as he shaved and dressed in formal morning suit, and foresaw correctly that it would be a long-drawn-out fight. He knew that the state constitution provided

cool relationship: Curley and President Roosevelt at Brockton Fair Grounds, October, 1938.

A warm discussion: Postmaster-General Farley and Curley, October, 1938.

Curley tells his Tammany Club he will run again for governor, July, 1938.

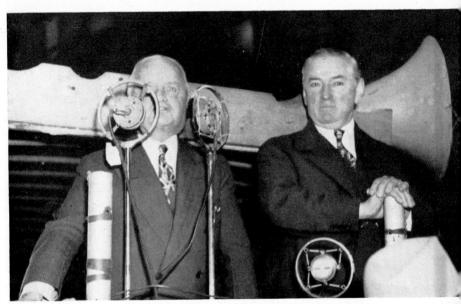

Honey John Fitzgerald sings "Sweet Adeline" as he endorses Curley for Govern
November, 1938.

that "the governor shall take office in the presence of the president of the Senate and before both legislative houses," and that he would be expected to cool his heels and wait until a Senate president had been chosen.

"I won't do it," he told the members of his family, and they knew he meant it.

When he arrived at the State House shortly before high noon, the moment when he should be sworn in, the Senate was still deadlocked. Battery A of the National Guard Field Artillery stood at alert on Boston Common waiting for a signal to announce by cannon salute that a new governor was in office. Curley went directly to the governor's office. Governor Ely sat there patiently waiting for the sergeant at arms in silk hat, frock coat, formal dress, ribbon across chest, carrying a mace and escorting a joint committee to escort the new governor into the chamber and relieve him of office. He, too, knew it would be a long wait.

Massachusetts has a century-old dust-thou-art-and-into-dust-thou-shalt-return tradition. It requires that when a governor retires from office and the twenty-one-gun salute begins to boom, he shall walk alone and unescorted from his office down the wide marble staircase, through the Hall of Flags, out the front door and down the long flights of steps that divide the terraced lawn of the State House to Beacon Street. Still alone, as the gunners continue to fire their battery, he walks through Boston Common until he becomes lost as an ordinary pedestrian among the common people. It symbolizes that his authority derives from the people, and when it ends, he becomes again merely one of them.

As Ely waited, Curley and not the sergeant at arms came into the room and closed the door behind them. What was said and what happened there probably never will be recorded. It is known that there was a dispute and physical conflict. Both men were somewhat disheveled when the door was opened. A breaker of precedent by wilful and sometimes whimsical choice, Curley summoned Secretary of State Frederic Cook, took the oath of office and ordered the cannon to boom.

That was the signal for the retiring governor's last long walk. Ely sauntered out the door, down the marble steps, through the Hall of Flags, out the door and down the terraced steps. Ten thousand spectators watched him silently. His head was high, his shoulders back. He looked above the murky, low-hanging smoke of Boston toward the far horizon of the Berkshires. He was, in truth, walking back into private life to join Al Smith, and for the same reason, through with politics forever, disillusioned and disgusted. And yet, there was born that day a new respect on the part of each for the other. Curley never again would criticize Ely, nor would Ely criticize Curley.

His public administration got under way that night in a burst of splendor that was blinding. Hitherto an inaugural ball had been a perfunctory thing, a reasonably quiet affair in the Copley Plaza where the governor, party workers and friends gathered to banquet and dance. Curley's inaugural ball was held in the Armory for twenty-four thousand guests. Almost everybody to whom he had spoken a passing word was on hand. He loved it and they loved it.

Next day he showed up bright and early at the executive offices, in the State House, and things happened so fast that for the next two years newspapers covered him night and day in three shifts. Sometimes each paper had a corps of from three to six men working on far-flung ends of executive actions. Even Jamaicaway had to be covered in a co-operative lobster watch.

Just as Curley had always invited almost everybody he met to drop in at City Hall and see him about any problem, so he invited everybody to drop in at the State House. The executive suite had always been a quiet place with an art gallery of paintings of the governors of three hundred years, anterooms, deep blue carpets, soft easy leather chairs, glistening brass, blue ropes and the dignified atmosphere of a chapel. For the next two years the corridors were jammed every day with mixed, noisy crowds. Scores of policemen were on hand to keep them in order. Curley followed the same routine as he had at City Hall, walking through the rooms, saying a crisp word to one, two, or to delegations of a dozen or scores at a time. He had corps of secretaries interviewing them. Almost everybody got in to see the governor. Men, women and children outlined their troubles to secretaries who kept more secretaries busy sorting and attending to them.

The unemployed stormed him at every appearance. They began crowding around his Jamaicaway house early in the morning, trampled down his shrubbery and the lawns and flowers of the neighbors. He had cards printed, referring the holders to the state employment office, and distributed them after breakfast as he left his home. They were given preference. That did not last very long, though, because alert mayors of other cities learned about it and gladly paid ten cents' carfare for each of their own unemployed, sending them to the governor's house at breakfastime. The daily jams became such a problem that streets were roped off and police details called to break them up.

He embraced C.W.A., P.W.A. and later W.P.A., every program that offered federal money for wages, and kept the pressure on Roosevelt for more and more money. He built roads and bridges on almost any excuse. People in little villages and hamlets who never thought they'd see a curbstone woke up to find trucks and crews laying them. He probably laid more miles of curbstone than any executive in history. When he ran out of jobs he invented them. Every department was stocked with as many persons as could be jammed into available floor space, and if department heads complained that they didn't have anything for these people to do, they were told to find something. More than eighteen hundred were sidetracked into the department of mental diseases. Some hospitals had more help than patients. If the help didn't have patients to care for, he told the superintendents to put them into the fields to till the soil and plant potatoes. He didn't care what they did as long as they worked.

Thirty-six of them were unloaded on the tax commissioner (where they were known as "Wooden Indians"). He set them to work checking the arithmetic on the tax returns of 1910, so that they would not interfere with the regular work of his department; but he couldn't get rid of them, and out of them ultimately he fashioned one of the most efficient tax departments in the country.

Patronage was just as frantic. Curley honored political debts. That was part of his code and one of the chief factors in his success. If he promised a campaign worker an appointment, he got it—or he got something just as good; but under the pressure of unemployment, he had no time to check qualifications. He made appointments quickly and they were final.

As governor, Curley was a strange combination of clockwork efficiency, a silver-tongued Solomon, a political Machiavelli, a civic planner with frightening vision, a Great White Father behaving like a footpad while easing the burden of a troubled people, a stealthy schemer as naive as a child, playing poker with one hand and chess with the other to the utter bewilderment of scores of assistants who never knew what he was doing or what he was about. He worked sixteen to eighteen hours a day, day in and day out, wore out secretaries, stenographers and typists. When they had nervous breakdowns, he sent them home with full pay, showered them with flowers and medical attention, became very sympathetic and continued to wear down the next batch. He was tireless and nerveless. He could take a drink or let it alone. He lived and loved every minute of every day. He wondered why so many people around him cracked up, and could not understand it.

He could put in fourteen hours at his desk, talk to four hundred persons in four hundred individual conferences, speak to sixty or seventy more on the telephone, taking five or six to luncheon or dinner, disposing of five hundred problems or making decisions, and at midnight he would put on his frock coat and hat, look around at a staff that he could not understand was exhausted, and, just as he and they were about to go home, spot a sentence or a phrase in a report on his desk that gave him a new idea.Then, in inspired impulse, he might assign one, five, ten or a hundred persons to a job that it would take them six months to complete.

When twelve to twenty-five employees around him were fagged out, their minds blank, he could think of funny stories, play them out, acting every character in the story, and look at his audience in puzzled wonder because they did not laugh. None could equal him for stamina and endurance. He never thought the job required either. Temperamentally and physically it suited him. He was often thoughtless of those around him because it did not occur to him that they would tire. He used up photographers and reporters fast, but that was not his concern. Managing and city editors would replace them. He used up state police and motorcycle officers fast, too, and that brought wrath upon his head because there were accidents. One was hurt and one was killed. After that he eased up on police.

He could be hilariously funny, although he seldom clowned, and he could be the master of satire and subtle wit. Sometimes those around him had the uncanny feeling that they were acting out parts in a comedy without music, and occasionally even that was furnished; but they never knew what their lines or stage business would be. He wrote the plot and created complications as he went along. He hated Harvard and the Brahmins, and delighted in placing them in awkward juxtaposition to the Boston Irish.

When the term of Commissioner of Education Payson Smith, a noted educator, expired, Curley infuriated Harvard and the Brahmins by appointing an obscure Irish schoolmaster, a superintendent of schools in a little town, and he knew when he did it that it would infuriate the Boston Irish, too, not so much because the Irish superintendent was not up to the job, but because he had changed his name from Reardon to a more dilettante Reardan. The appointment was, nevertheless, payment for the school superintendent's work during the campaign. Educators were shocked. They decried it and said it would ruin the state's educational system. Ten years later no bad effects could be discerned. Continued underpayment of teachers did far more harm.

As commissioner of agriculture he appointed an Irish grocery salesman who joined the Grange, had himself adopted by the Mashpee Indians, and as his first official act promptly put in a bill for a $490 radio so that he could listen to the daily farm and garden-hour and market reports.

Countess Elektra Rosanska had made a singular contribution to his campaign. She would sing the national anthem at the drop of a hat at rallies anywhere at any time. He rewarded her by creating a job and appointing her to teach folk songs to the inmates of the Women's Reformatory at two thousand a year.

His appointment of Margaret O'Riordan as state librarian wiped out both a personal political debt to her and also one of long standing to the Ancient Order of Hibernians. Mrs. O'Riordan, an officer in the Hibernian Auxiliary and a member of the Democratic State Committee, had worked hard for his election. Curley asked the United Democratic Women at their annual banquet whom they would select for the job. They picked Mrs. O'Riordan. When reporters interviewed Mrs. O'Riordan to find out what kind of librarian she would make, she had no books in her living room and acknowledged that her favorite reading was *Spy Stories* and *True Romances*. However, this appointment turned out to be an Indian gift. She got it, but she could not have it. The Governor's Council turned her down.

He lived up to his political code meticulously. If it was established that an appointed office or job holder, who could be reached, had worked against him, that office or job holder was transferred or removed so that the office or job would become available. If it was established that the office or job holder had been impartial and had not taken sides, Curley left him severely alone and showed no interest in him. His chance for a raise or advancement in his job was forfeit. If it was established that an office holder or employee had worked for his election, the office holder or employee was rewarded. If a supporter or campaign worker was not a state employee and did not want a job, he got an honor.

Persons in that category were appointed to trusteeships in state institutions, to unpaid boards and commissions. When these were used up, Curley revived the defunct Massachusetts Volunteer Militia (replaced in 1917 by the War Department with the National Guard) and as commander in chief of the state's forces, he handed out commissions of all ranks like Kentucky Colonelcies. The state was peppered with generals, colonels, captains and lieutenants. There were no noncommissioned officers or troops. Military strategists were hired to teach these warriors how to salute, how to wear a visored cap and Sam Browne belt, and how to strike the correct pose for cameramen. Booted and spurred, they climbed into automobiles to attend all official functions, and when none was available hired taxicabs. Some would not walk three hundred yards from the State House to the Parker House, but rode up to its doors in state.

All of this was outside the jurisdiction of the Boston Finance Commission, still investigating Curley's acts as mayor;

but investigating Curley had long been standard practice in any job he held. The House of Representatives' Ways and Means Committee took over the job of investigating Curley as governor forthwith, beginning with the minute he was sworn in, and there was some doubt about that. A defendant named DiStasio, appealing a case that had nothing to do with Curley, protested that a judge who ruled on it was not validly appointed because the governor was improperly in office. The Superior Court ruled that it made no difference whether Curley was governor de jure or de facto, and went no further to decide which.

The limitations of patronage frustrated him. Even with federal help he could not put enough people to work. In normal times, with his disregard and contempt for rules and regulations that proscribed and circumscribed employment, he could have put everybody in need to work. When civil service stood between him and hundreds of jobs that he could fill if it were not for regulations and requirements, he could not wipe out the laws or the civil-service administration, but he found it easy to control, merely by appointing as civil-service commissioner one of his own men, Thomas Green, one-time boss of Charlestown, who had joined him. It became Green's responsibility to hold and supervise examinations, and immediately almost anybody could pass, qualify and be appointed. Civil-service rules, Curley held, were all right in times of prosperity but no good during a depression.

Not all spoils went to the victor. When a new governor takes office, department heads in the opposition party usually resign, certain that they will not be reappointed, but some, by reason of long service in a particular job, acquire "tenure of office" and can be removed only for cause. Others, appointed for a term that overlaps into the new governor's administration, hang on stubbornly, determined to fill out their time in the hope that a public opinion favorable to them will compel a governor to reappoint them—and sometimes that happens.

These two classes gave Curley the most trouble. He couldn't throw them out. He could remove them only for cause. His removal proceedings were always dramatic, and in some aspects they resembled his more bewildering tongue-in-cheek appointments. Chairman of the Metropolitan District Commission, for example, is a lush political plum, and at the same time an important administrative office. It was held by Eugene Hultman, tall, bald, eminently dignified. He always wore formal dress, black ribbon falling from pince-nez glasses. He was a successful engineer who had spent most of his life in public service. He had made quite a reputation as Commissioner of Necessaries of Life in World War I. He had been Boston's commissioner of police. He was an anti-Curley Republican holding a job that Curley could very nicely fill, so he put him on the carpet before his council and charged him with "moral turpitude."

Boston and the state were puzzled. Such a charge applied to Hultman was unthinkable. Hultman was placed on trial before the council, prosecuted by one of the best criminal lawyers in the state, with Curley and the council sitting as judge and jury, and as the case unfolded the moral turpitude reduced itself to specific charges that Hultman had sampled a bottle of confiscated champagne and had spread manure taken from the city stables upon the lawn of his summer home. The people of the state laughed. The trial became a circus. Spectators jammed the State House. The proceedings would have been a daily sellout in a theater, but the governor went stubbornly ahead until the drama of bubble water and horse manure filled eleven hundred pages of testimony turned over to the district attorney with public instructions to prosecute. Hultman's job was saved by the public ridicule of his trial. Long afterward, it was discovered that during the proceedings, Curley had euchred the council into taking away

$65,000,000 Hultman had to spend on a project, and turning it over to him to administer, but by that time everybody was happy. The people had been entertained. Hultman kept his job. Curley got the money and put about three thousand more persons to work with it. They were happy, too.

On the night before Memorial Day, Curley summoned the adjutant general of the National Guard to his office. "To-morrow," he said, "the cemeteries of this state will be crowded as people remember the soldier dead and their own departed relatives and friends. I'd like to have a private and fitting memorial for a man who served me well, a good man—whatever his shortcomings. Only myself on earth and his own loyal, understanding soul on the other side of the border will understand it fully. I want you to have a band and a detail of soldiers at the grave of Standish Willcox. I want a volley from a firing squad and I want taps sounded to echo from the hills nearby."

"Very good, Governor," the adjutant said.

"There's one more detail, General," he went on. He picked up an oblong package from his desk. "I am placing in your hands a bottle of Sauterne," he said. "Standish loved Sauterne. I want you, General, to place this bottle of Sauterne gently and softly among the flowers upon his grave."

The general nodded, clicked his heels and departed.

A few days later Curley's chauffeur, Charles Mannion, was driving the governor home in his big, black limousine "Mass. S-1" and as they were passing the cemetery where Standish was buried, the governor called: "Stop here for a minute, will you, Charlie?" Mannion brought the car to a halt at the curb. It was a cold, raw night in early June, raining with a biting wind from the east.

"Go over to the cemetery," he directed, "to Standish Will-cox's grave. You'll find a bottle of Sauterne in a long package by the headstone. I had it placed there on Memorial Day.

There's no point in letting it go to waste. Bring it back to me."

Mannion left, returned with the bottle of Sauterne and handed it to the governor. That night he drank a toast to the faithful departed Standish Willcox. Standish, he was sure, would appreciate and approve.

Twenty · How to Lose a Senate Seat

He was called a dictator. It was a handy, convenient and popular word, but it did not properly apply. He did not intend to do so, but he made of Massachusetts a test case and proved, among other things, that the people of a state were temperamentally unfitted for dictatorship, and would die, perhaps, defending their rights and snarling at anyone who seriously tried to abridge them. With all his talent, equipment and ability, he could not herd state employees whom he controlled, let alone the public at large, which he governed.

The power of his oratory and voice was as abundant as that of Hitler and what he had to say far more literate. He had the same power to induce mass hypnosis. He spoke the King's English so flawlessly that it was a delight to listen to him. He had complete control of the state and all of its machinery. He spent millions of dollars in state and federal money in his own state-wide New Deal. He put more than sixty thousand persons to work. He did much more than his share in borrowing and spending the way to prosperity, and yet he could not become a dictator. He became instead, even as governor of the state, an elected fugitive from justice.

He made one mistake after another until they multiplied into a long series, became stubborn, and refused to correct them. He had imagination and daring and ignored the need for caution. He played to the majority in the Boston Irish gallery, forgot the Boston Irish minority, and forgot the rest of the state and the nation.

He set out to show Roosevelt who was boss in Massachusetts and within six months he had a lion by the tail. He could not bury the sins of omission and commission of his subordinates while he had been mayor of Boston, although he tried desperately to do so in the second act of a comic opera amid plots and counterplots that deserve a place in any textbook of practical politics.

Patiently and painstakingly the Boston Finance Commission had been tracing and tracking down all the transactions of City Treasurer Edmund Dolan, the Mohawk Packing Company, the Legal Securities Corporation and the settlement for water damage to the General Equipment Corporation. The Commission felt that it had built up such an airtight case against the city treasurer that it could send him to jail, and its case against James Michael Curley was a formidable one to present to a jury. The members of the Finance Commission had been appointed for a term of years by Governor Ely, and they were about ready to bring Governor Curley and his treasurer into the courts on both civil and criminal charges. Newspapers were speculating about the affair on front pages. It looked as if Curley would go on trial before a jury as governor of the state for something that he was alleged to have done as mayor of the city.

The elected Governor's Council in Massachusetts is a people's barrier. It stands between them and any arbitrary, unscrupulous despot. Elected according to councilor districts, the Council had always been Republican, even under successive Democratic administrations. Curley wanted to do away with it, but could not. Its function is to place a restraining hand upon a governor, particularly in important appointments, and say: "You can't do that." Its approval is necessary. Its veto defeats him. Curley could not change or capture the Finance Commission without first changing or capturing the nine-man Council. This is how he did it.

He appointed one member of the Finance Commission a Superior Court judge and replaced him by appointing a friendly Republican who had at one time been his corporation counsel for the city. The Council approved both the appointment of the judge and the appointment of the Republican. He demoted the chairman of the Finance Commission and designated the new appointee as the new chairman. He brought two more members of the Finance Commission before the Council on ouster proceedings, charging that each had acted as legal counsel for clients engaged in public activity and had, therefore, disqualified themselves for positions on an investigating body like the Finance Commission. Four Democrats and five Republicans made up the Governor's Council. One of the Republicans deserted his party and voted with the Democrats. The two members of the Finance Commission were ousted by a five to four vote. The Republican who voted with the Democrats was given a lush job on the Fall River Finance Commission, and the governor appointed a Democrat to succeed him on the Council.

All of this was done just in the nick of time, with but hours remaining before the case would be moved on legal processes into the courts. Throughout the proceedings, Edmund Dolan could not be reached. He was in Florida. Two faithful Democrats were appointed to the vacancies in the Finance Commission. The Council approved, and when the Democrats moved into the Finance Commission, the files on the case against Dolan disappeared. Dolan, however, reappeared. He came back from Florida.

There was still some resistance to later Curley appointments. Five to four was not a sufficient majority in the Council. Another Republican councilor was appointed to the bench, and from his district Curley appointed another Democrat. For the first time in three hundred years, the Governor's Council now had a six to three Democratic majority and Curley had no further trouble with it.

Mayor Mansfield watched this take place and was powerless to prevent it. The Finance Commission was now disarmed, its years of work destroyed and Mansfield asked the legislature to create a new Commission to "investigate the financial affairs of the City of Boston," a rival body with a specific mission. The legislature agreed that this ought to be done. The bill was rushed through the House and Senate and came to the governor for his signature. It was expected that Curley would veto it and the legislature promptly would pass it over his veto. He surprised everybody by signing it. He surprised everybody further by appointing as chairman of that special Commission the one man who knew more than anybody else about the finances of the city and the activities of Edmund L. Dolan as its treasurer. He appointed Edmund L. Dolan.

Mansfield, like a spider spinning a new web where one had been swept away, started painstakingly at scratch again with his own city law department to prepare the same case against them. He was persistent, impervious to pressure. He could not be bought, persuaded or frightened. It might take the remainder of his four years in office to backtrack, retrace steps and rebuild the case. The governor attacked him and ridiculed him, but Mansfield could not be diverted. The ousted members of the Finance Commission gave him all the help they could, but it was clear that it would be years before the case would reach the courts.

Curley knew he was wrong. It seemed as though he had been jinxed from the moment he blew up before Roosevelt.

He had broken now with James Roosevelt and told his few remaining intimates that the president had sent him a warning that one day he would "get" him. Now he seemed to handle everything badly. Nothing came off as he planned it. He achieved what he wanted in the Council, the Finance Commission and the Dolan case. He could do things like that and had done them regularly, within the confines of a city, but on a state-wide scale they missed fire.

In his interminable fight with the Finance Commission and what he called his Brahmin and High Irish enemies, the Boston Irish had always been on his side. Now that he had vanquished the Finance Commission he thought the Boston Irish would cheer, but they did nothing of the sort. To his consternation they turned up their noses as though something smelled.

Ever since he entered politics he had been threatening to throw the Brahmins out of office. Now, as governor, he bounced them out unceremoniously. One by one, as their terms expired, or as they quit under his pressure, he appointed Irish descendants. For years he had been promising to do this at rallies, banquets and wherever he spoke, and the Boston Irish had applauded. He was keeping his word, but the Boston Irish were looking at him with cold eyes, and they were not applauding; they were silent.

"You can't do that, Jim," they told him. "That's not what we wanted. We didn't elect you to do that. There's been a misunderstanding somewhere along the line. You'd better cut out this nonsense. We don't like it."

This made him all the more angry. He thought he knew better what they wanted. His reaction was like that of a petulant, spoiled and stubborn child. He would not only show Roosevelt who was boss in Massachusetts, but he'd show the Boston Irish, too. The result was a nightmare in which he piled bad taste upon outrageous judgment, making himself a constant target and inviting incessant criticism and attack.

When he made a bad choice, a bad decision, a faulty snap judgment, he emphasized it and sometimes perpetuated it by standing by what he had done in spite of contrary public opinion. He acknowledged mistakes when it was too late. Sometimes when he was crossed by opposition, a capricious retaliation led him to a sound and sensible reform.

There is no question, for example, that the courts in every state are cluttered up to some extent by judicial deadwood, superannuated senile septuagenarians, some of them in their dotage, no longer capable as judges, referees or arbiters, unable to give or write competent decisions. When the courts got in his way, he proposed to sweep all judges over seventy off the bench, thus in a way anticipating Roosevelt's own court-packing scheme, and proposed that all such submit to mental and physical examinations by doctors and psychiatrists before the Governor's Council. Apparently he forgot that three of the councilors were over seventy. He anticipated the defiance of the bench and bar, but the size of the whirlwind and storm that followed was spectacular in its flashes and cracklings. No judge was removed. A couple resigned, but the unexpected result was that the bench and bar turned the searchlight of criticism back upon itself and cleaned house, while the judges, for the first time, got an adequate pension system.

He never moved about without bands, fanfare, salutes, military aides, motorcycle outriders and all of the trappings of office. His critics called this heraldry arrogance and ego, but they were not entirely correct. He knew what he was doing. He was entitled to it under the law and he made the most of it. The Irish born and older American born of Irish descent loved it. To them, he was a poor boy elevated to the nobility, the king of the people of his state. They wanted him to look, act and dress the part. He was their Jim, one of them, with his head above the clouds. Second- and third-generation

American born considered this sort of thing harmless, were amused by it and enjoyed the show.

As governor of the state, he was invited to participate in Harvard's tercentenary commencement in 1935. He made such a show and spectacle of it that Harvard and the Boston social set covered faces that were red in painful embarrassment. He arrived at the Harvard Yard with an escort of lancers, an impressive display of National Guard, pomp, ceremony, gold braid, panoply, the blaring of trumpets and beating of drums. Actually, he was following in minute detail the pattern of colonial governors, true to the tradition in a stricter sense than the graduates, recipients of honorary degrees, guests, officers and fellows of the corporation.

He spoke his piece in the accent of an Oxford don, the best orator of the day, making one of the best speeches of his career, stealing the show and making headlines as usual. It was the only Harvard commencement for which the Boston Irish turned out en masse. Most Boston Irish children are taught almost at their mother's knees to root for Irish Boston College first, and then for Yale. The Boston Irish stood on the side lines, arms folded, grinning, enjoying it, saying: "That's our Jim. He did it again."

So many things happened to and around Curley as governor that newspapers used up tiers of special filing cabinets to document and accommodate the mass of material written about him. There were uncounted plots with mysterious characters who never materialized—unfinished stories. A plot to kidnap his son, a plot to tap his wires, a hidden microphone attached to his house radio that turned out to be a toy, a time bomb arriving at the office. It all turned out to be harmless. Another infernal machine turned out to be a box of peppermints wrapped up in the Boston *Herald* with an alarm clock attached, a practical joke by a group of Harvard boys. Most of these things happened in the nick of time to divert public attention from the revelations in various investigations, like one made by the Ways and Means Committee which showed that the governor's office spent $85,206 in one year for taxis, flowers, luncheons, cigars, refreshments and trips for himself, his secretaries and guests. Sample expenditures were: $2,786.58 for flowers, $5,461.05 for taxis, $7,658.68 to hotels, $8,776.68 for railroad travel, $7,022.89 for a three-day convention of the Atlantic Deeper Waterways Commission.

But these things did not deter him. In midwinter he moved his entire staff to Florida where he saw to it from the golf links that they administered the affairs of the state of Massachusetts. His popularity in Boston and Massachusetts had sunk now to about the same low as when he abandoned Al Smith for Franklin Roosevelt. And yet he became a hero and had the people cheering him again over night.

New England had had an exceptionally hard winter in 1936. Deep snow was piled high over hundreds of acres of Maine, New Hampshire and Vermont. Massachusetts had had its heaviest snowfall in years. An early spring with temperatures in the seventies for days melted it fast, and the worst floods in seventy-five years came. Farms, factories and homes were swept away throughout western Massachusetts, in the Berkshires and along the banks of the Connecticut River. Uncounted thousands were homeless.

Those who saw Curley during the flood saw him at the height of his power. There was something magnificent about him as he came into emergency camps, praising doctors and Red Cross nurses, giving a chuck and a pat under the chin to the nearest youngster and a tender word of sympathy and encouragement to the men and women. He was magnificent as he turned to address those forlorn thousands who sat crowded together on cold, bare army cots, their homes and their jobs gone, their aged sick. He promised them new homes, new jobs, food and shelter, medical care and state protection; pledged that he would personally see to it that not one suffered; urged them to be strong in adversity. As his magic oratory swelled through halls, faces lighted with the first glimmer of hope in many cruel hours. When he finished, men and women who thought they would never again speak above a whisper leaped to their feet and cheered him to the rafters.

He used up reporters, photographers, state troopers and chauffeurs, leaving them exhausted by the roadsides. Four of the state's bridges had been swept down the Connecticut, miles of highways were washed out, and homeless, hungry refugees were pouring into state armories and school buildings. For four days and nights he toured the flood area, traveling by automobile, walking miles on foot, flying by plane to towns and places that were isolated. He went without sleep for ninety-six hours, picking up a bite of food here and there, visiting every school building, armory and shack where more than three refugees were gathered to talk to them. It is probably a fact that he talked to every person who had suffered in any way in the flood.

He returned to organize the state and did it well, declared a condition of emergency and martial law, called out the National Guard and kept law and order, supplied beds and blankets, organized a flood-fund drive and formulated plans for clearing farms of silt and for cleansing homes of muck, for reopening factories and for securing emergency bank loans for reconstruction work. Every doubt as to his courage was dispersed when he ordered his chauffeur to drive him in his twelve-cylinder Lincoln across a condemned bridge, which was swept away twenty minutes after he crossed it. He kept his word to those people and committed his successors to a program for reconstruction. For a time, at least, the flood had cleansed him. In spite of his past, at that time he could have been elected to any office within the gift of the people of the state.

But four months later Curley announced himself a candidate for United States Senator opposing Henry Cabot Lodge, Jr., grandson of the Woodrow Wilson hating Senator. Curley was sixty-one, Lodge thirty-four. In that short period of time, Curley had slipped in popularity. The Boston Irish were surprised at his decision, certain that his feud with Roosevelt was responsible for it. He had asked for no advice, sent up no preliminary trial balloons, and mistook the praiseful and laudatory echoes of multiple yes-men who now surrounded him as an accurate sounding of public opinion. He had come down to the level of his people during the flood, but within a few months he had taken off and was soaring above them, completely out of touch with the rank and file. The people of the state had expected that he would be a candidate to succeed himself as governor. Almost all governors ran for a second term and most were successful. He had disconcerted them, compelled them suddenly to change their sights.

In spite of his awful mistakes and excesses as governor, he might have been re-elected for a second term, but by picking the higher office, he changed political relationship with the voters. The scores of thousands who had benefited by his wild administration were disappointed. As a United States Senator, he could no longer be the Great White Father to them. While he was governor, their jobs and wages were secure. He would be no good to them in Washington. They sensed that he wanted to go to Washington chiefly to wreak vengeance upon Franklin D. Roosevelt; and as between Curley and Roosevelt they were sure to choose Roosevelt.

His Republican and Democratic opposition throughout the state at first were unbelieving, fearful that he would repair the blunder and retrieve himself. They were actually timid about it, hoping desperately that he would stand by his decision. The fancies, fantasies and follies of his administration that might be tolerated for two more years of doing the greatest good for the greatest number made him utterly impossible as a Senator. His defeat was inevitable. Many of the Boston Irish felt that he was overreaching himself, deserting his own political league.

Henry Cabot Lodge, Jr., was a political neophyte. His chief recommendation was an historical name. His political training and experience had been meager. Born in Nahant, son of author George Cabot, he had been given the usual training of the blueblood wealthy: Middlesex School, 1920, Harvard, A.B., 1924. He had married socialite Emily Sears two years later, and they had two sons. He had been Washington correspondent for the Boston *Transcript* during 1923 and joined the staff of the New York *Herald Tribune* a year later. He returned to Nahant, became a candidate for the lower branch of the state legislature in 1932, was elected and re-elected in 1934. He was still serving his second term when he decided to try to pole-vault over all other intermediate offices into the United States Senate. Seasoned politicians in both parties looked askance at him. Sinclair Weeks and Republican big wheels concluded that the name Henry Cabot Lodge was worth the trial, and young Henry had the money. They adopted, nurtured and promoted him.

Curley dismissed Henry Cabot Lodge airily as a boy dispatched on a man's errand. He refused to take him seriously, dubbed him "Little Boy Blue," and as he could not very well fight Junior, he fought the memory of the Senior Lodge. Curley told rally after rally how many Jews he had appointed to public office, and recalled that the Senior Lodge had led the fight in the Senate against the confirmation of Louis D. Brandeis for appointment to the Supreme Court.

The campaign had minor complications. Father Charles E. Coughlin had been making some impression upon the Boston Irish. The Union party had organized locally. Congressman William Lemke of North Dakota had announced himself as a candidate for president and picked Thomas C. O'Brien, well-known in Boston as a former district attorney of Suffolk

County but little known throughout the rest of the country, as his running mate. Curley, whose friendship for Coughlin had been cooling fast, broke with him then and attacked him at rallies and on the air.

It was a Roosevelt year. A Republican did not have a chance. Curley took his election for granted. There was never any doubt in his mind that he would beat Henry Cabot Lodge and go to the Senate. Toward the close of the campaign, he was stricken with influenza, took to his bed and stayed there. His children, Mary, Leo, Paul and seventeen-year-old George, carried on for him at rallies and on the air.

When the votes were counted, Roosevelt had swept Massachusetts among the forty-six out of forty-eight states that he carried. Charles F. Hurley, an efficient state treasurer under Curley and his choice for governor, had been elected along with a Democratic panel of officers, except state treasurer. All Democrats had been elected by overwhelming majorities and pluralities—but Curley. He was defeated by Henry Cabot Lodge by 136,000 votes, and was dumbfounded by the result. The Boston Irish in the Metropolitan District had deserted him en masse.

Gertrude Casey Dennis was a widow with two grown sons in school. She was eminently respectable and deeply religious. She loved music, played the piano well and had been swept into Curley's women's political auxiliary by women friends, singers, who persuaded her to accompany them on the piano at rallies. She was quiet, conservative and far removed from the excitement that attends rallies. While Curley was governor, Gertrude Dennis often was seen with him, and it was no surprise to the people of Boston when the announcement was made toward the close of his term that they were to be married.

Curley's marriage at any time, whether he was in or out of office, would attract wide public attention, but his marriage while in office would have been a spectacle. Both Curley and Mrs. Dennis knew that they could not be married quietly. The people of Boston would not permit it. Their marriage was certain to be one of the few occasions when popularity would trespass and intrude upon privacy. They decided to be married as soon as he had left the governor's office and retired to private life.

Curley broke precedent when he took office. He broke it regularly while in office. He broke it as a final salute to the office. He and Gertrude Dennis were married that morning at ten o'clock in Saint Mary's Chapel of Boston College by the then Bishop Francis J. Spellman, pastor of the Sacred Heart Church, Newton. After the ceremony, the governor went directly to the State House to turn the reins of office over to Governor Charles F. Hurley. As he came down the terraced stone steps on the long walk, crowds lined it to cheer and congratulate him on his wedding. His bride awaited him in a limousine at the foot of the stone steps. He stepped into the car and was whisked away to a reception, stealing the show and the headlines from his successor as his final act in office. They left that day on a honeymoon.

The couple received an avalanche of wedding gifts and a bale of telegrams and letters. The prize of the day, though, was this telegram from the White House: "My congratulations to you and your bride on your wedding day. All the happiness and good luck in the world. Franklin Delano Roosevelt."

Twenty-one · Defeats by Tobin and Saltonstall

His POPULARITY and prestige were now at their lowest ebb. Voters remembered his errors and absurdities, forgetting entirely what he had done during the flood, forgetting, too, that he had compelled the legislature to sweat through a torrid summer to wrest from them amendments that liberalized extensively the Workmen's Compensation Act; to pass an anti-injunction law which labor leaders everywhere called the country's best; to provide a forty-eight-hour week and a wage increase to state institution employees. The bad lived and was perpetuated to plague him. The good died when his term expired.

He returned to Boston chastened and determined to recover that ground quickly. He did not go into private business this time. There was no place for him there. His experience had been entirely in public business. Most governors have little difficulty finding lush, dignified jobs for themselves when they return to private life. They are in good demand, particularly among banks and insurance companies. Curley's reputation precluded that. None was offered. He went right back into politics, preparing the way to get back into City Hall. There were two very vital reasons why. First, he was broke. He had been so sure that he would beat Henry Cabot Lodge that he had thrown most of his own funds into the campaign kitty. Second, Mayor Mansfield was making such headway in the preparation of the General Equipment case against him that if some hand did not restrain him or the case, both he and Dolan would probably find themselves in court before a judge and jury. Finally, the election for mayor was only nine months away.

This time he found himself opposed by a young man whom he had trained in his own organization, Maurice J. Tobin, thirty-six years old, a New England Telephone Company employee, whose political experience had been limited to the Boston School Committee and minor, unpaid political and party offices. Tobin was good looking—he later turned down movie offers—a good public speaker, although he could never compare or compete with Curley. He was a new, fresh face. Smiling, amiable, affable, he had made friends among the younger men and women in Curley's loose machine.

Like Curley, he was a first-generation American born of Irish parents who were recent immigrants, far removed from the potato famine. His father had arrived in Boston from Clougheenofishogue and his mother from Mitchelstown in Ireland just before the turn of the century. They met and were married in Boston, and Maurice was the first born in 1901. He had attended parochial school on Mission (Cork) Hill and the High School of Commerce. He worked for a while in the leather business and at twenty-one became a rookie relay adjuster for the New England Telephone and Telegraph Company and joined the union. He remained there until politics began to interfere with his job.

This was a family row, personal, bitter, at times laden with

the vicious domestic acrimony that results when members of
the same household split apart and become enemies. Tobin
had learned politics at Curley's knee. He had been a regular
visitor at Jamaicaway, a member of the inner circle, as close
as Curley ever got to a cabinet. The house had always been
open to him. Curley had helped him, advised him, encouraged
him. Tobin got his training in public speaking campaigning
for Curley. Curley felt that Tobin had betrayed him, and
said so. Tobin knew and understood Curley's campaign technique. Almost all his workers had been Curley workers.

Tobin never lost the initiative and always had the advantage. There was little doubt that he would win, but Clifton
Carberry, editor of the Boston *Post*, made sure of it. For many
years the *Post* had carried a single-line sermon, a proverb or
an axiom across the very top of page one. Election day came
on the feast of All Souls, a holy day when Catholics are
obliged to attend mass. As the faithful poured out of churches
that morning, on their way home or to work, they could not
miss the sermon in big black type atop the morning *Post*:

"Anyone who votes for a person they know to be dishonest
or otherwise unfit for office, commits a sin."—WILLIAM CAR-
DINAL O'CONNELL.

They walked dutifully into the polling places and marked
a cross beside the name of Maurice J. Tobin, astonished that
at last the cardinal had raised his voice in local politics. They
could look through the *Post* with a magnifying glass, if they
cared to take the trouble, and not find the statement supported by a news story. It had been lifted out of the text of
an address by the cardinal before the Holy Name Society in
Holy Cross Cathedral six years earlier. When the votes were
counted, Curley was badly beaten by the neophyte.

The next upcoming election, a year away, was for governor.
Curley immediately set about preparing for that. Charles F.
Hurley, who succeeded Curley as governor, thought he was

entitled to another term, and although Curley had failed now
in two elections, he still could dominate the primary, where
he polished off Hurley handily enough and again became
Democratic nominee for governor in 1938.

That was a black year for James Michael Curley, and perhaps it was the first false dawn of a new era for the Boston
Irish and Boston. If the end of a cycle can be determined as
arriving at a specific time, a political epoch ended that year
and another one began. It was then that tough, rugged South
Boston discovered that Yankee Brahmins were human beings,
and the Yankee Brahmins discovered the new Irish. If it
takes four generations to go from shirtsleeves to shirtsleeves,
regardless of wealth, distinction and ancestral backgrounds,
both discovered suddenly that they were upon the same
level.

They found that they were now swept into the same stream,
politically, economically and socially. Each discovered that
they needed the other. For years, Yankees had the money and
the Irish had the votes. Yankees controlled the financial structure, while the Irish controlled the political structure. Both
had been bled white, and a time came when it was now wise
for them to coalesce. Many of the bluebloods were broke and
had to go to work. Small families, deaths and wars had deci-
mated their numbers, and the depression had concentrated
their wealth into fewer hands. For years, money had fought
votes. Now the Irish had both money and votes, while many
of the Yankees had money and could not get at it. They were
prevented from doing so by spendthrift trusts.

The spendthrift trust is a peculiar Massachusetts legal device. It was designed more than a century ago when Yankee
money barons (many of whom founded their fortunes in a
triangular trade trafficking in rum, molasses and slaves) foresaw the possibility of profligate sons, grandsons and great-
grandsons ad infinitum who might squander these fortunes,

and tied their wealth and holdings up in wills and special trusts that preserved the principals and bequeathed only the interest to heirs in limited amounts. Under this Massachusetts law, the only such in the country, a principal so protected against spendthrifts can never be touched. Many Boston socialite millionaires are thus limited to ten thousand a year or less. If they live beyond their incomes and cannot pay their bills, there is nothing creditors can do about it. Only the interest can be attached—never the principal that provides it. The Yankee buccaneers, privateers and pirates who made these fortunes from the War of 1812 up to and after the Civil War could not foresee inflation as it would occur in a world of a century or more later. These Boston fortunes must grow in perpetuity until the end of the world, while heirs and beneficiaries are limited by the terms of the trust.

One thing that the Yankees brought to politics was integrity, and although integrity is sometimes a poor substitute for intelligence, the Irish needed it desperately. Robert Bradford, nine generations removed from the original Colonial Governor Robert Bradford, was now district attorney of Middlesex County and doing a thoroughgoing job of cleaning it up. Henry Parkman, Jr., was Mayor Tobin's corporation counsel. Leverett Saltonstall became the Republican candidate against James Michael Curley, and the Boston Irish adopted him.

Sir Richard Saltonstall arrived on the *Arbella* in 1630, and to most Bostonians, Saltonstall was merely a *Mayflower* name until Leverett bobbed up in the legislature a few years after World War I. He started from the bottom of the political escalator as a member of the Newton board of aldermen. He had a war record, overseas service and a commission as a lieutenant in the 301st Field Artillery. He had married Alice Wesselhoeft, daughter of Boston's leading surgeon. He met her at dancing school when she was eleven, and from that time on she was his girl. They settled in a big house to raise a large family—more like the Boston Irish than the Boston Brahmins.

Nobody paid much attention to him in the State House of Representatives. He was just another blueblood, another Saltonstall lawyer in a long line of them in a state where old families are a drug on the market. A Harvard-trained conservative, he spoke with the approved accent and, like a true Republican gentleman, voted precisely as he was told by the Republican whip. Massachusetts Republicans that year wrote one of the worst labor records in decades. The American Federation of Labor damned them to hell; even the State House scrubwomen held their noses when one passed by. At the end of the session, Saltonstall looked around to find out what caused the odor. He knew he didn't mean to do anything like that; but there it was. That's how the liberal education of Leverett Saltonstall began.

That kind of record hurt him not a bit in his district, a bedroom of Boston bankers, brokers and bond salesmen, but he disliked the character his party had made for him. He felt as if he were in the right church but the wrong pew, and next term he began to ask questions of the Boston Irish and of the Boston Italians in the legislature. To his astonishment, he discovered they had a lot to say. Before long, he was patiently interpreting the Boston Irish and the Boston Italians to the Boston Brahmins and upstate Yankees, and trying desperately to make the Boston Irish, particularly, understand that they could do business with Brahmins and Yankees.

More and more he found himself walking down the middle road of compromise, and he began to learn how the Irish regularly captured city and state offices at election time. He was getting a clearer and more accurate idea than most Republicans of the anatomy of Democratic machines and began to develop skill in recognizing the bait that attracts votes. He was utterly honest, painfully so at times. He could not

shut his eyes to corruption around him, but he shut his mouth
in grim disapproval and refused to play stool pigeon. Reform,
he was sure, would never come that way. At the end of his
third term, he was the only representative in the House whom
both sides would trust and he was elected Speaker in 1929,
a job he held for the next eight years.

One of his first acts as Speaker was to hire as his secretary
a tough-fibered, hard-boiled newspaper reporter, Daniel J.
Lynch of the South Boston Irish. Lynch knew all the twisting
ways of Boston politics and the leavening of Leverett was
about complete. He crossed swords with Governors Curley
and Hurley, tangled with Democratic leaders and with leaders
of his own party. When either tried to put something over,
he became the state's angry man, direct and disconcerting.
He cleaned up dirty legislation quietly by backing sponsors of
shakedown bills into corners and forcing them to withdraw.

When a particularly outrageous piece of shakedown was
on the verge of passing, he rose in wrath, slammed the gavel
and adjourned the House, taking the gavel with him so that
nobody could carry on in his absence. When members
swarmed into his office shrieking "Dictator!" he set them back
on their heels with language that no Brahmin should ever
use. They understood him perfectly and the bill died. Whenever his decisions as Speaker were questioned, Democrats
joined Republicans to support him. It was inevitable that he
would be a candidate for governor. Labor now approved him.

James Michael Curley elected him. He didn't intend to.
That was the furthest thing from his mind. Curley was being
funny—always a disastrous thing for him in public. He forgot
that Saltonstall had come to know the Boston Irish and
their ways.

Saltonstall's face does not mean as much to the rest of
the country as it does to Boston, where people are familiar
with it. It is one of the most unbeautiful heads that God
ever set on a man's shoulders, long and angular with long

teeth and cowcatcher chin. He looks like an American Indian named "Horse-face," and he wears his clothes in a way
that accentuates the illusion. People in Boston have been
poking fun at Saltonstall's face for years. He doesn't mind a
bit; sometimes he contributes original ideas of his own about
it. It has been described as a well-worn antique and the most
distinctive face in American public life. During the 1938
campaign the Boston *Transcript* characterized Saltonstall as a
man with a Back Bay name and a South Boston face. That
did it.

Before South Boston had a chance to get mad about it,
Curley quipped on the radio: "Saltonstall may have a South
Boston face, but he doesn't dare show it in South Boston."
Curley should have known better and ruefully admitted it
later. Saltonstall did exactly what Curley would have done
if the situation had been reversed. He appeared in South
Boston early next day, walking up Broadway, dropping in at
bars and taverns, making himself known. He said hello to the
local pastors and clergy, to kids on sand lots and back lots.
People on the streets knew him. They couldn't miss him.
He talked like Back Bay but acted like South Boston, and
invited them to hear him speak that night at his South Boston rallies. "I may have a South Boston face," he told one
cheering audience after another; "if so, I'm proud of it. But
one thing you may be sure of—I'm not two-faced. It's the
same face before and after election."

Saltonstall came down to the Boston line with a whopping
plurality and the Metropolitan District magnified it for him.
Throughout the campaign he had been something of a political maverick. He had made the Republican party in Massachusetts one in which Leverett Saltonstall was the left wing,
a definition that made Boston bluebloods shudder and the
Boston Irish grin. He spoke brashly of Roosevelt as "Our
Great President," and meant it—a heresy to coupon-clipping

Fourth-term inauguration, January, 1946.

The Mayor returns from Danbury, November, 1947.

Victory, 1948: Rep. John W. McCormack, Mayor Curley, President Truma
Secretary of Labor Maurice J. Tobin, Governor-elect Paul A. Dever.

Republican Roosevelt haters but music to the ears of the
Boston Irish. Both voted for him, but some bluebloods closed
their eyes when they did so, while the Boston Irish kept
theirs open.

A problem child to his own party in the state, he now dominated it. To the social set on Beacon Hill, he was still "Lev,"
a wonder boy whose political eccentricities made them cheer
and choke. To the rugged Boston Irish in South Boston, he
became "Salty," and although he was never properly baptized,
they forgave and forgot it. His lack of Irish ancestry was an
impediment that was forthwith corrected. He was elected a
member of the Charitable Irish Society by virtue of an obscure Irish ancestor somewhere in a distant and almost in-
visible branch of the Saltonstall family tree. If he hadn't
found one to qualify himself, the Boston Irish would have
found one for him. He became their boy.

He all but annihilated the master in that election. Curley
was stunned and groggy—beaten now three times in a row.

And now the mistake he made in Dolan came home to
roost. Mayor Mansfield had succeeded in channeling two
separate cases into the courts, one against Edmund L. Dolan,
charging him with the theft of $178,000 from the city treas-
ury, and another jointly against Curley and a companion on
the state Democratic ticket, Dr. Joseph Santosuosso, a candidate for secretary of state. This was a bill in equity demanding an accounting of the $85,000 received in the General
Equipment case.

Indicted by the Grand Jury, Dolan thought he knew how
to fix things for a not-guilty verdict, but it did not work, and
he was brought into court on a charge of conspiring to cor-
rupt the traverse jurors in that he did offer and give bribes
to them. That was enough for Judge Frederick W. Fosdick.
He held him in contempt of court and sentenced him to two

and a half years in the county jail; but the perversion of county government, as compared with city government, was so much greater that the judge might as well have sentenced him to two and a half years in Boston's swank Copley-Plaza.

Twenty-Two · Hospitality Hall

When erstwhile City Treasurer Edmund L. Dolan arrived at the Charles Street Jail, he shook hands with High Sheriff John F. Dowd—and was home free. The jail under High Sheriff Dowd ought to be immortalized in a modern political Aesop's fables as a heavenly dream-prison, the kind of a place perfidious politicians hope to go to when they die. High Sheriff John Dowd, who wore an eighteenth-century coat and vest, bearing a wooden mace as he escorted the black-robed supreme-court justices in somber dignity to the bench to open the season, was the archangel who made it that way—a jail where the prisoner was always right.

"Johnny" Dowd, as he was known, was born in Curley's ward, attended grammar school there, and went to work without further schooling to support his mother. He sold papers, ran errands and even at that age gained a reputation as a juvenile sharpie, a youngster who would bear careful watching, particularly when he was handling money. He developed a calculating, scheming mind, always selling raffle tickets for prizes won by the lucky in other cities and towns, making collections for charitable causes for which there was never an accounting, the first to suggest a fund for anyone in the district burned out of house and home and to collect it personally without helpers. He did all the work. Such funds, when they were delivered, always seemed to be outrageously small, considering the amount of time and effort Johnny put into these causes.

He became a street-corner gangster, learned to live by his wits and did quite well at it. He absorbed the ward version of politics in poolrooms and bowling alleys, and even before he was twenty-one had become versed in all the angles and the cunning ways to play them. He served eighteen months in the army during World War I, wangled his way into the motor transport corps and by "using my head," as he put it, contrived a way to get a commission as a second lieutenant. After the war, he was advanced to first lieutenant in the quartermaster reserve corps. His record was bare of combat service. This qualified him to become director of Americanization for the city of Boston, and Curley appointed him to that office. Eight months later he had maneuvered himself into the mayor's secretariat.

Dowd chose politics deliberately as a short cut to wealth and an easy life. Always on the lookout for a chance to make a quick dollar, he had become skilled in sneaking up on opportunity and seizing it. Trained to live by his wits as a juvenile, he now padded out his income by advising, directing and counseling number and baseball pool salesmen, bootleggers, petty thieves and juvenile delinquents, assuring them of a protection that he was seldom able to provide, and lamenting that somebody had double-crossed him when they got caught. He had a wide acquaintance among hoodlums and gangsters, the best people to promote his political success. With that background and skill, he measured up to the norm of the average city councilor.

He became one of Curley's battery of public speakers, mastered the customary Boston political speech format, a stereotyped saga of a poor boy, born in a humble home, denied opportunities for an education, pleading for the sympathy of the voters. He became a good speaker and impressed Boston voters with his earnestness and sincerity. At the same time, he acquired two very profitable side lines. He became a florist, providing flowers for city celebrations, and he put an annual Christmas-basket fund for the poor of old Ward Seventeen on a business basis. The philanthropic Christmas-basket business did some good for the poor of the ward. Dowd collected large sums of money from the merchants of the ward and neglected to distribute it to the poor, and as Christmas approached, he solicited meat and provisions from the whole-salers and distributed it.

The poor were well supplied at Thanksgiving and Christmas. They got baskets from Dowd, from the Salvation Army, the Volunteers of America, the Saint Vincent De Paul Society and from various other agencies. Three and four turkeys were given to one family. The foresighted promptly swapped the excess with local butchers for corned or roast beef and hams. The rest ate turkey three meals a day for a week and got very tired of it.

Curley had assayed Dowd early in his career as useful but dangerous, the kind of a campaign worker who would de-mand, or chisel, more than his pound of flesh. When Dowd told Curley toward the close of his second administration that he was going to be a candidate for the city council, Cur-ley asked for his resignation and told him that he would not endorse him. This did not deter Dowd. He became a candi-date and was elected. The salary of a city councilor was $38.38 a week ($2,000 a year). Dowd spent an estimated $8,000 to be elected.

Scanning the political horizon for the right get-rich-quick opportunity, Dowd trained his sights on the office of county sheriff, an exceptionally lush one. County government in Massachusetts is an extraneous structure superimposed upon cities and towns. It serves no useful purpose and duplicates many of the functions of the cities and towns. In any intelligent streamlining of government, it would be swept away, a reform that is not easy to accomplish except on paper. Its extra wheels in the machinery of government require an excessive amount of legitimate and illegitimate financial grease. The county sheriff lives an easy and languid life. He has more help than he can keep employed. He has a beautiful house, provided by the state, and pays no rent, water, gas or light bills. Trusties tend his garden and shine his shoes. He has a trusty chauffeur and his choice of prison cars—and he had a budget of $3,500,000 to spend. All of these things made the job exceptionally attractive to Johnny Dowd.

Sheriff John A. Kelliher was growing old. He had been in public office for forty years as state representative and senator, congressman and sheriff. In 1932, Dowd became a candidate against him, but the old sheriff was popular and Dowd was badly beaten. He wound up in the bankruptcy court, owing the owners of sound trucks, automobiles, halls, hotels, printers and advertising novelty makers. This was no new experience for Dowd. He seemed to have the notion that a city councilor need not pay for anything, ordered gold and silver cups over the years to award at field days and beauty contests, collected money by public subscription to pay for them, but never did. Three times he had been brought into court to take a poor debtor's oath which shrived him of the responsibility to pay.

Kelliher's six-year term expired in 1938 and again Dowd became a candidate for sheriff. It was clear to everyone but Kelliher that he had not long to live. He was seventy-one, ailing and failing fast. His friends shook their heads and knew that a strenuous campaign would kill him; and it did. Political scandals in Dowd's background were revived: the sale of jobs to W.P.A. and to welfare workers in his ward, and questions of welfare slips in Dowd's possession that had disappeared; nevertheless he was elected. Sheriff Kelliher died while the vote was being counted, and a few days later Governor Hurley appointed Dowd to fill out the balance of Kelliher's unexpired term.

When Dowd took over as high sheriff, he had more than two hundred permanent employees: deputy sheriffs, deputy jailers, guards, gate officers, clerks, stewards, a pharmacist, matrons for the women's wing, power-plant engineers and firemen, scrubwomen, a few part-time experts and professionals, like the jail physician and dentist, and an average transient prisoner population of 271 serving two and a half years or less.

The regular salaried employees were chiefly married men with families. Many of them had already had long years of service in the jail and owned their own homes or were buying them. The scrubwomen were widows or wives of invalid husbands. Dowd let them know right away that all ought to consider themselves lucky to have jobs in days of such widespread unemployment, and pointed out that they would have trouble finding jobs if they were discharged from the jail.

He put a price on every job, and the price varied according to the size of the employee's salary, his estimated bank account and whether he owned his home or an automobile. Twenty-six scrubwomen getting eighteen dollars a week, were ordered to pay from two hundred to two hundred and fifty dollars each to keep their jobs. One of them, an East Boston widow supporting a twenty-two-year-old son, a victim of infantile paralysis, was fired because she could not raise the money. The cost of security among deputies and guards was higher, scaled from five hundred to twenty-five hundred dollars.

The employees were helpers. They had to pay or be fired. They withdrew their savings from banks. Some of them mortgaged their homes. Others went to loan sharks or pledged their automobiles. A number of them failed to raise the money and were fired. One was driven insane by his dismissal and was removed to State Hospital. In three days Dowd netted eighteen thousand dollars from those who remained, not counting the money he would collect in selling the jobs left vacant by those who could not meet his requirement. These went at fancy prices. A jail officer's berth brought three thousand dollars, almost two years' salary. He even sold jobs that he did not have to give. A number of prospective purchasers paid him for a promise and he did not return the money.

He was an unscrupulous charlatan who cut the salaries of deputies and raised his own in an underhanded way. In Massachusetts courts, the fees paid deputies for serving writs and legal processes are part of their legal compensation and are not turned in to the court or county. They keep it. It is common practice for Massachusetts deputies to turn their fees in to a pool. The pool is divided equally among all deputies once a month. The reason is that deputies assigned to judges and court sessions would be prevented by their duties from serving profitable processes, and those not so assigned would be making all the money. Dowd told the deputies that he would take five hundred dollars a month from their pool.

The demoralization and corruption of the jail was swift, bold, brazen and complete. Few respectable persons ever go behind prison walls. Inspections and examinations are perfunctory, and because of the very nature of the place, official visitors can be channeled and guided through in such a way as to see only what the custodian wants them to see. Dowd felt absolutely safe, sure that he could get away with anything. What he did with the jail, the ingenuity and inventiveness that he used to bring it about would make a screen writer's eyes pop with envy.

He made it a rule that anybody in the jail could have anything he wanted any time he wanted it. He put the jail on a hotel basis, opened a service bar, turned guards, deputies and trusties into waiters, and ordered them to serve the prisoners at any time and to turn in their tips to him. He put food and liquor checkers at the service bar and in the kitchen. Any prisoner could order a scotch and soda, a rye highball, cocktail or mixed drink and have it served in his cell. He ordered the doors between the men's and women's wings, which had always been closed, opened so that men and women prisoners could intermingle and fraternize. He ordered that cell doors of all prisoners who paid the price be left open so that they could wander around the jail at will.

He hated jail guards, had a gangster's contempt for them and made no secret of it. He was the prisoner's friend whether the prisoner had money or not, and as between guards and prisoners, he was on the side of the prisoner. He berated and ridiculed the guards and deputies before the prisoners and reprimanded them publicly for failing to do a prisoner's bidding promptly. Guards, turnkeys or "screws" were, in his opinion, stool pigeons and cops at heart, and as such he had nothing but hatred for them, and he said so. He dressed a jail officer down in blunt, sulfurous language for refusing a drug to a prisoner, ordered him to do so and stood looking on while he administered it.

When City Treasurer Edmund Dolan arrived at Dowd's jail, he was greeted with open arms. "Make yourself at home, Eddie," Dowd invited, as he showed him through the jail. "You'll find the service good here, even if I do say so. You're a hell of a fellow and I like you. You're going to enjoy it here, but just to keep the record straight, so there'll be no misunderstanding, it's going to cost you about as much as staying at the Ritz. You can stand that, can't you?"

"Sure, Johnny," Eddie agreed. "Anything you say."

Dolan picked out a nice, comfortable, sunny room for himself in the hospital wing and settled down for a pleasant stay in the happy little jail. There were three other Boston politicians there for taking bribes. He knew them well, and there was a continuous poker game to interest him any time he wanted to sit in. Dolan looked around, amused and astonished, and nodded in approval. He knew he was going to like it.

Visiting hours had been abandoned. Prisoners were invited to have friends come at any hour of the day or night, to drop in at two in the morning after leaving night clubs. It was all so nice and cozy. The visitors were good spenders, bought drinks lavishly and ordered food. The best gambling games for miles around were in the jail. It offered everything— roulette, poker, Canfield, dice. All a prisoner had to do was name it. The sheriff had it. The jail "bookie" was William Forgrave, former head of the Anti-Saloon League in Boston, now an inmate. He made the rounds of the cells registering bets on horses at all tracks.

Prisoners had free access to the telephone. One prisoner carried on his established insurance business. When he was sentenced, he swapped a desk in a downtown office for a desk in the jail with trusties as office boy, clerk and stenographer. He had his clients come to the jail by appointment to see him. Prisoners could leave the jail by arrangement with the sheriff. Those who were not so well known and not likely to be recognized were allowed to taxi to the municipal golf links, to return at an appointed hour at night. Trusties were driving jail cars all over the city and surrounding country. A girl inmate was undecided whether to go to the country or the seashore one day. She came out into the jail yard, stepped into a car and said to a trusty chauffeur: "Where'll we go?"

He shrugged his shoulders indifferently. "You name it, lady," he said. "I don't care. I've got ten gallons of gas and two years. Where do you want to go?"

One of the political prisoners asked permission to attend the funeral of a mayor in an adjoining city. The sheriff agreed to let him go if he would pay the expenses of a jail guard to accompany him. The prisoner did so and the two set off for the funeral. At suppertime that night, they had not returned, but no one worried. About two o'clock the following morning, the gate bell clanged. A deputy answered to find the prisoner and his guard on the steps, both very drunk.

"I've been trying to get this guy to come back since four o'clock yesterday afternoon," the prisoner complained, "but no. He wanted to go night clubbing."

At about that time there was a minor escape scare. A trusty, polishing the sheriff's car in the front yard, disappeared. The grounds, the house and the jail were searched, but he could not be found. Dowd was chary about sounding an alarm. That would bring the police. Word spread from tongue to tongue along the main and side streets that a trusty had taken it on the lam. The trusty came running back, breathless, to find out who had been silly enough to run away from that jail.

"Where've you been?" the sheriff demanded angrily.

"Who, me?" The trusty was surprised. "That polish parches my throat. I only went down to the corner for a glass of beer."

"Next time"—the sheriff shook a warning finger—"ask permission! Now get back on that car and finish it."

Prisoners threw lavish champagne parties for themselves and their friends, parties that began early in the evening and lasted until the following morning. Visitors came to the jail for dinner and stayed for breakfast. During one such party, the sheriff, utterly exhausted by hard work, was sleeping in the residence provided by the state adjoining the jail yard. One of the girls in the jail chortled: "Let's go across the yard and up to his bedroom and tickle Johnny's toes. We'll wake him up and get him over here to the jail and have some fun."

At night, petters were all over the place, in the executive offices and the rooms reserved for daytime consultations between prisoners and counsel. A minister, summoned there for a Sunday-afternoon shotgun wedding with organ music, flowers, best man, bridesmaid, reception and buffet, complained later that he was disconcerted when, at the most solemn point in the ceremony, a golf ball bounced through the chapel window, shattering the glass. He was sure it did not land in his hat. He characterized it as "vexing." Inmates were playing miniature golf in the prison yard.

The prisoners were, perhaps, the best fed in the world. They ate like kings, not because Johnny was that generous, but because with such a large budget to spend, he had awarded contracts to meat and provision wholesalers for more food than he could use. They had steak and potatoes, with a wide variety of vegetables, fruits and pastries whether they wanted it or not. The sheriff's contract for butter alone was such that each prisoner had to have at least a quarter of a pound on his plate at every meal.

In the underworld from coast to coast Charles Street (or Suffolk County) Jail came to be known as "Hospitality Hall." It was a haven and sanctuary for criminals in hiding. If they could but reach Boston, they knew they were safe—safe from the F.B.I., from G-men and T-men, safe from detectives, private, city and state, safe in the arms of Johnny. They paid his price, put the money on the line, got a comfortable room in the hospital wing, disappeared from sight. They were well fed, had a lot of fun and were secure. Nobody would ever think of looking for them in a jail. How many he harbored, and their identities, may never be known. Eddie O'Hare, the Chicago race-track figure and gambler, came frequently to go into a huddle with City Treasurer Dolan, and New York mobsters moved in to make the jail a headquarters for a laundry racket.

The prisoners approved and applauded Dowd's attitude toward guards, turnkeys, deputies and jail employees, and reflected it. They treated them with scorn, ordered them around arrogantly, had them rustling up drinks and food, making telephone calls, mailing letters, and rewarded them with insults. Prisoners had ready access to arms and ammunition, but none had any intention of making a break for freedom. They had freedom—and this was a comfortable and painless way of paying a debt to society. The normal position of guards and prisoners was reversed. The nerves of the guards were rubbed raw and they came to be afraid for their lives. The characters of some of the prisoners were bad enough, but those of transient criminals who came there for protection were worse. The guards had arms, but they were useless. They had keys, but these, too, were useless. Cell doors were never locked, but the locks on all doors and gates of the jail were changed, nevertheless, once a month, because Dowd had a contract with a locksmith who contributed his share to Dowd's income.

Each guard and deputy was fearful that he might be pushed a little too far and lose his temper. He might throw a punch at a prisoner, and he knew that if he did it would not only cost him his job, but it might cost his life. Men going off duty on the day shift looked with speculative eyes upon men coming on for the night trick, and wondered if they would see them in the morning. The jail had become a high-compression chamber waiting for the spark that would explode it.

That was the state of affairs on an afternoon in summer, almost a year after Dowd had taken over, when Attorney Ruben Lurie walked into a vault in the office of Clerk of the Court John Patrick Connolly and found two women crying. The clerk of the court has no direct connection with the jail, its administration or the sheriff. The two weeping women were not employees of the sheriff. They were employees of the clerk of the court. Lurie looked down at them, puzzled and sympathetic.

"What's the matter?" he asked.

"We've just been fired," one of the clerks explained.

"What for?" He was surprised. He had seen the girls in the clerk's office for years.

The explanation came piecemeal. Clerk Connolly's term in

office was soon to expire. He would have to campaign for re-election. He would have opposition and he needed money. Everybody in the clerk's office had to pay for his job, and theirs had been sold over their heads to higher bidders.

"What have you done about it?" Lurie asked.

"Nothing," one of the girls answered. "What can we do? Other girls have been fired. They went to the attorney general about it, and he sent them to the district attorney. They went to the district attorney and he said: 'You've got nothing but suspicion and no evidence of graft,' and that ended it."

Ruben Lurie is a man of wide and solid reputation in many other fields than law. At that time he was an auditor for the Superior Court and his business took him into the clerk's office regularly. He had an office of his own, across the hallway from the pressroom, and on that day he came back to that office burning with indignation at a system that permitted faithful employees to be tossed around, shaken down and bled for their savings or whatever money they could raise. The more he thought of it, the madder he got. He went into the pressroom, where he was known, to make a few inquiries. Courthouse reporters knew what Connolly was up to, but they couldn't print it without a reasonably substantial peg to hang it on. Lurie promised them that peg. He went back to the clerk's office and invited the two girls to come to his downtown office (where he conducted his private law practice) for a talk, and as they had no other place to turn for relief, he decided to help them.

For years, Ruben Lurie has been associated, one way or another, with controversies. An instinctive defender of civil rights and human dignity, tyrants intrigued him for academic and clinical study. He seemed never to have known fear, although he could understand its presence in others. He was forever retrieving lost causes, for the sheer fun of saving them. To him the Bill of Rights was a catalogue of fundamental privileges, and when his interest was persuaded in a violation of any one of its doctrines, he sacrificed lush fees to follow it through to its finish. Sometimes he was the advocate of the popular majority, sometimes of the unpopular minority. He had a mathematical mind that reduced human equations to algebraic and mathematical equations. Scrupulously ethical, he was highly respected in his profession, frequently an arbitrator and mediator.

He presided at the New England Town Meeting of the Air where he brought college professors and public officials together to discuss current topics and answer extemporaneously the questions fired at them by the audience. He did much the same thing at Ford Hall Forum, one of the last surviving temples dedicated to free speech, where anyone might say anything. In Boston he is bracketed in the public mind with Arthur Garfield Hays and Morris Ernst. The weeping women could not know that the lawyer who stumbled upon them had the intellect, the inclination and the skill to spin their cause.

Lurie is small and slight, about five feet five inches tall, weighs about 135 pounds, and has steel-gray eyes. When preoccupied with a problem he smokes cigarettes down to his fingertips. As a student at Harvard he wrote fiction that was published in national magazines. After he was graduated in 1919 he did a tour of duty in the newspaper business as reporter, rewrite man and editorial writer, then went back to Harvard to study law and was admitted to the bar in 1926.

He knew his way around politically and in a few days he had uncovered some rather startling things about the conduct of the office of the clerk of the court. Studious by nature his researches and the studies of others examining the vagaries of government had led him to these human equations expressed in mathematical form:

graft + gratitude = no exposure
graft + resentment = exposure + security

In the first problem, graft never can be exposed because the graft payer (graftee) is perfectly happy in the possession of the job or with the contract that his bribe purchased. He is satisfied that he got his money's worth. He would not inform or give evidence against the grafter, because by so doing he would lose his job or contract. Continued enjoyment of the benefits of his purchase depend upon silence.

In the second problem the grafter can be exposed if (1) the price is exorbitant, (2) continued payments become blackmail, or (3) the graftee is resentful. On the other side of the equation, exposure can result only if the prosecutor can guarantee to the graftee continued security in his job or continued possession of his contract.

Lurie's investigation was careful, painstaking and thorough. Inevitably it was noised around the courthouse that he was making one. This made all politicians nervous, the more so because they did not know why Lurie should be investigating, or for whom. It was inconceivable to politicians that a man might undertake an investigation on his own hook, and immediately there were references to the mysterious power behind Lurie, unknown reformers who were financing it. An air of the sinister about the investigation gave politicians the jitters.

The grievance committee of the Bar Association had been receiving complaints about the office of the clerk of the court. Both Massachusetts and Boston Bar Associations are, fortunately, islands of integrity, so strict and impersonal that they have no hesitancy or compunction about investigating themselves. The complaints had been set aside and were awaiting attention when Damon Hall, president of the Bar Association, heard that Lurie was investigating. He sent for him.

"Are you making an investigation of the clerk of the court?" he asked.

"Yes," Lurie answered.

"Good." Hall approved. "Perhaps you'd better get together with the grievance committee so that we can co-operate and get behind you."

This arrangement was made, and when the official announcement came that Lurie was investigating for the Bar Association, a few grafters packed their bags and left town. With the Bar Association behind him, Lurie applied his formula. He called all the employees of the clerk's office before him, interviewed them separately, and gave each his own personal assurance that he would remain undisturbed in his job, that future payments of money would stop instantly if the employee would tell how much he was paying and to whom. He got signed affidavits from each. When the case was completed, he put it in the lap of the district attorney.

While talking with one of the women employees of the clerk's office, she said to Lurie: "If you think things are bad in our office, you ought to drop around to the jail. They're much worse there. My cousin works in the boiler room and I know."

That statement was all Lurie had to go on. It was the first hint to newspapermen or anybody outside the jail that anything was wrong there. Lurie went back to President Hall at the Bar Association. "I'm told that things are just as bad at the jail," he said.

"Then you'd better go right after it." He was given the nod, and when it became known that Lurie was calling jail officers to his office the storm broke. For the time being, Lurie ignored what the jail officers told him about the laundry and other rackets operated there from New York. In a few days he had all the evidence he needed, filed it with the supreme court and Dowd was ordered to appear to show cause why he should not be removed.

Before the time for the hearing Dowd disappeared and was picked up the next night by New York police on East Seventy-seventh Street. His head was badly battered and bleeding.

He refused to identify himself to police at the Sixty-seventh Street station. He had six thousand dollars in his pocket and a gold sheriff's badge. New York police wired Boston police to find out about him and removed him to Bellevue Hospital where doctors found he was suffering as well from alcoholism.

While New York and Boston reporters waited at the front door of the hospital for him to come out after his discharge the following day, Dowd, master hand at receiving graft, paid some. His head swathed in bandage and a strip of adhesive across his nose, he gave a hospital attendant a twenty-dollar bill and was permitted to slip out the back door. He stepped into a waiting cab and sped away, like so many of the gangsters he had befriended, taking it on the lam. He was reported for weeks in various parts of the country and finally in Texas. Boston police, the Federal Bureau of Investigation and five insurance companies were looking for him. His life was insured for $126,000.

Governor Saltonstall appointed a young, honest school committeeman, Frederick R. Sullivan, to fill out the five years remaining of Dowd's term. When Dowd was finally brought to book, he was a helpless invalid, and the court was considerate enough to sentence him to another jail, in Norfolk County. Connolly also went off to jail. The two investigations and prosecutions were the least expensive the county ever had. They didn't cost the taxpayers a dime.

Twenty-Three · Pay or Go to Jail

THE TIDE was running heavily against Curley now. Tragedy reached into his home again. His son Paul died. His luck appeared to have run out. Some of his best friends and closest associates were in jail. He had lost temporarily his skill in mass mind reading. He timed his moves badly. His political strategy was ineffective. Still the champion orator, his persuasion was not as lasting among listeners. They crowded halls because he always put on a good show; and they listened on the radio, but they would not vote for him.

His public reputation was primarily responsible for this slump in public opinion, but of almost equal importance was the cold-blooded conviction of the Boston Irish that they could profit more by electing somebody else. Curley's break with Roosevelt was now well known. Federal aid and patronage had been shut off. David I. Walsh was not particularly popular at the White House and could get them little. New Dealers who did not even hold public office were dispensing patronage. There was an impression throughout the city that Boston and Massachusetts were being penalized because of Curley. Voters measured him by a selfish yardstick, and although they were grateful to him for what he had done for

275

them in the past, they wanted no part of him for the balance of Roosevelt's administration.

Curley was broke and out of a job, living on borrowed money. This time he had invested most of what he had in a quicksilver mine in Nevada. He was sure it was going to make him rich. He had learned nothing by his earlier experiences. An expert in city government with a thorough understanding of it in all of its ramifications, he could understand businessmen and bankers in their relationships and dealings with the city and state. He could sense their motives and foresee their profits on any deal. He could jockey one against the other, get what he wanted and leave them with the uncomfortable impression that they were as amateurish as children. Yet out of office and on his own in business he was as rank and unskilled as a high-school freshman, lost and helpless. Nobody could fool him in the building of magnificent holes in the ground, such as Sumner vehicular tunnel or the Kenmore subway extension, yet out of office he still bought them with childish, trusting confidence.

He was not as well dressed; his jaw and face were taut. Walking through Boston's streets, he was saluted and greeted as cordially as ever by almost everyone he passed. But he was not followed by the usual mob that crowded about him when he was in office. He could have used one of the scores of overcoats he gave away so impulsively when he was riding high. The one he wore was threadbare and its velvet collar was mottled with gray as he lunched occasionally in Thompson's Spa, a popular stool and counter restaurant on Newspaper Row.

He was plagued, at the same time, by the General Equipment investigation. The mill of justice had been grinding slowly for four years and he was still on a conveyor belt inching toward it. When he was a candidate for governor against Leverett Saltonstall, a court had already ruled that he owed the city of Boston $37,500 and must pay it, but Curley appealed the ruling and now the case was moving through the upper court, and by this time the case was so confused that strictly on the evidence, if the defendant had been a man of good reputation outside politics, it is doubtful that a court could have found against him.

Chief witness against Curley was Frederick H. Graves, an admitter perjurer, later indicted, tried and found guilty of it. He told three separate stories of the transaction, one to the Finance Commission and two in court. He changed his testimony so often during the trial that nobody knew whose side he was on. The facts, as presented in superior and supreme courts, were these:

Ernest W. Brown, Inc., a New York insurance firm, sued the city of Boston in two proceedings, one an action in tort, the other a petition for an assessment of damage to the General Equipment Corporation building. Graves was an insurance adjuster employed by the company. The company hired Joseph Santosuosso as its counsel to effect a settlement with the city. A meeting was arranged in the mayor's office. Curley, his corporation counsel, transit commissioner, auditor and head of the city water department were present.

Santosuosso reminded them that a jury had estimated the damage to the building at $119,000, although the verdict had been set aside. He said the damage might run higher, even to $140,000. They talked it over. Corporation Counsel Samuel Silverman, according to Santosuosso, offered $50,000. Santosuosso refused.

Negotiations spread over a period of weeks and a number of conferences. Santosuosso finally asked $90,000. Silverman offered $80,000. They compromised on $85,000. Santosuosso told Graves that he would take $25,000 counsel fees out of this for himself and $10,000 for his office partner, George L. Cohen. Cohen later testified that this was scaled down to $6,000 for himself and $10,500 for Santosuosso.

The settlement attracted no public attention. It might have

been filed and forgotten had not the Finance Commission and Mayor Mansfield become interested in the matter. Curley had brought suit against the Boston *Herald* for $500,000, charging libel because the newspaper had published an earlier Finance Commission report which he felt reflected maliciously upon his honesty. Whether the *Herald* was responsible for the interest of the Finance Commission and Mayor Mansfield in this settlement is not clear. Curley claimed the newspaper's attorneys had located Graves, traveling about the country, and brought him to Boston, where he told a different story of the settlement to the Finance Commission.

Mayor Mansfield had brought a bill in equity to compel Curley and Santosuosso to return to the city $50,000, alleging that the case had been settled with the Brown insurance company for $20,000. This time Graves said that he met Curley late in 1933 in the Mayflower Hotel in Washington and talked with him for less than a minute as he stepped off an elevator. Graves said he fell in step with Curley through the lobby for about fifty feet and asked: "Can't we settle this General Equipment case?"

He said Curley's reply was: "How much is there in it for me?"

"I replied," Graves testified, "$40,000, and he said: 'Go back and see Santosuosso and tell him to go ahead and settle.' "

Two police officers of the Boston Bureau of Criminal Investigation testified that while they had Graves in custody he told them he had been offered $15,000 to "frame" Curley and that he had told the truth to the Finance Commission the first time when he had confirmed and verified the story of the settlement as told by Curley and Santosuosso.

After wrestling with the matter for some time, Judge Frederick Fosdick decided that Curley did get $30,000 and Santosuosso $20,000 and ordered them to return the money to the city. Both appealed. With added interest and costs, Curley's bill to the city came to $42,629.

Curley did not have $42,629. It is doubtful that he had $42. The court looked high and low for caches of money in banks and safety-deposit boxes that Curley was supposed to have. Detectives scurried to Montreal and Toronto looking for $1,000,000 or more that his daughter Mary was believed to have in her name, and they returned empty handed. The banks would have been the first to turn the money up if they had it in their possession. They had no love for Curley. There was nothing to seize or attach. The city law department was chagrined; and a myth or legend that had been ballooned about Curley for years—that "he had made a millionaire of himself in city and state government"—was punctured. He had plenty of doubtful promise, but no liquid assets. Even the agents of the Internal Revenue Department, who sat patiently in the courtroom during the trial anticipating a haul, turned their backs in disappointment. The search was exhaustive. There was nothing to be found.

He needed a job badly and he was fitted by training and experience only to run a government. While the case was still pending in the supreme court, he became a candidate for mayor against Maurice J. Tobin. The city charter, amended to prevent Curley from succeeding himself, had been amended again to permit Tobin to succeed himself, a device expressly directed against Curley to be turned on and off by the legislature and a rare commentary on its ingenuity. Tobin beat him again in a campaign of youth versus age. Tobin was forty, Curley sixty-seven. It was his fourth defeat in a row. It appeared that the reign, the power and the glory of Curley had now ended; and to overflow his cup of bitterness, the supreme court now ruled that Curley must pay the judgment of $42,629. He was brought into West Roxbury District Court (the jurisdiction of his domicile) and ordered to do so at the rate of $500 a week.

The quality of justice in Boston is of rare design, its consistency plastic; and it can be stretched to fit almost any figure or contour of misfeasance, malfeasance, criminal or civil offense. The position in society or politics of the offender often determines the seriousness of the offense and the severity of punishment. A codefendant with Curley in the General Equipment suit was the defeated candidate for secretary of state, Dr. Joseph Santosuosso, who was ordered in the same ruling to pay back $28,419.82 to the city of Boston. Brought before another judge in an adjacent Boston jurisdiction, equally responsible with Curley in what the court had characterized as a fraud, Santosuosso was ordered by the central municipal court judge to pay the money back at the rate of two dollars a week. This was not done at the discretion of the judge. Because of Santosuosso's legal situation of the moment, the judge could follow no other course. Curley was allowed 86 weeks to settle with the city at $500 a week. Santosuosso was allowed 250 years at $2 a week. There was no public clamor about the disparity.

Had Curley and Santosuosso been tried before a jury, there is little doubt that the result would have been different. There is no right to a trial by jury in Massachusetts in a case of this kind. In an equity action, Massachusetts follows the English common law established under the reign of Queen Anne. Curley asked for a trial by jury on the facts. Under English common law, his petition was not granted and he was tried by a judge.

Curley had to pay or go to jail. The newspapers headlined his predicament; and almost everybody in Boston knew now that Curley was broke—he could not pay.

Now that the chips were down, an impressive segment of Boston decided that it did not want Curley to go to jail, and within twenty-four hours, newspapermen assigned to keep track of Curley witnessed a puzzling and strange phenomenon. On the morning after his court appearance, two lines began to form outside his house on Jamaicaway, each one small and unimportant at first, alternately growing and shrinking in size as the morning wore on. Trucks, limousines, pushcarts, delivery wagons, automobiles of all sizes, shapes, makes and models were pulling up to the door, a leaderless, unorganized army of the grateful coming to his rescue. When they were questioned by reporters, they had little to say, except for occasional variations of the response: "Well, I read in the papers that the guy's behind the eightball. He's been pretty good to me. I figured he could use some dough, so I thought I'd drop by and kind of help him out."

The demonstration was spontaneous. It could not have been otherwise. There had not been time to organize it. There was no person to organize it. No one was aware of it until it was discovered. Curley and the members of his family were as astonished as the newspapermen outside his house. It got no help either from newspapers or radio commentators, who reported merely that a number of Curley's friends had called at his house. Lines outside Curley's house were not uncommon. There had been a number of them when he had been mayor, and there had been a succession of strange and fantastic ones there when he had been governor. Those lines had been spontaneous and unorganized, too, lines of persons who had come to get something from him; but this line, a random harvest for psychologists, came to give him something.

In this line, day after day and in substantial numbers for a week or more, were the Boston Irish, the Boston Italians, Jews, Chinese, Poles, Lithuanians, a complete cross section of the city, filing into the breakfast room or library, store-keepers, merchants, contractors, city employees, filling-station owners and attendants, laundry-truck drivers, messengers, office boys, firemen, policemen, waiters, a large number of doctors and registered nurses, elevator operators, almost every trade and profession, coming into his breakfast room or library to hand over bills, change, checks, and even nickels, dimes and quarters in rolls.

He did not ask for the contributions and no one asked for it in his behalf. In the beginning it had been the quick reaction of perhaps a couple of hundred persons who read in the newspapers or heard on the air that Curley would have to pay five hundred dollars a week or go to jail. During his forty years in public life he had done favors for a great number. He was in trouble now and they were repaying him. Within a month about fifteen hundred people called at his house. There is no record of the mail count during that period. He received enough money to meet the five hundred dollars a week payments without trouble for the next six months, and on the basis of this response it was estimated that Curley's loyal political cadre in Boston, a nucleus of votes that he could command, depend upon and deliver to any candidate, must be in the neighborhood of thirty-five thousand.

They had purchased freedom for him and he made use of it immediately. Since he could not be United States Senator, governor or mayor, he took the next step down the ladder and decided to go back to Congress, a not too difficult achievement for him. In Massachusetts it is not a requirement that a congressman be a resident of the district he represents. Thomas Hopkinson Eliot—son of the Reverend Samuel Eliot of Boston's Arlington Street Church and grandson of Five-foot Shelf President Charles W. Eliot of Harvard—represented rough, tough Charlestown and part of Cambridge (the 11th district). Eliot had been a reporter for the Boston *Globe*. A New Dealer, he was a favorite with both Franklin and Eleanor Roosevelt. He was much farther to the left than Irish Charlestown liked him to be and a pushover for Curley. Charlestown was one of Curley's citadels.

His election was so certain that Curley went to Washington to talk things over with John McCormack. In the lobby of the Mayflower Hotel, he met a man with a plan, another political goldbrick—not a gold mine, a silver mine or an oil well, but an expert service to business and industry. Both were crying for it. It was very simple. The United States was at peace but Europe imbroiled in war, and America was an arsenal of democracy. Washington was overcrowded with supersalesmen, carrying briefcases, ready to describe and sell raw materials and finished products to the government, but they got lost in the labyrinth of Washington bureaus, the multiplicity of purchasing agents, orders in duplicate, triplicate, quadruplicate, ad infinitum. There were contracts to be awarded to manufacturers, but the confusion was so great that the proper manufacturers' representatives could not get together with the proper Washington bureau heads. What the place needed was a central clearinghouse, a Washington representative for all manufacturers to channel the right persons to the right places and obviate in many cases the need for manufacturers to come to Washington.

The man with the plan was James G. Fuller. He had organized the "Engineers' Group, Inc," and he had persuaded Donald Wakefield Smith, a former member of the National Labor Relations Board, Marshall J. Fitzgerald of Chicago, David E. Desmond, a Boston stock broker, James B. Underwood of Louisville, Kentucky, and Bertram Hall of Dallas, Texas, to join him in the venture.

The project needed only the prestige of well-known names and a little financing, Fuller told Curley. The Engineers' Group, like any sales organization, would charge a commission for its services. "It will be a gold mine," Curley was assured.

Fuller was a fast and convincing talker, an answer to a bankrupt politician's prayer. Curley listened to him attentively. A miracle like this, he thought, might get him out of the woods and make enough money to wipe out the balance of his fine in Boston. There was only one hitch.

"I'm about forty-two thousand dollars short of being broke,"

Curley confessed. "At the moment, I could use a little quick money myself."

Fuller was disappointed. "You mean you haven't got anything? No stocks, no bonds—nothing you can convert into cash?"

"I've got some brewery stock," Curley said, "but I've never been able to convert it into cash. It's worth thirty-five thousand dollars on paper, but in my situation at the moment, I don't think I could get even thirty-five hundred on it as security for a loan."

"Have you tried?" Fuller asked.

"No," Curley told him.

"I'll tell you what I'll do," Fuller said. "Come along with the rest of us in the Engineers' Group setup, and I'll lend you thirty-five hundred on that stock."

"It's a deal," Curley snapped him up, and he sent to Boston for the stock.

Fuller was very happy about it. Curley, a former governor of Massachusetts and a former mayor of Boston, was the best name he had in the group, and it was not very difficult for Fuller to persuade Curley to become president of the organization. He accepted the nomination and his name appeared as such on the corporation stationery.

Fuller gave Curley his personal check for thirty-five hundred dollars. When Curley presented it at the bank, it was refused. "No funds."

Furious, Curley stalked Fuller with fire in his eyes, but Fuller's hair-trigger, rapid-fire tongue disarmed him. He had deposited it too soon. The funds would be available after organization was completed. It was all very simple and everything would work out all right. Curley returned to Boston to go through a routine formality of being elected to Congress. He surprised Boston by his careful, almost tender treatment of Tom Eliot, a political lamb foredoomed to slaughter. There was no contempt in his voice when, just before election, he

summoned a select Charlestown group to his headquarters
and asked them to see to it that Tom Eliot got enough votes
in Charlestown to spare his pride. It would be an insult to
a great Boston name, he told them, if Tom did not make
some kind of showing. Charlestown voters did not comply
very well. Eliot was swamped.

Investigation revealed that James G. Fuller was a confidence man with a long record who had spent a good part of
his life in jail. Curley had enough. Another chimerical project
faded. He had a lot of trouble getting his stock back and
severed his connection with Engineers' Group six months
after he joined it. He was still a private citizen waiting to
begin serving his term in Congress when Pearl Harbor was
attacked. He became a wartime congressman. Two of his
sons, Leo and George, served in the navy.

Out of sight, he was out of mind in Boston. The army of
anonymous volunteers who came to his rescue when they
were afraid he might go to jail lost interest or became en-
grossed, diverted and distracted by the war. For a while, after
he went to Congress, they got the money up every week, but
this relief had never been organized, and there was no way it
could be organized. Voluntary gratitude cannot be molded
that way. Donations fell away. His plight, compared to that
of his constituents whose sons and daughters were going to
war, could not be dramatized and it became more and more
difficult for his family to raise the five hundred dollars every
week. He could not pay that kind of fine on his salary as a
congressman. He became delinquent, fell in arrears and had
to remain in Washington, at times, where his office gave him
immunity from arrest. Twice, when his Boston cadre learned
that he could not come home because the fine had not been
paid, they raised the money for him. Nevertheless, he spent
a number of lonely weekends.

Twenty-Four · A Congressman Buys a Gold Brick

SIX YEARS and thirty-four court continuations after the city of Boston had obtained a judgment of $42,629 against him in the General Equipment case, Congressman James Michael Curley fulfilled his obligation with a final payment of $12,-461.96 on December 27, 1944. It turned out that he overpaid the city $96, and that was returned to him. He was in the clear; but not for long. The Truman committee, investigating war contracts, got a tip from a well-known white-haired character who made the Mayflower Hotel bar a headquarters for cadging drinks that the files of the Engineers' Group, Inc., would interest them, that James G. Fuller, its promoter, was a notorious confidence man who had spent a good part of his life in jail. The files were seized and an investigation was begun.

The case was of no great or immediate importance. As an organized swindle it had not been very successful. The war contracts involved were chiefly for stoves and building materials. A war contract in time of war apparently can be stretched to include everything, but the country was not at war during the period in question. Engineers' Group, according to the evidence, had no success in channeling any contracts or scarce materials to anybody. It subtracted nothing from the stockpile of the nation's raw materials. Fuller, operating behind the front of well-known names on a letterhead, might have subtracted money from the corporations and business organizations that became his clients. If they were scotched financially they deserved it. They should have been ashamed of themselves. Their purposes in paying him money were selfish and unpatriotic, and to that degree they were just as crooked as Fuller—but they were not prosecuted.

Curley, serving in Congress while awaiting another city election, had announced that he would be a candidate for mayor of Boston, and the Engineers' Group file before the Truman committee did not become important until the thirty-five-hundred-dollar rubber check, which Curley had returned when he got his brewery stock back, was found in it. Then it became of far greater importance outside the Truman committee than within it. The committee's investigation had been fruitless but for that. Had the check been made out to an unknown, it is doubtful that anything would have been done about it. The Truman committee, after examining the file and the evidence, did not even bother to call Curley. The check became an interesting bit of gossip that got into newspaper columns. Before the Truman committee even got around to Fuller he was already in jail for passing bad checks.

From that point the procedure became so unorthodox that the record, in places, is mystifying. Curley had been persona non grata at the White House for years. Every city boss who had helped to elect Roosevelt was having a hard time of it. The Indian sign had been placed on Tom Pendergast in Kansas City and he went to jail. Ed Kelly and Frank Hague were now either in the administration doghouse or on their way there. When Curley heard that the Department of Justice

had seized the Engineers' Group file he became apprehensive
that his own number was up. "What's all the shooting
about?" he asked Harry Truman. Curley's association with
Engineers' Group had been short-lived and of such a flimsy
nature that he had not even been called before the committee.

Truman answered that his committee had been unable to
find anything against him. Nevertheless, rumor began to build
up that an indictment of Curley was contemplated, and some
of it was soon substantiated. The attorney general's office
asked the Truman committee for its file on Engineers' Group.
Attorney General Anthony Drexel Biddle was in Mexico City
when he heard about the Curley check. Curley's friends told
him that Biddle had telephoned Assistant Attorney General
Tom Clark instructing him to bring the evidence before a
grand jury and to insist upon an indictment. Curley said he
was told that orders for indictment and prosecution had come
from the White House.

He began to worry. He called on Majority Leader John
McCormack and asked him to go to the White House and
find out from Roosevelt what was going on. McCormack's
district was South Boston, where Curley's vote was heavy.
McCormack went to the White House and talked with
Roosevelt, who gave him one of his most charming smiles and
told him to "forget it," that Tom Clark would not ask for
an indictment. McCormack reported the conversation to
Curley. Curley was relieved for five or six hours until he
learned on the radio that he had been indicted.

Where criminal charges are involved, ordinary legal procedure is to assign the case to the district attorney of the
District of Columbia, but since Curley was a congressman
the case was given special treatment. Two special assistants
from the attorney general's office had been assigned to the
case. The evidence was brought before a grand jury and there
were signs of haste and pressure to persuade the grand jury

to indict. It was marked up for quick trial and the machinery of justice moved so fast that it jammed. A defense could not be prepared on such short notice, and objections to a delay were so adamant and persistent that even the court noted it in the record.

Even after his indictment, David I. Walsh, who had no love for Curley, scoffed at it when he came to Boston. Ordinarily he would have been quick to condemn Curley. Instead, he told his intimates that there was nothing to the case. He was sure that it would blow up, that the indictment would boomerang and elect him mayor. An intense and purposeful determination to "put Curley in jail" soon became so apparent that an impression grew in Boston of something sour and smelly about it.

His indictment meant little to the people of Boston. In or out of office he was always in trouble. He had tangled with courts before and had won and lost. That affected his reputation throughout the country, but it did not bother the voters who elected him. Whether the indictment would result in a trial was then doubtful, and the people of the city did not contemplate what would happen if he did not come to trial and was found guilty. He took out papers on a day late in May, and that night stepped before a microphone in a studio of WMEX, a small independent station, to broadcast that Boston would be a ghost town after the war if he were not elected and business and politics were not divorced.

It became a typical Curley campaign, except for one omission. He could not and would not discuss his indictment. The case might, after all, come before a court and whatever he might say would place him in contempt. The city was in an unprecedented political dilemma at that time. Seven months earlier Maurice J. Tobin had been elected governor and had vacated the office to go from City Hall to the State House. He had been succeeded in the interim by John Kerrigan, president of the city council who became a candidate for mayor to succeed himself. Kerrigan had been elected mayor by the members of the council, and not by the people.

There was a scramble for the office, and to join Curley and Kerrigan came a fire commissioner who had been in the music-publishing business; an Italian-descendant governor's councilor who felt sure of the Italian vote; the son of one of the city's noted philanthropists, whose interests seemed to be chiefly in sailboats in a sleepy lagoon on the Charles and in off-center ideas of civic reform that people could not understand and he could not make clear; and an unknown with an Irish name under a lightning rod hoping it would strike.

President Roosevelt died. Atomic bombs were dropped on Hiroshima and Nagasaki and the war in the Pacific ended before election day, and as the city sat back to readjust itself and take stock, Curley's prediction that it might become a ghost town began to make sense. The huge Fore River shipyard closed. War contracts were canceled. Textile, shoe and leather, clothing, machinery and precision-instrument workers were being laid off by thousands. More thousands were released by the navy yard. Thousands who had come to the city from other parts of New England and outside of it began trekking home again. All but four of the city's twenty-six night clubs folded quietly. Excess activity slowed down and stopped. Wartime excitement died away.

The people of the city knew what Curley could do. They could only guess at the ability of the others. Once again he became the old campaigner dramatizing the city and its troubles. The war had left it in a sorry state. Its streets were in bad shape, its parks, roads and beaches neglected. Material and labor had been scarce and repairs had been impossible. Prices were climbing. Food was short, and in spite of the horde of war workers who deserted the city, housing had never been more critical. Whatever Curley's reputation, part of it was that he was a builder, employer, spender. He had the answers, the others did not and the voters listened. When the votes were counted on the morning of November 7, 1945, Curley had defeated his nearest rival Kerrigan almost two to one with an impressive total of 111,799 votes. In a field of six, he polled 45 per cent of the total vote.

They voted him back into office for a fourth term as mayor in spite of the fact that as the campaign progressed and election day came closer it had been made perfectly clear from Washington that Curley would go on trial charged with using the mails to defraud and with conspiracy to use the mails to defraud.

The louder and more threatening the news from Washington became, the stronger his support became. Less than two weeks after election, his trial opened in Washington.

The reaction of Boston was understandable to people of Massachusetts but bewildering to those outside the state. As the testimony unfolded, Curley voters became indignant. It was one thing for those who knew him to kick him around and punish him, which they did quite frequently whenever he got too smart, strayed from the reservation or did something that offended them. It was quite another to realize that the rest of the nation outside of Boston had fashioned him into a spurious Frankenstein, a fascist leader who controlled a city and the people in it. If Boston wanted to get rid of Curley it would do so very handily. It didn't care to have anybody in Washington do it for them.

Nor were the people of Boston particularly stupid. Until Roosevelt died, Curley honestly believed that the case would never come to trial, but Harry Truman was now president and Tom Clark had become attorney general. A very odorous situation had developed in Kansas City—vote frauds, indictments, subversion of jurymen and stolen ballot boxes that had been impounded. In comparison to Kansas City in Truman's home state, Boston was a place of pristine purity. Tom Pendergast died, and Truman went to Kansas City in the

Sacred Cow to attend his funeral. Newspapers and newspapermen were needling Clark and the president. Curley
provided an excellent diversion—a good way to change the
subject.

Although newspaper reports were complete and accurate,
Boston newspaper readers found it impossible to discover
what it was that Curley had done. It was made clear first that
Curley never had received any money from the Engineers'
Group. He did get a rubber check for thirty-five hundred dollars. He was charged with using the mails to defraud, and yet,
according to the evidence, he had never posted a letter or
signed his name to one, or to any other document or piece of
paper that went through the mails. The prosecutor admitted
it. The only thing he did was to give his verbal consent to
the use of his name on stationery, as did the head of a well-
known encyclopedia, a former member of the National Labor
Relations Board and a group of prominent and well-known
businessmen. Some of these were not even indicted.

All of this happened before Pearl Harbor. Curley and three
others were brought to trial three years later, when the nation
was at war, and the transactions in which Engineers' Group
was engaged in time of peace were labeled "War Contracts."

Engineers' Group was ahead of its time. Identical organizations appeared almost overnight in Washington after Pearl
Harbor. They were reprehensible. They thrived on actual war
contracts. Some of the best-known people in Washington
were identified with them. Members of Congress co-operated
with them, but these were never investigated, nor has anyone
ever been indicted.

Throughout all the pages of testimony there is no evidence
anywhere that Curley ever received any money from Engineers' Group. Auditors for the Federal Bureau of Investigation
testified that they had examined the books and could find no
such evidence. If Curley had never signed or mailed a letter

for Engineers' Group, or received any money or made any profit on it, why was he on trial? The people of Boston wanted to know and could not find out. It was not revealed in the testimony. Curley's lips were sealed and under penalty of contempt he could not tell them.

Engineers' Group was damned by the character of its principal promoter, James G. Fuller. A speculator all his life in the kind of business gold mines that had landed him in jail often, he had finally conceived a legitimate child and was too crooked to realize and appreciate it. It is no reflection upon the intelligence or business judgment of the encyclopedia publisher that he was duped by Fuller. His proposal made good sense and there was nothing illegal about it as Fuller outlined it. There was no reason, then, why they should question the honesty and integrity of Fuller; nor was there any reason for Curley to do so, either.

There was one Negro on the jury. In Washington, D. C., where the Negro was emancipated, the pigment of a man's skin still colors jurisprudence. It is not legal practice there to lock up juries made up of Negroes and whites. This was a criminal, not a civil case. Most states require that a jury be locked up from the time it gets a criminal case until a verdict is reached. The practice is generally followed above the Mason-Dixon line.

Conspiracy was charged against James Michael Curley, Donald Wakefield Smith, James B. Underwood of Louisville, and Bertram Hall of Texas. The rights of a defendant charged with criminal conspiracy are so easily abridged that it is common practice in Massachusetts to lock up a jury from the beginning of a trial until a verdict is reached.

In this case, the jurors listened to the evidence and were permitted to go home at night, to visit their clubs, bars, taps, taverns or lounges, to attend lodge meetings or to mingle with others anywhere. At the outset of the trial Justice James M.

Proctor gave them the customary abjuration not to read about
the case, nor to listen to it discussed, and not to talk about it
to others.

The law is still naive and blind in that respect. The pre-
tense that such instruction will be observed still persists,
although it is doubtful that there ever was a juror who did
not discuss a case with his wife, his family, his intimates, in
some cases talking it over strictly in confidence with anywhere from three to thirty persons. The courts still pretend
to believe that a juror so instructed will dutifully abstain from
reading what is written about a case they are hearing and
upon which they must ultimately deliberate. No judge has
yet devised a prescription or enunciated one in court telling
jurors how to plug up their ears, to shut out radio or how to
cast their eyes down modestly, humbly and reverently to avoid
looking at an episode in a newsreel or on television affecting
a case they must decide.

Once during the trial it was necessary to caution the jurors
not to look at copies of *Life* and *Time* magazines. Each juror
was polled and the court inquired whether the jurors had
looked at pictures in these magazines, and the jurors declared that they had not. Any juror who admitted that he
had looked at the magazines (both contained pictures and
text highly unflattering to Curley) would be confessing his
own serious offense. The juror might be jailed, in contempt
of court, and a mistrial would result; and anyone not troubled
with Charley horse between the ears must realize that the
same jurors who accidentally had not seen the newspaper or
magazine would get it forthwith and have a look.

Congressmen are not popular among the citizens of the
District of Columbia and are likely to get very little sympathy
from them. Curley's political reputation in Boston had been
thoroughly and nationally publicized. The jury heard evidence
that established conclusively that James G. Fuller was a thief

and a swindler. He was brought into the courtroom each day handcuffed to a guard—and they knew about Curley, whether they could read or merely looked at the pictures. When they heard about the meeting between Curley and Fuller in the lobby of the Mayflower Hotel, it would not be unnatural for them to reconstruct the colloquy something like this:

"I'm James G. Fuller, and I'm the best crook you ever met; served time in some of the best jails in the country, and of course I know what a big crook you are. How about you and me getting together to rob a lot of businessmen who want to rob the government?"

"Sure, Fuller. Glad to meet you. Get on your horse and get some stationery printed right away."

One of the most pathetic figures in the trial was Donald Wakefield Smith, a lawyer of good reputation who had served with some distinction on the National Labor Relations Board. He was almost stone deaf and sensitive about it. It is doubtful that Smith ever knew what Fuller was up to, or what was going on, but he had to take the rap and go the distance because of Fuller's genuine and Curley's popular reputations.

The government's case against Fuller made sense. It was clear from the testimony and the record that he was guilty. The case against Curley and Donald Wakefield Smith seemed to make little sense. They were tied to Fuller in a prosecution package. It was established that Fuller collected all money paid by clients to Engineers' Group. It was established that Curley and Smith did not receive any money from clients or from Fuller. The evidence against Curley was that he had been president of the group for six months preceding the war, that he had referred three contractors to Fuller, telling them merely that Fuller was the man to see in connection with the procurement of construction work, that he personally discussed with a bank official on the telephone a matter of a loan to the group, which was to be left on deposit.

The banker testified that the loan was not an unusual one nor contrary to good banking principles, that he had six or seven similar applications for loans of that type from other concerns, that he had refused to make the loan and the matter was dropped. Curley made no further attempt to secure a loan to the group from any other bank. The only other evidence against him was that he was seen in the offices of the group. During the six months that he was president, he was carrying on a campaign for mayor of Boston against Maurice J. Tobin and could devote but a minimum of time to the business of Engineers' Group. He made but two short visits to Washington.

The Curley case went to the jury shortly before noon on January 17, 1946, and the assumption of the people of Boston was that the jury, although not locked up during the trial, would be locked up until it reached a verdict or confessed deadlock in their inability to agree. At ten o'clock that night, after nine and a half hours of deliberation, Justice Proctor sent for the jurors, made certain that they had not been able to agree, and discharged them for the night to go home and sleep on it, an unheard-of procedure in any criminal case in Massachusetts.

He had warned them during the trial not to read the Washington newspapers. He repeated the warning and told them: "I feel confident that I can impose the necessary trust in you to go to your homes tonight. Do not talk to anyone, for that might interfere with your continued deliberations. Be on your guard. If any untoward situation arises, report it to the court."

Every American home, of course, has an acoustically soundproof room, where menfolk doing jury duty can retire in cloistered silence; and a juror whose wife, listening to the radio and reading editorial comment about it in the newspapers, observed, for example, "If you don't find that bandit from Boston guilty, you ought to have your head examined," would instinctively turn her in to the court next morning so that she could be locked up for contempt.

Next day they deliberated for twelve and a half more hours, a total of twenty-two hours in all, and finally came into court. The foreman was asked if the jury had reached a verdict. He said they had and recited the counts upon which Curley, Fuller and Smith had been found guilty. The jurors were polled for their individual understandings of the verdict, and when this was concluded an unusual thing happened. Three of the jurors got up and said they had made mistakes. They couldn't even recall the correct counts.

Justice Proctor, after giving Curley a sentence of from six to eighteen months in prison and a fine of one thousand dollars, had this to say:

"Frankly, I want an appeal in this case. I have told counsel, though I acted to the best of my judgment and ability, I appreciate the fact that there are some rulings as to which other men may differ, and in view of that I much prefer that other jurists as competent or more so than myself take this record and pass upon it before the defendants actually suffer any punishment I have imposed."

Convicted of using the mails to defraud, Curley returned from the courtroom in Washington to a hero's tumultuous welcome in Boston. More than a thousand persons who waited more than an hour in bitter January cold milled around him in Back Bay Station. Above the din of cowbells and horns, cheers and shouts of encouragement, he told them: "They've had me dead before, but I've always come back." From the moment he stepped off the train he had to force his way through people who wanted to touch him, to speak to him, encourage him and assure him: "You'll come through all right, Jim."

His wife, his daughter and his son George, recently discharged as a navy lieutenant, were there. He had to be pushed and pulled through to them by a detail of police. He managed to get up the stairs to the main level where another crowd waited. There were more than five thousand persons gathered around the station on upper and lower levels and in waiting rooms. They were not herded there. It was not an organized demonstration. There had not been time for that. They read in the afternoon newspapers or heard on the radio that he was coming home. The din increased; the demonstration mounted. It took a half hour for him to get to his limousine and another half hour to get the limousine away from the station, and there was another crowd outside his Jamaicaway home when he arrived there. To the world outside Boston that seemed to be a disgraceful spectacle, a curious way to greet a man who had just been found guilty of a federal offense.

Twenty-Five · Five Months in Danbury

CURLEY WAS seventy-one years old when he took office in January, 1946. He had been suffering from diabetes for four years and required a daily injection of insulin. His eyes were beginning to go bad. He had an operation on one and was under the regular care of a doctor. He turned up, nevertheless, every day in City Hall and put in a full day's work, but on a day to day basis because the Court of Appeals might decide his case at any time. He worried about it and that impaired his health all the more.

Curley's attorneys appealed to the United States Circuit Court of Appeals for the District of Columbia. There are other circuits, but this particular one had once ruled in a similar case that "where all the substantial evidence is as consistent with innocence as with guilt, it is the duty of the Appellate Court to reverse the judgment against the defendant."

He had been in office a year when the three judges reached a decision. It was two to one against him. Justices Edgerton and Prettyman said in their decision: "We agree, as Curley contends, that upon the evidence reasonable minds might have had reasonable doubt. As much might be said in many, if not most, criminal cases. The jury, within the realm of reason, might have concluded that it was possible that Curley was merely a figurehead, that he had complete faith in Fuller, that he never asked any questions, that he was never informed as to the contents of the contracts with customers or the financial statements or the use of the money; in short, that it was possible that he was as much put upon as the customers. If the jury had concluded that such was a reasonable possibility, it might have had a reasonable doubt as to guilt. . . . If we ourselves doubted Curley's guilt, that doubt would be legally immaterial, in view of the evidence and the rule of law applicable. However, we think it proper to add, under the circumstances of the case, that to us, as to the jury, there is no doubt."

Justice Wilbur K. Miller wrote this dissenting opinion:

"It is my view that the jury should have been instructed to find the appellant, James M. Curley, not guilty. The wrongs were done by Fuller. Curley made no representations to anybody. He did not participate in negotiations with customers. He signed no letters, executed no contracts. He did not know of the 'brochure' [an advertising prospectus] or the 'financial statement.' He received no money or any other thing of value. All of this is admitted, even recited, in the court's opinion."

Curley's lawyers took the last step. They brought a writ of certiorari (a petition for review) before the United States Supreme Court. The justices discussed the petition and ruled that no matter what had happened to Curley in the courts beneath them, his case did not deserve review or consideration by them. Justice Felix Frankfurter refrained from voting. He did not explain why. Justice Murphy sent down a dissenting rescript, which meant that he disagreed with his associates on the bench and felt that the Curley case should have been reviewed. He was alone, outvoted seven to one.

The case was over. The only thing left was to execute sentence. It was June now. It had taken the Supreme Court six months to reach the case and thus dispose of it.

Curley's blood pressure had been alternately going up and down for weeks. He had been in bed and out. His family had been worried and had called in Doctor Edward H. Schott, director of near-by small-town Cohasset Hospital, not far from the Curley summer home. Dr. Schott had no interest in politics and less interest in Curley. He looked upon him impersonally as a man of seventy-two years suffering from the ailments that are likely to occur in a patient with such a history at that age. The doctor was indifferent to the law, to newspapermen and to the curious who asked questions. Curley was in bad shape. He said so. Blood pressure had increased alarmingly after the decision. There was a possibility of cerebral hemorrhage. The doctor ordered complete rest and quiet, a difficult condition to fulfill under the circumstances.

Curley's illness brought a curiously mixed reaction in Boston. His critics refused to believe that his condition was that serious and hinted that it was another trick to evade the law. It was too late now for tricks of any kind, except a medical one, and Dr. Schott went as far as he could to work that.

When Curley grew worse and the doctor thought there was some danger, his family assembled at his bedside—his wife, his daughter Mary, his sons Leo, George and Francis, whose name had appeared but rarely in Boston newspapers since a day years earlier when he had left his home to study for the priesthood. As a Jesuit scholastic at Weston College, Francis is far removed from the excitement of politics.

A priest was summoned and Curley was given the last rites of the Catholic Church. That was his privilege and he had availed himself of it because he could not be sure. The doc-

tor, Mrs. Curley and the members of his family had been
selling him death. He knew that he was not going to die.
He did not feel like dying. He had a number of scores to even
before that happened, so he settled on the last rites to appease
them. He knew what political capital his enemies would make
of that. They'd say he was a faker, making a play for public
sympathy, trying to influence the judge to go easy on him.
Perhaps it might have that effect. He was too weary and too
indifferent to quarrel about it and he knew that excitement
might push his pressure up higher, closer to the danger mark.
Let them have their way for now. He had had these attacks
before and got better. He'd get better again and he did.

When the danger subsided, Mary, Leo and George, familiar with all of Curley's ways, took over to continue the
fight until the doors of a penitentiary should close upon him.
They opened headquarters in the Parker House, assembled
the stock political workers by using the telephone, and within
twenty-four hours the Parker House suite was crowded with
lawyers, judges, members of both branches of the state legislature and yeoman workers. Out of it grew a petition to Judge
Proctor designed to persuade him to be lenient. The petitions
were rushed to a printer and next day workers appeared everywhere in Boston, on street corners, in the shopping district,
hotel and theater lobbies, and going from house to house in
the suburbs. In less than a week they had gathered 172,000
signatures. This petition had no effect. Judge Proctor would
not even look at it. There were also uncounted letters to the
judge. Whatever Curley did, the signatures showed that at
least one quarter of Boston's population did not want him
to go to jail for it, and if the workers had had more time, the
number would have been much larger.

When Doctor Schott decided that Curley was up to it, he
went to Washington by train to appear before Judge Proctor
on June 26, 1947. The proceedings were brief. Curley wanted

to make a statement, but the court would not hear him. He was ordered to serve the six to eighteen months already imposed. Curley was not so sure that he could survive six months in jail. "You're sending me to my death," he told Proctor, but the Judge appeared not to have heard. He looked at Curley coldly and indifferently, and turned away.

A guard took him by the elbow and led him from the courtroom. They went down one floor below to a room where Gertrude, Mary, Francis, Leo and George were waiting to say goodbye. He smiled and they tried to smile. He assured them that he would not be in prison long. Truman would pardon him. John McCormack would circulate petitions among congressmen and senators. Truman couldn't refuse. After all, hadn't he given him a clean bill of health as head of the Truman committee? There was a wide area of legal doubt. The Appellate Court had not been in agreement. He repeated things that they all knew, and again they were convinced. They assured him that it would be all over soon. Gael Sullivan and Bob Hannegan had been very encouraging.

He turned away with the guard and knew that they cried after he left. He knew that they would follow him to the gates of the Federal Penitentiary in Danbury, Connecticut, even though he told them not to. He knew and he knew they knew that the assurances and reassurances that he would be pardoned quickly made a chorus of whistling in the dark. It would not be quite that easy.

As the limousine turned into the drive to deliver him to the warden, reporters and photographers were gathered on the lawn to record what they thought might be his last appearance. He looked them over, saw familiar faces and could picture the big black headlines on Boston front pages: "Curley Goes to Jail."

He could imagine the chop-licking satisfaction of the editors of the Boston *Herald* that at long last they could print that headline. The woes of Boston were ended. Curley was finally finished. How often had they printed it? And how often had they prophesied it during the past two score years and seven?

As he walked into the warden's office, his shoulders were drooped forward, but he was too tired and too sick to be conscious of poise and posture; his eyes were badly bloodshot again and he could not see very well. He hoped they'd get the routine preliminaries over quickly. He wanted to lie down. He needed a shot of insulin and further medical attention.

The warden was cold and distant and that in itself was a shock. The interview was brief, to the point and painfully revealing to Curley. It was made clear to him that he was just another prisoner and would be treated as such. He sensed that the warden looked upon him as an undesirable and would have been far happier if he had been sent to another penitentiary. He was not the kind of prisoner any warden wanted to have around. There had already been too much publicity about his coming there. If he favored Curley and relaxed rules even slightly, Curley's critics in Washington would hear of it. If he did not, there was the possibility that Curley's friends would remember it. The warden was a practical man and Curley was an unpredictable person. He might be an inmate today and a political power of considerable importance a year from today. To the warden, Curley was a problem and not an opportunity. He would have to solve the problem, and either did not know how or did not care to take advantage of whatever opportunity his presence might offer. Curley had said publicly that he would run the city from jail. The warden told him he would not be allowed to conduct official business. He would not be permitted any more visitors or privileges than other prisoners.

He found out what that meant a few minutes later. He was escorted to a bare room except for bench and table. Two guards stripped him of his clothing and he stood before them in his nakedness as they sized him up. As governor of the state of Massachusetts, he had appointed a commissioner of correction and had seen to it that a warden and jail guards had been appointed. These men before him were like thousands who jammed the anteroom of the State House, looking for just such jobs. Now he was naked, helpless and powerless before them.

The doctor who came in to give him a cursory physical examination had in his hands the papers that had come along from the Cohasset Hospital with him, detailing his condition. The doctor looked him over quickly, asked a few questions and ordered him to bed. He would give him a more complete examination later. The guards gave him a khaki prison uniform. He put it on and was taken to the hospital wing where once again he undressed and got into bed. The doctor gave him a sedative and now, in the sunset of life, James Michael Curley stared at a ceiling in a prison, just as he had at the sunrise of his political career.

The cries in Boston for a new election that would pre-empt Curley while he was in jail were stilled from a strange source. The descendant of the first Governor Bradford, *Mayflower* name, a perfect symbol of the Brahmins whom Curley had attacked for half a century, put a stop to it. Governor Robert A. Bradford proved his courage and integrity when he cleaned up Middlesex County as its district attorney. That helped catapult him into the State House. The overwhelming majority of Republicans in the Massachusetts legislature had no love for Curley, but when Bradford cracked the whip, they not only put through the legislation that would protect and preserve Curley's job as mayor of Boston, but also would pay him his salary while he was in jail. Curley donated his salary to the prisoners on Boston's Deer Island.

Bradford went even further. The president of the Boston city council, who would normally be acting mayor while Curley was in jail, was already under indictment by a Boston grand jury, charged with graft—another reason for a special election—and the legislation provided that the Boston city clerk would be acting mayor. Bradford thought of everything. Lest City Clerk John Hynes get the idea of building a political machine to contest against Curley at any time in the future for mayor of Boston, Hynes was given a raise in pay and life tenure that ceased the moment he became a candidate for office. The Republican Brahmin had done as masterful a job for Democrat Curley as Curley could have done for himself had he been sitting in the governor's chair.

Politically Bradford had much to lose and little to gain by his act, but he had a good deal of affection for Curley and loved to hear him speak. As a prosecutor Bradford had made a sound and solid reputation for himself. He knew the law, and he, too, had followed the case. A Republican legislature opposed Curley politically and would work to defeat him, but they wanted no vengeance wreaked upon him.

Curley got no special treatment in Danbury Prison. He carried a tray in the mess hall, clearing dishes from the table where the prisoners ate. He met his fellow inmates in the jail yard, where he was usually the center of a knot of them. Like any audience they liked to listen to him and came to like him. They poured their troubles into his ears in the hope that when he got out he might do something to help them or the members of their families; and they were kind and good to him. His closest companion was a Harvard graduate in there for stealing from the mail, and all the ivy-league colleges were represented.

As often as they were permitted, his daughter, his wife and sons came to the jail to see him, but only one was admitted at a time, and they could talk to him only through screen and glass. His son George was stricken with phlebitis and confined to a hospital. Curley was permitted to come home under guard to see him and within twenty-four hours was returned to Danbury.

Both the prisoners in Danbury and the people of Boston had one common idea: that Curley never would serve either his full or minimum term, and they were right. From the day that he went in the pressure of Democratic leaders had been upon Truman to release him. Many of them had been asking for clemency, but Robert Hannegan had been insistent. Curley's condition did not improve much. The prison medical officer reported that he had an acute heart condition and diabetes. On the day before Thanksgiving, five months after he entered Danbury, President Truman commuted the sentence. Who was responsible for persuading him was in doubt. It may have been a gift to Robert Hannegan as he was leaving the Cabinet, although John McCormack quoted the president as saying: "I did it for you, John."

The members of his family met him at the jail. He was driven out the back door. He looked thin, wan and sickly. Next day he cut a Thanksgiving Day birthday cake, surrounded by his family in his home in Jamaicaway.

Two days later he was back at his desk in City Hall.

Two months later Jamaicaway was back to abnormal—a normal condition in the Curley house. People were coming and going. A quartette from Harvard, friends of George, were harmonizing at the piano in the music room. A company of politicians, lawyers and newspapermen were paying no attention to piano and voices. Lawyers and politicians were gnawing at their lips, deep in thought, rubbing their foreheads occasionally, memorizing their lines. Curley was closeted with one of them, talking privately in his library. At least seven among the lawyers and politicians were there to tell Curley how each one of them, separately, and single-handed, had managed to tip the scales in Washington by reaching the attorney general or the president by way of a private pipeline to get him out of Danbury before Thanksgiving, and each would petition him for a suitable reward for doing it.

Among the guests that night were a small handful whom

Curley could trust, a few intimate friends who had been close to him for almost half a century and those who disagreed with him almost entirely but could, nevertheless, get on common ground with him. The rest were on the silver standard, prepared to sell him for thirty pieces of it. He knew it and could understand them, and played political poker with them, calling a bluff with an inscrutable face when it suited his purpose. A few would be permitted to get away with it because he wanted it that way. Newspapermen there knew who got Curley out. They remembered his daughter Mary and his son Leo camping on doorsteps in Washington while he was in prison. They remembered a message that Mary managed to have delivered to Truman in person, asking him to see her, and a verbal reply from him that he would not see her because he knew how such a plea would affect him. He had a daughter of his own.

Eight months after Curley was back on the job, headlines in Boston newspapers were back to normal. Curley was extending the rapid transit subway under Boston harbor to Boston airport and beyond. In complete charge of the project was Malcolm E. Nichols, the Republican who had once relieved Curley for four years as interim mayor of Boston. The Finance Commission was investigating and was shrieking about outrageous payroll padding on the construction job. Democrat Curley was defending Republican Nichols, saying in effect to the Finance Commission: "Tut, tut! Gentlemen, stop this nonsense," and saying to the people of Boston through the newspapers: "Why doesn't the Finance Commission do something constructive and investigate itself? One of the Finance Commission's investigators is a law student, being paid for the time he spends in classrooms. He hasn't been around for months. Another can be found every day hanging around the bars and taverns near City Hall. What kind of a way is that for a Finance Commission to investigate a city job?"

Boston Brahmins and the Boston Irish want reform and progress, but they want them to come as beautiful and natural phenomena, like a breath-taking sunrise, the glory of spring or the splendor of autumn foliage. They want it to come without pain, without inconvenience, and the Brahmins want it to come only and positively without expense. Both groups unanimously and definitely do not want to bring it about. Upsetting the status quo is unthinkable, and as the status quo goes back some three hundred years, upending it now would be a Herculean job, anyhow. Kings Charles I and II and George III set the stage, and since that time, in spite of the fact that the Cabots talked to Him, God alone has not changed the scenery much, but James Michael Curley has.

King James I, plagued by Communal Separatists, the Puritans and a pressure group of merchants who had lent him considerable money, got them out of his hair by authorizing them to settle in the new world. The Puritans landed on Plymouth Rock and thought they were in Virginia, where they belonged. They organized a colony that ultimately embraced Boston and elected John Carver governor, but the job and the climate killed him in less than a year. He was succeeded by William Bradford, who begat a long line of Bradfords down to and including Robert, the Republican friend, champion and protector of James Michael Curley in 1946.

The Puritans had no sense of order, staked out land holdings apparently by tearing up the first crude maps, and the jagged edges of the pieces became boundaries. The pieces were of all sizes and shapes, and they became a pattern for the cities and towns of Eastern Massachusetts and Metropolitan Boston. There isn't a straight line between any two. Perhaps the map was torn on a windy day.

Three centuries later the arrangement of cities and towns was just as confusing, divided into Boston Proper and the Metropolitan District. There were few Proper Bostonians left in Boston Proper. The Bureau of Census listed it as ninth in population with 770,816, without explaining that this is Boston's nighttime population when an equal number or more have gone to their suburban bedrooms outside the city proper. The Metropolitan District has a population of 2,307,897.

The Metropolitan District's thirty-nine cities and towns each has its own separate government—a mayor or board of selectmen. Each is completely autonomous and independent of the City of Boston, an advantage that none ever would think of surrendering. Each depends upon Boston and if Boston went into bankruptcy, they would inevitably follow, but it is impossible to make that clear to the people who live in them. The Metropolitan District supplies their water. A Metropolitan Transit Authority provides their transportation. They work in Boston, use its cow-path streets in such numbers that sidewalks are not wide enough for them. Their automobiles jam the city and choke it with traffic, and almost unanimously they hate Boston's government, its mayors and its politics.

Boston's government is phenomenally expensive because it cannot tax or assess the people who pour into it to make a living. That expense is borne chiefly by Boston real estate, although some of it must be borne by the state itself, so that people in the faraway Berkshires must make up part of the deficit created by the free-riders in the Metropolitan District outside Boston Proper. This suburbanite bedroom population boasts about its low tax rates and efficient governments, and turns up its nose scornfully at mismanaged Boston, critical of all of the services Boston provides for them for which they pay nothing.

Because of them, Boston must build bridges and overpasses, tunnels and subways. Because of their automobiles, Boston's traffic is unmanageable and the problem defies solution. They will never vote to surrender their independent governments, elect Boston's mayor or share Boston's burden, and as a result Boston resembles an antiquated, anemic cow, milked every day by milkmaids who come from green pastures, irked and indignant because the stream from the udder is condensed and evaporated, screaming: "This is an outrage. I come from green pastures," while all the old cow can do is say wistfully: "I wish I did."

In the daily unfolding of the comedy of Boston, everybody wants to get into the act. The legislature—sometimes it seems out of sheer whim or caprice—clips the powers of its mayors, assumes some of the powers of city government for itself, creates boards and commissions to exercise other powers and sometimes invites rank outsiders to take a hand. Commissions and boards get new ideas and are authorized to impose them on the city. As a result, Boston is a fatherless, sometimes helpless bastard, unwanted and deformed, constantly being corrected and reproved by multiple foster parents. Its area of home rule is limited.

It has no control over the water that it uses, or over part of the sewerage system. The Finance Commission is appointed by the state to police the city's administration. The state sets the city's borrowing limit, and limits its spending for public schools. Its police commissioner is appointed by the state, not by the mayor. As a result, a career man can never aspire to be police commissioner of Boston. That plum is usually awarded by a governor to one of his supporters. As police commissioners, Boston has had in recent years the editor and publisher of a Boston newspaper, two businessmen, two engineers, a contractor, and the advertising manager of a Boston newspaper. To add to the confusion the Metropolitan District police conflict with city police within the city-proper area.

The chief cause of graft and corruption in government is the niggardly salaries paid by the American public to its elected and appointed executives and officials and employees. As employers they expect an executive administering a $300,-

000,000 budget to turn in a $100,000 a year job for $20,000. They expect a graduate engineer, who ought to be able to command $12,000 in private industry, to turn in the same kind of job for a city or state for $6,000. They expect a teacher with a master's degree to be happy on a salary of $45 a week or less. The result is, the city tends to get the mediocre, the incompetents, the misfits and the failures, or those who use the position merely for temporary interim training. Society rewards its servants with pennies and ingratitude.

Business and industry have been forced by competition and labor unions to raise wages and salaries. There is no competition between cities, and strikes against the public service are seldom effective. The professions, except teaching and law, have been able to take fairly good care of themselves with rules, regulations and scales of fees. Business and industry compete for the best and most talented executives and pay them fabulous salaries to manage. Government has lagged woefully behind them in accommodating itself to a changing world and revising salaries upward. The deterrent, of course, is fear of the voter at the polls. Increased salaries mean increased taxes.

To provide proper and adequate fire and police protection, schools and hospitals, water (in some cities gas and electricity), drainage, sewerage, extend streets and highways and keep them in good repair in a city of one million population requires at least one employee for every hundred of population, or ten thousand employees, and this contemplates only the most efficient city organization making the best use of trained executives, skilled specialists and personnel. The public, as employers, selects its elected executives from among a small group, narrowed during the past twenty-five years by industrial and business expansion, new techniques and scientific progress, from those among the wealthy who have an inclination for public service, the retired, and the uneducated, unskilled and untrained failures, the street-corner loafers and bums who have tried everything and finally wound up happily in politics. And in any contest for election the uneducated, incompetent bum always has the edge over the wealthy or well-to-do retired.

The reason is: Minor elective offices pay such small salaries that no one of intelligence wants them, except a man of means to whom government is attractive as a pastime, and the bum to whom twenty-five hundred per year as a city councillor, for example, is a big attraction, not to mention its known potentialities for kudos and petty graft. There is no competition for such offices among the great middle group because all of them are already more gainfully employed. The salary does not attract them and they disdain graft either because they are men of integrity or because they look upon it as too hazardous, or not worth the time and trouble involved.

The average city council, a board of directors of a municipal corporation, is therefore made up chiefly of men whose minds cannot comprehend more than four digits and go blank beyond that, a council of twenty-five hundred a year base-pay career men, too lazy for a Fuller-brush route, too slow witted to keep books straight as weekly life-insurance debit collectors, but smart and brilliant enough to determine the policies of a city. Men such as these rise to become state legislators and provide the pool from which governors, major office holders and mayors are drawn; and inevitably they thump their breasts as examples of what an uneducated selfmade man can become in a democracy, while the intelligent in their audiences ponder how much better government might be if they had at least a smattering of organized knowledge.

Twenty-Six · The Return of the Native

In the interminable feud between Curley, the dwindling Brahmins and his Boston Irish adversaries, there are unwritten articles of war and rules of the game. His antagonists either could not or would not remove him from office while he was in jail. That would not have been fair. When he was back in office, the battle to get rid of him was resumed. Any tactic was permissible then, including political trickery on either or both sides.

A council-city manager form of government had been successful in Cambridge. Influenced by the experience of that city, several others in Massachusetts had adopted it. Almost all city governments cry for modernization. Their charters were contrived during an era of national growing pains. Original models have changed but little since Samuel Morse invented the telegraph. They have been amended and patched, partially dismantled and reformed upon the same old structures.

There are only five charter forms designated by statute in

Massachusetts. They are Plan A: A mayor with much authority and a city council with little; Plan B: A city council with much authority and a mayor with little; Plan C: A commission form of government, like a board of selectmen; Plan D: A commission form of government with a city (or town) manager; Plan E: A city council operating like a board of directors, with one member as a ceremonial mayor without authority and a liaison between it and the school committee who hire a city manager to administer the affairs of the corporation.

The chief improvement of Plan E over all others is that it doubles, triples and quadruples the salaries of elected and appointed city officials, a feature that makes the penurious taxpayer sick when he first hears of it, but larger salaries draw the experienced, talented and able from private business and industry into government. Honest and efficient business administration makes up the difference in salaries, reduces the tax rate, provides better government and extends public services.

Plan E, though, is complicated by a system under which councilors are chosen according to proportional representation, elected not by marking a cross, but by numerical choices on the ballot. It requires a complete re-education of the voter in election practice. Any form of government can be perverted. Plan E depends for its integrity in operation upon a large, closely knit, intensely civic-minded bloc, usually organized as a civic association, to police politics and government constantly. Wherever that has occurred, Plan E has been phenomenally successful.

The Plan E committee of Boston, however, was neither large, closely knit nor intensely civic minded. A good many who joined the Plan E group looked upon it as a political gimmick that might banish Curley at long last to the political salt mines. The Plan E committee went to the Republican legislature for permission to place it before the voters of

Boston on the ballot for adoption at the next election. Curley's representatives in the legislature asked that Plan A be included, too. The city had been operating under Plan A since its last charter change in 1914. The only thing that E had to offer over A, as Curley saw it, was the increased salaries, and he approved of that enthusiastically.

The legislature was either hypnotized or otherwise bedazzled. At any rate, when the lawmakers looked back upon what they had done, they found that proponents of the first plan to file 200,000 signatures, certified by the election commissioners of the city of Boston, would be permitted to ask the voters to adopt a charter on a referendum question on the ballot. The defeated group would have to wait six years to ask the question again. Curley had appointed the election commissioners. Getting 200,000 signatures was easy for him. Certification of them was assured. Neither was easy for the Plan E group, and they went to court about it. As a device to get rid of Curley, like all others, it had backfired.

Organized opposition of all kinds had been trying to do that for fifty years and none had ever succeeded. Curley survived in public office because of his partnership with the Boston Irish who found that they could get along better with him than without him. Only they could control him. During the course of a century in Boston, from 1848 to 1853 to 1949, they, too, had changed. The Clover Club, for example, lists among its members the wealthiest, the most successful and the most exclusive among the Boston Irish. Their progenitors would look upon them in disdain as ultra-lace curtain. The Great Immigration spawned most of these elite, who gather in the biggest banquet room in the city once a year, close to Saint Patrick's eve, to wine and dine and listen to speeches, living momentarily in an Irish history that few of them ever trouble to consult.

Here gather the cream of the Boston Irish, resplendent in full dress and tuxedos, indulging in the kind of ancestral worship for which they had scorned the Brahmins of Mayflower descent—and the most active of the city's Brahmins in politics, government, business and finance are there to help them. During these one hundred years, the Boston Irish had gathered local antiquity, tradition and money. They had all but pre-empted the Brahmins and substituted for them an identical society and caste system. The Clover Club is similar in many aspects to the Brahmin Union Club of fifty years ago— men of means, stout, complacent, smoking expensive cigars, with expensive wines and liquors on tables before them. The size of the tab each would pick up would be a matter of complete indifference. Some maintain big estates and have large summer places along exclusive New England shores. Most are college graduates. Their sleek and shiny cars fill a parking space near by, and their college-student or graduate sons and daughters have similar cars.

Their fathers and grandfathers had loaded and unloaded ships, swung picks and shovels, worked in mills and sweatshops; built railroads, railways and canals with their brawn; but after all the Brahmins had an equally humble beginning. A hundred years later, the cycle was now complete. The size of the average Irish family had shrunk to two, three or four children. Larger families were exceptions. The women had their own exclusive clubs and were sharing society pages with the Brahmins. The Boston Irish were now inclined to be snobbish and to look down their noses, shuddering in horror at the idea of opening the immigration gates to refugees, "those impossible people," oppressed and hungry, who wanted to come here just as the ancestors of the Irish came and for much the same reason. The Society Irish could see nothing inconsistent in that. Curley was at least consistent. All he wanted from the rich was money; all he wanted from the poor was votes. He got both.

The new Boston Irish were inclined to be scornful of Curley and to join the chorus of his critics. His white-collar vote among them is small, but the men in overalls, their wives and families, in populous South Boston, Dorchester, Charlestown, the middle- and lower-class suburbs, still would march to the polls and vote for him. The municipal buildings he built were their clubrooms, with showers and swimming pools. Their children played on the playgrounds and beaches he made. The transient, successful Boston Irish would pass, or go the way of the disappearing Brahmins, but, barring atomic destruction, his imprint would remain upon the city for centuries on roads, bridges, subways, on the shorefront and the hinterland. Whatever it cost, and whatever he made on them personally, there they are.

Outlanders surveying the Boston scene seldom understand it. "How can you tolerate a man like that?" they ask. Visiting newspapermen ask the same question, and as they can't get an answer that makes sense, they investigate, determined to isolate the cause and place the blame. Every master and journeyman critic, even those who stop off for a few hours between trains, takes a whirl at it. More often than not they blame the city's six newspapers and have made them the most criticized press in the country.

Crusading journalism cannot remove Curley. It has been going on in Boston for thirty years and never has made a dent. If nothing is done about bad government in Boston, it is not because of the character of its newspapers. They turn up more column inches of scandal daily than the newspapers of any other city in the country; not because there is more of it, but because competition for circulation in an overpapered city brings more of it to light. There is a saturation point where the power of the press ceases. It arrives when political scandal becomes so commonplace that a reader takes it for granted, is disappointed when he does not find it and is no longer moved to indignation by it. A series of stories that might win a Pulitzer prize in any other city, not accustomed to such a diet, are editorial features in Boston.

Most of the criticism of Boston newspapers originates with Boston newspapermen themselves. Unable to do anything effective in achieving reform, not because of the newspapers that employ them, but because of the curious indifference of the people, they pour their exasperation and frustration into the ears of visiting journalists, who are sometimes both astonished and entertained; but they are not telling the exact truth. The visitors write it as truth and give it wider circulation.

Curley, at seventy-four, was putting in a ten- to fourteen-hour day at City Hall. He was contemplating building an overhead highway to bridge the city from North to South. Planning and drafting had already been done by state engineers. He was also thinking of another project, a wide highway along the Boston shore of the Charles River. It would involve a good deal of land taking and underwater construction.

He had made his peace with Harry Truman and campaigned for his election, one of the few Democratic politicians in the state who were confident that he would win. Truman helped clear the local political picture for Curley when he appointed Maurice Tobin secretary of labor, removing him as a candidate for governor against Paul Dever, Curley's choice. A week before election, Curley was taking all the odds-on-Dewey bets he could find. His friends cautioned him, certain that he would lose everything he had, and he looked at them unbelieving.

"How can Truman lose?" he asked. "Are you blind? Can't you see what's going on? Truman is right about the polls. They're all crazy. This state will go for him in a landslide, and it will elect Dever."

It did.

The American Prison Association held its annual convention in Boston and it was Curley's duty to welcome them to the city. He looked down at an audience of jail administrators, including some who had been at Danbury. "I know a good deal about jails," he said. "I've been on the inside looking out, and I met some of our best people in the penitentiary in Danbury." At Christmastime he sent a message to Harry Truman asking amnesty for all veterans of World War II, except those who had deserted under fire.

Within a year, Danbury was forgotten. The tide that swept Truman and Dever into office had elected a Democratic State House of Representatives and an evenly divided Senate for the first time in three hundred years. He was certain that he could beat Plan E and was plotting how to persuade a Democratic legislature to return to Boston the powers that had been shorn from its mayor over the centuries. What he could not accomplish as governor, he might as mayor: the end of the Finance Commission and the Metropolitan District Commission. He might yet get the state out of Boston's business, regain the right to appoint his own police commission, control it and retrieve authority over parks, roads, reservations, water and sewerage.

Social life returned to Jamaicaway again on the old scale. His family was around him, giving dinners and parties. His son George had a costume party for his friends there one night. Pretty girls in hoop-skirts whirled around the floor at the bottom of the winding staircase. When the orchestra rested between sets, a pianist took over and the talented among the guests entertained. Curley sat on the steps with a few friends and looked on. Fire Commissioner Russell Codman and his wife were there. Codman was the only blueblood Curley had appointed to office, an efficient and businesslike executive, well liked by his firemen.

"Stop the music!" Curley said, looking down at the pianist,

not realizing that he was using a command made famous by
Jimmy Durante and a radio give-away show. The music
stopped. He looked over the heads of the guests at his tower-
ing, slender commissioner.

"Russell," he said, "do your imitation of John L. Lewis!"

Codman grinned, stepped out into the middle of the floor.
His eyebrows were bushy. He looked something like Lewis
and he delivered a fighting speech to miners in the Lewis
manner. The irony was not in the impersonation of Lewis
but in the fact that a Brahmin *Mayflower* descendant was
pinch-hitting as court jester for a mayor and former governor
who had come up from the mud flats. The irony became
poetic justice when one remembered what Curley and his
wife, early in his career, had had to put up with in the homes
of Brahmins on Beacon Hill.

Curley left his limousine one morning in late winter to
go into City Hall and saw a black, sweep headline across page
one of an afternoon paper: "Demands Million for New Social Service Center." He grinned. It was not his headline.
He had nothing to do with it. It summarized the report of
an independent committee studying the community fund
and the agencies participating in it. He could picture the
frantic consternation of the heavy taxpayers of the city,
spitting and choking over the news, and probably babbling
it into telephones before they found out what it was all
about.

That night he was a guest on a telecast. The brilliant light
beat down upon him. An interviewer discussed city problems
with him and ended by asking: "How long do you expect
to live, Mr. Mayor?"

Curley thought it over a moment and looked from television screens upon an assortment of those who loved and
hated him. He smiled and said: "I expect to live to be one

hundred and twenty-five years old, and I also expect to be mayor of Boston all of that time," and his image faded out on the screen; the last of the political buccaneers, ungovernable, unmanageable, irrepressible, incorrigible, apparently indestructible.

Chronological Tables

VITAL STATISTICS

Born November 20, 1874.

Married Mary E. Herlihy (d. 1930), June 27, 1906; Gertrude (Casey) Dennis, January 7, 1937.

Children: twins, 1907; James, Jr., 1908; Dorothea, 1910; Paul, 1913 —all deceased. Mary, 1909; Leo, 1915; George, 1921; Francis, 1925.

PUBLIC OFFICES AND CAMPAIGNS

1900–01	Boston Common Council
1902–03	Representative (State Legislature)
1904–09	Alderman
1910–11	City Council
1911–14	Congressman
1914–18	Mayor
1917	Defeated for Mayor by A. J. Peters
1922–26	Mayor
1924	Defeated for Governor by Alvan T. Fuller
1930–34	Mayor
1935–36	Governor
1936	Defeated for U. S. Senate by Henry Cabot Lodge, Jr.

1937   Defeated for Mayor by Maurice J. Tobin
1938   Defeated for Governor by Leverett Saltonstall
1940   Defeated for Mayor by Maurice J. Tobin
1943–46   Congressman
1945–   Mayor

Index